WOMEN AND RELIGION

WOMEN AND RELIGION

Nitin Doshi

CYBER TECH PUBLICATIONS
4264/3, Ansari Road, Daryaganj, New Delhi-110002 (India)
Ph.: 011-23244078. Fax: 011-23280028
E-Mail: cyberpublicationsdelhi@yahoo.com

Women and Religion

First Edition 2009

Published by G.S. Rawat

For Cyber Tech Publications

4264/3, Ansari Road, Daryaganj, New Delhi-110002

Ph.: 011-23244078. Fax: 011-23280028

E-Mail: cyberpublicationsdelhi@yahoo.com

Printed at

Asian Offset Printers

Preface

Over the centuries, billions of people have fallen prey to religion run amok. How many Jews and Gypsies suffered in Nazi concentration camps while churches in Germany turned their heads? How many people were murdered in the Crusades during the middle ages—in the name of God?

This research is urban-based, as we're looking at young urban women to provide us with a picture of change and transformation. The activity and public role of these women are key: they are working women and young students who embody and illuminate issues of sexuality, marriage and paid employment (rather than motherhood, children and housework). The challenge for us is to "read" these discussions in a way that brings out the empowering factors in young women's testimonies, to look at how they are reframing the cultural contours that surround them. These women's negotiation of the new spaces that religion has created can be empowering, but the nature of these spaces remains defined by patriarchy. This element is not being contested or denied; rather, what women seem to be doing is negotiating for greater rights within patriarchal structures.

Every care has been taken to include material in accordance with the course contents of the students at various levels of their studies. We are indebted to the various authorities on the subject. We gratefully acknowledge them.

Last but not the least my publishers who appreciated this book and brought this work out in a record time.

—Editor

Contents

CHAPTER ONE

What is Religion?

A religion is a set of beliefs and practices, often centered upon specific supernatural and moral claims about reality, the cosmos, and human nature, and often codified as prayer, ritual, or religious law. Religion also encompasses ancestral or cultural traditions, writings, history, and mythology, as well as personal faith and religious experience. The term "religion" refers to both the personal practices related to communal faith and to group rituals and communication stemming from shared conviction.

In the frame of European religious thought,[1] religions present a common quality, the "hallmark of patriarchal religious thought": the division of the world in two comprehensive domains, one sacred, the other profane.[2] Religion is often described as a communal system for the coherence of belief focusing on a system of thought, unseen being, person, or object, that is considered to be supernatural, sacred, divine, or of the highest truth. Moral codes, practices, values, institutions, tradition, rituals, and scriptures are often traditionally associated with the core belief, and these may have some overlap with concepts in secular philosophy. Religion is also often described as a "way of life" or a Life stance.

The development of religion has taken many forms in various cultures. "Organized religion" generally refers to an organization of people supporting the exercise of some religion with a prescribed set of beliefs, often taking the form of a legal entity (see religion-supporting organization). Other religions believe in personal revelation. "Religion" is sometimes used interchangeably with "faith" or "belief system,"[3] but is more socially defined than that of personal convictions.

Etymology

Religion by country

North America

- Canada • United States • Mexico
- Cuba • Dominican Republic
- Trinidad and Tobago • Nicaragua

South America

- Colombia • Peru • Bolivia
- Brazil • Argentina Paraguay

Europe

- Iceland • Ireland • United Kingdom
- Portugal • Spain • Italy • France
- Netherlands • Belgium • Germany
- Switzerland • Luxembourg • Austria
- Denmark • Sweden • Norway • Finland
- Poland • Lithuania • Moldova • Russia
- Albania • Serbia • Montenegro
- Bulgaria • Romania • Greece • Malta

Middle East

- Egypt • Israel • Lebanon
- Jordan • Armenia • Azerbaijan
- Iran • Iraq • Syria • Turkey

Africa

- Nigeria • Sudan • Ethiopia • Seychelles
- Uganda • Zambia • Kenya • South Africa

Asia

- Afghanistan • Pakistan • India
- Nepal • Sri Lanka • Vietnam
- China • Hong Kong • Macau • Taiwan
- North Korea • South Korea • Japan
- Malaysia • Singapore • Philippines

Oceania

- Indonesia • Papua New Guinea
- Australia • New Zealand • Fiji

The English word religion is in use since the 13th century, loaned from Anglo-French religiun (11th century), ultimately from the Latin religio, "reverence for God or the gods, careful pondering of divine things, piety, the res divinae".[4]

The ultimate origins of Latin religio are obscure. It is usually accepted to derive from ligare "bind, connect"; likely from a prefixed re-ligare, i.e. re (again) + ligare or "to reconnect." This interpretation is favoured by modern scholars such as Tom Harpur and Joseph Campbell, but was made prominent by St. Augustine, following the interpretation of Lactantius. Another possibility is derivation from a reduplicated *le-ligare. A historical interpretation due to Cicero on the other hand connects lego "read", i.e. re (again) + lego in the sense of "choose", "go over again" or "consider carefully".[5]

Definitions of Religion

Further information: Sociology of Religion, Transcendence, Theism, Sacred (comparative religion), Religion and mythology, and Myth and ritual

Religion has been defined in a wide variety of ways. Most definitions attempt to find a balance somewhere between overly sharp definition and meaningless generalities. Some sources have tried to use formalistic, doctrinal definitions while others have emphasized experiential, emotive, intuitive, valuational and ethical factors. Definitions mostly include:

* notion of the transcendent or numinous, often, but not always, in the form of theism
* cultural or behavioural aspect of ritual, liturgy and organized worship, often involving a priesthood, and societal norms of morality (ethos) and virtue (arete)
* set of myths or sacred truths held in reverence or believed by adherents

Sociologists and anthropologists tend to see religion as an abstract set of ideas, values, or experiences developed as part of a cultural matrix. For example, in Lindbeck's Nature of Doctrine, religion does not refer to belief in "God" or a transcendent Absolute. Instead, Lindbeck defines religion as, "a kind of cultural and/or linguistic framework or medium that shapes the entirety of life and thought... it is similar to an idiom that makes possible the description of realities, the formulation of beliefs, and the experiencing of inner attitudes, feelings, and sentiments."[6] According to this definition, religion refers to one's primary worldview and how this dictates one's thoughts and actions.

Other religious scholars have put forward a definition of religion that avoids the reductionism of the various sociological and psychological disciplines that reduce religion to its component factors. Religion may be defined as the presence of a belief in the sacred or the holy. For example Rudolf Otto's "The Idea of the Holy," formulated in 1917, defines the essence of religious awareness as awe, a unique blend of fear and fascination before the divine. Friedrich Schleiermacher in the late 18th century defined religion as a "feeling of absolute dependence."

The Encyclopedia of Religion defines religion this way:[7]

In summary, it may be said that almost every known culture involves the religious in the above sense of a depth dimension in cultural experiences at all levels – a push, whether ill-defined or conscious, toward some sort of ultimacy and transcendence that will provide norms and power for the rest of life. When more or less distinct patterns of behaviour are built around this depth dimension in a culture, this structure constitutes religion in its historically recognizable form. Religion is the organization of life around the depth dimensions of experience – varied in form, completeness, and clarity in accordance with the environing culture."

Other encyclopedic definitions include: "A general term used... to designate all concepts concerning the belief in god(s) and goddess(es) as well as other spiritual beings or transcendental ultimate concerns"[8] and "human beings' relation to that which they regard as holy, sacred, spiritual, or divine."[9]

Religion and superstition

In keeping with the Latin etymology of the word, religious believers have often seen other religions as superstition. Likewise, some atheists, agnostics, deists, and skeptics regard religious belief as superstition.

Religious practices are most likely to be labeled "superstitious" by outsiders when they include belief in extraordinary events (miracles), an afterlife, supernatural interventions, apparitions or the efficacy of prayer, charms, incantations, the meaningfulness of omens, and prognostications.

Greek and Roman pagans, who modeled their relations with the gods on political and social terms scorned the man who constantly trembled with fear at the thought of the gods, as a slave feared a cruel and capricious master. "Such fear of the gods (deisidaimonia) was what the Romans meant by 'superstition' (Veyne 1987, p 211). Early Christianity was outlawed as a superstitio Iudaica, a "Jewish superstition", by Domitianin the 80s AD, and by AD 425, Theodosius II outlawed pagan traditions as superstitious.

The Roman Catholic Church considers superstition to be sinful in the sense that it denotes a lack of trust in the divine providence of God and, as such, is a violation of the first of the Ten Commandments. The Catechism of the Catholic Church states superstition "in some sense represents a perverse excess of religion".

The Catechism clearly dispels commonly held preconceptions or misunderstandings about Catholic doctrine relating to superstitious practices:

Superstition is a deviation of religious feeling and of the practices this feeling imposes. It can even affect the worship we offer the true God, e.g., when one attributes an importance in some way magical to certain practices otherwise lawful or necessary. To attribute the efficacy of prayers or of sacramental signs to their mere external performance, apart from the interior dispositions that they demand is to fall into superstition. Cf. Matthew 23:16-22 (para. #2111)

History

Detail from Religion, Charles Sprague Pearce (1896). Library of Congress Thomas Jefferson Building, Washington, D.C.Main article: History of religion

Development of religion

Main articles: Origin of religion, Development of religion,

Anthropology of religion, and Prehistoric religion

There are a number of models regarding the ways in which religions come into being and develop. Broadly speaking, these models fall into three categories:

Models which see religions as social constructions;

Models which see religions as progressing toward higher, objective truth;

Models which see a particular religion as absolutely true.

In pre-modern (pre-urban) societies, religion is one defining factor of ethnicity, along with language, regional customs, national costume, etc. As Xenophanes famously comments:

Men make gods in their own image; those of the Ethiopians are black and snub-nosed, those of the Thracians have blue eyes and red hair.

Ethnic religions may include officially sanctioned and organized civil religions with an organized clergy, but they are characterized in that adherents generally are defined by their ethnicity, and conversion essentially equates to cultural assimilation to the people in question. The notion of gentiles ("nations") in Judaism reflect this state of affairs, the implicit assumption that each nation will have its own religion. Historical examples include Germanic polytheism, Celtic polytheism, Slavic polytheism and pre-Hellenistic Greek religion.

The "Axial Age"

Main article: Axial Age

Karl Jaspers, in his Vom Ursprung und Ziel der Geschichte (The Origin and Goal of History), identified a number of key Axial Age thinkers as having had a profound influence on future philosophy and religion, and identified characteristics common to each area from which those thinkers emerged. Jaspers saw in these developments in religion and philosophy a striking parallel without any obvious direct transmission of ideas from one region to the other, having found very little recorded proof of extensive inter-communication between the ancient Near East, Greece, India and China. Jaspers held up this age as unique, and one which to compare the rest of the history of human thought to. Jaspers' approach to the culture of the middle of the first millennium BCE has been adopted by other scholars and academics, and has become a point of discussion in the history of religion.

In its later part, the "Axial Age" culminated in the development of monism and monotheism, notably of Platonic realism and Neoplatonism in Hellenistic philosophy, the notion of atman in Vedanta Hindu philosophy, and the notion of Tao in Taoism.

Central Asian (Tocharian?) and East-Asian Buddhist monks, Bezeklik, Eastern Tarim Basin, 9th-10th century.

Middle Ages

The present-day world religions established themselves throughout Eurasia during the Middle Ages by: Christianization of the Western world; Buddhist missions to East Asia; the decline of Buddhism and rise of Hinduism in the Indian subcontinent; and the spread of Islam throughout the Middle East, Central Asia, North Africa and parts of Europe and India.

During the Middle Ages, Muslims were in conflict with Zoroastrians during the Islamic conquest of Persia; Christians were in conflict with Muslims during the Byzantine-Arab Wars, Crusades, Reconquista and Ottoman wars in Europe; Christians were in conflict with Jews during the Crusades, Reconquista and Inquisition; Shamans were in conflict with

Buddhists, Taoists, Muslims and Christians during the Mongol invasions; and Muslims were in conflict with Hindus and Sikhs during Muslim conquest in the Indian subcontinent.

Many medieval religious movements emphasized mysticism, such as the Cathars and related movements in the West, the Bhakti movement in India and Sufism in Islam. Monotheism reached definite forms in Christian Christology and in Islamic Tawhid. Hindu monotheist notions of Brahman likewise reached their classical form with the teaching of Adi Shankara.

Modern period

European colonisation during the 15th to 19th centuries resulted in the spread of Christianity to Sub-Saharan Africa, the Americas, Australia and the Philippines. The 18th century saw the beginning of secularisation in Europe, rising to notability in the wake of the French Revolution.

In the 20th century, the regimes of Communist Eastern Europe and Communist China were explicitly anti-religious. A great variety of new religious movements originated in the 20th century, many proposing syncretism of elements of established religions. Adherence to such new movements is limited, however, remaining below 2% worldwide in the 2000s. Adherents of the classical world religions account for more than 75% of the world's population, while adherence to indigenous tribal religions has fallen to 4%. As of 2005, an estimated 14% of the world's population identifies as nonreligious.

Classification

The statistics in this section rely primarily upon a single source (adherents.com), whose reliability is also not established.

Please help improve this article by introducing appropriate citations of additional sources.

Major religious groups

Further information: Comparative religion and Sociological classifications of religious movements

Religious traditions fall into super-groups in comparative religion, arranged by historical origin and mutual influence. Abrahamic religions originate in the Middle East, Indian religions in India and Far Eastern religions in East Asia. Another group with supra-regional influence are African diasporic religions, which have their origins in Central and West Africa.

Major religious groups as a percentage of the world population in 2005 (Encyclopaedia Britannica). In summary, religious adherence of the world's population is as follows: "Abrahamic": 53.5%, "Indian": 19.7%, irreligious: 14.3%, "Far Eastern": 6.5%, tribal religions: 4.0%, new religious movements: 2.0%.

The main Religions of the World, mapped without denominations.Abrahamic religions are by far the largest group, and these consist primarily of Christianity, Islam and Judaism (sometimes Bahá'í is also included). They are named for the patriarch Abraham, and are unified by their strict monotheism. Today, around 3.4 billion people are followers of Abrahamic religions and are spread widely around the world apart from the regions around South-East Asia. Several Abrahamic organizations are vigorous proselytizers.

Indian religions originated in Greater India and tend to share a number of key concepts, such as dharma and karma. They are of the most influence across the Indian subcontinent, East Asia, South East Asia, as well as isolated parts of Russia. The main Indian religions are Hinduism, Buddhism, Sikhism, and Jainism. Indian religions mutually influenced each other. Sikhism was also influenced by the

Abrahamic tradition of Sufism.

Far Eastern religions consist of several East Asian religions which make use of the concept of Tao (in Chinese) or Do (in Japanese or Korean). They include Taoism, Shinto, Chondogyo, Caodaism, and Yiguandao. Far Eastern Buddhism (in which the group overlaps with the "Indian" group) and Confucianism (which by some categorizations is not a religion) are also included.

Iranic religions originated in Iran and include Zoroastrianism, Yazdanism and historical traditions of Gnosticism (Mandaeanism, Manichaeism). It has significant overlaps with Abrahamic traditions, e.g. in Sufism and in recent movements such as Bábísm and Bahá'í.

African diasporic religions practiced in the Americas, imported as a result of the Atlantic slave trade of the 16th to 18th centuries, building of traditional religions of Central and West Africa.

Indigenous tribal religions, formerly found on every continent, now marginalized by the major organized faiths, but persisting as undercurrents of folk religion. Includes African traditional religions, Asian Shamanism, Native American religions, Austronesian and Australian Aboriginal traditions and arguably Chinese folk religion (overlaps with Far Eastern religions). Under more traditional listings, this has been referred to as "Paganism" along with historical polytheism.

New religious movements, a heterogeneous group of religious faiths emerging since the 19th century, often syncretizing, re-interpreting or reviving aspects of older traditions (Bahá'í, Hindu revivalism, Ayyavazhi, Pentecostalism, polytheistic reconstructionism), some inspired by science-fiction (UFO religions). See List of new religious movements, list of groups referred to as cults.

Demographic distribution of the major super-groupings mentioned is shown in the table below:

Name of Group Name of Religion Number of followers Date of Origin Main regions covered

Abrahamic Religions

3.6 billion Christianity 2.1 billion 1st c. Worldwide except Northwest Africa, the Arabian Peninsula, and parts of Central, East, and Southeast Asia.

Islam 1.5 billion 7th c. Middle East, Northern Africa, Central Asia, South Asia, Western Africa, Indian subcontinent, Malay Archipelago with large population centers existing in Eastern Africa, Balkan Peninsula, Russia, Europe and China.

Judaism 14 million 1300 BCE. Israel and among Jewish diaspora (live mostly in USA and Europe)

Bahá'í Faith 5 million 19th c. Dispersed worldwide with no major population centers

Indian Religions

1.4 billion Hinduism 900 million no founder Indian subcontinent, Fiji, Guyana and Mauritius

Buddhism 376 million Iron Age (1200–300 BCE) Indian subcontinent, East Asia, Indochina, regions of Russia.

Sikhism 25.8 million 15th c. India, Pakistan, Africa, Canada, USA, United Kingdom

Jainism 4.2 million Iron Age (1200–300 BCE) India, and East Africa

Far Eastern Religions

500 million Taoism unknown Spring and Autumn Period (722 BC-481 BC) China and the Chinese diaspora

Confucianism unknown Spring and Autumn Period (722 BC-481 BC) China, Korea, Vietnam and the Chinese and Vietnamese diasporas

Shinto 4 million no founder Japan

Caodaism 1-2 million 1925 Vietnam

Chondogyo 1.13 million 1812 Korea

Yiguandao 1-2 million c. 1900 Taiwan

Chinese folk religion 394 million no founder, a combination of Taoism, Confucianism and Buddhism China

Ethnic/tribal

400 million

Primal indigenous 300 million no founder India, Asia

African traditional and diasporic 100 million no known founder Africa, Americas

Other

each over 500 thousand

Juche 19 million North Korea

Spiritism 15 million

Neopaganism 1 million

Unitarian-Universalism 800,000

Rastafarianism 600,000

Scientology 500,000

Kumbh Mela, a Hindu religious festival is the Largest religious gathering on earth. Around 75 million Hindus from around the world gathered in Varanasi, a Hindu holy city. Geoeye.com

Religious belief

Confucianism, Taoism, and Buddhism are one, a painting in the litang style portraying three men laughing by a river stream, 12th century, Song Dynasty.Religious belief usually relates to the existence, nature and worship of a deity or deities and divine involvement in the universe and human life. Alternately, it may also relate to values and practices transmitted by a spiritual leader. Unlike other belief systems, which may be passed on orally, religious belief tends to be codified in literate societies (religion in non-literate societies is still largely passed on orally[10]). In some religions, like the Abrahamic religions, it is held that most of the core beliefs have been divinely revealed.

Religion and science

Relationship between religion and science

Religious knowledge, according to religious practitioners, may be gained from religious leaders, sacred texts (scriptures), and/or personal revelation. Some religions view such knowledge as unlimited in scope and suitable to answer any question; others see religious knowledge as playing a more restricted role, often as a complement to knowledge gained through physical observation. Some religious people maintain that religious knowledge obtained in this way is absolute and infallible (religious cosmology).

Early science such as geometry and astronomy was connected to the divine for most medieval scholars. The compass in this 13th century manuscript is a symbol of God's act of creation.The scientific method gains knowledge by testing hypotheses to develop theories through elucidation of facts or evaluation by experiments and thus only answers cosmological questions about the physical universe. It develops theories of the world which best fit physically observed evidence. All scientific knowledge is subject to later refinement in the face of additional evidence. Scientific theories that have an overwhelming preponderance of favorable evidence are often treated as facts (such as the theories of gravity or evolution).

Many scientists held strong religious beliefs (see List of Christian thinkers in science) and worked to harmonize science and religion. Isaac Newton, for example, believed that gravity caused the planets to revolve about the Sun, and credited God with the design. In the concluding General Scholium to the Philosophiae Naturalis Principia Mathematica, he wrote: "This most beautiful System of the Sun, Planets and Comets, could only proceed from the counsel and dominion of an intelligent and powerful being." Nevertheless, conflict arose between religious organizations and individuals who propagated scientific theories which were deemed unacceptable by the organizations. The Roman Catholic Church, for example, has in the past[11] reserved to itself the right to decide which scientific theories were acceptable and which were unacceptable. In the 17th century, Galileo was tried and forced to recant the heliocentric theory based on the medieval church's stance that the Greek Hellenistic system of astronomy was the correct one.[12, 13]

Many theories exist as to why religions sometimes seem to conflict with scientific knowledge. In the case of Christianity, a relevant factor may be that it was among Christians that science in the modern sense was developed. Unlike other religious groups, as early as the 17th century the Christian churches had to deal directly with this new way to investigate nature and seek truth.

The perceived conflict between science and Christianity may also be partially explained by a literal interpretation of the Bible adhered to by many Christians, both currently and historically. The Catholic Church has always held with Augustine of Hippo who explicitly opposed a literal interpretation of the Bible whenever the Bible conflicted with Science. The literal way to read the sacred texts became especially prevalent after the rise of the Protestant reformation, with its emphasis on the Bible as the only authoritative source concerning the ultimate reality.[14] This view is often shunned by both religious leaders (who regard literally believing it as petty and look for greater meaning instead) and scientists who regard it as an impossibility.

Some Christians have disagreed or are still disagreeing with scientists in areas such as the validity of Keplerian astronomy, the theory of evolution, the method of creation of the universe and the Earth, and the origins of life. On the other hand, scholars such as Stanley Jaki have suggested that Christianity and its particular worldview was a crucial factor for the emergence of modern science. In fact, most of today's historians are moving away from the view of the relationship between Christianity and science as one of "conflict" - a perspective commonly called the conflict thesis.[15, 16] Gary Ferngren in his historical volume about Science & Religion states:

While some historians had always regarded the [conflict] thesis as oversimplifying and distorting a complex relationship, in the late twentieth century it underwent a more systematic reevaluation. The result is the growing recognition among historians of science that the relationship of religion and science has been much more positive than is sometimes thought. Although popular images of controversy continue to exemplify the supposed hostility of Christianity to new scientific theories, studies have shown that Christianity has often nurtured and encouraged scientific endeavour, while at other times the two have co-existed without either tension or attempts at harmonization. If Galileo and the Scopes trial come to mind as examples of conflict, they were the exceptions rather than the rule.[17]

In the Bahá'í Faith, the harmony of science and religion

is a central tenet.[18] The principle states that that truth is one, and therefore true science and true religion must be in harmony, thus rejecting the view that science and religion are in conflict.[18] 'Abdu'l-Bahá, the son of the founder of the religion, asserted that science and religion cannot be opposed because they are aspects of the same truth; he also affirmed that reasoning powers are required to understand the truths of religion and that religious teachings which are at variance with science should not be accepted; he explained that religion has to be reasonable since God endowed humankind with reason so that they can discover truth.[19] Shoghi Effendi, the Guardian of the Bahá'í Faith, described science and religion as "the two most potent forces in human life."[20]

Proponents of Hinduism claim that Hinduism is not afraid of scientific explorations, nor of the technological progress of mankind. According to them, there is a comprehensive scope and opportunity for Hinduism to mold itself according to the demands and aspirations of the modern world; it has the ability to align itself with both science and spiritualism. This religion uses some modern examples to explain its ancient theories and reinforce its own beliefs. For example, some Hindu thinkers have used the terminology of quantum physics to explain some basic concepts of Hinduism such as Maya or the illusory and impermanent nature of our existence.

The philosophical approach known as pragmatism, as propounded by the American philosopher William James, has been used to reconcile scientific with religious knowledge. Pragmatism, simplistically, holds that the truth of a set of beliefs can be indicated by its usefulness in helping people cope with a particular context of life. Thus, the fact that scientific beliefs are useful in predicting observations in the physical world can indicate a certain truth for scientific theories; the fact that religious beliefs can be useful in helping people cope with difficult emotions or moral decisions can indicate a certain truth for those beliefs. (For a similar postmodern view, see grand narrative).

Religion, metaphysics, and cosmology

Please help improve this section by expanding it.

Further information might be found on the talk page or at requests for expansion.

Being both forms of belief system, religion and philosophy meet in several areas - notably in the study of metaphysics and cosmology. In particular, a distinct set of religious beliefs will often entail a specific metaphysics and cosmology. That is, a religion will generally have answers to metaphysical and cosmological questions about the nature of being, of the universe, humanity, and the divine.

Mysticism and esotericism

Man meditatingMysticism focuses on methods other than logic, but (in the case of esoteric mysticism) not necessarily excluding it, for gaining enlightenment. Rather, meditative and contemplative practices such as Vipassanâ and yoga, physical disciplines such as stringent fasting and whirling (in the case of the Sufi dervishes), or the use of psychoactive drugs such as LSD, lead to altered states of consciousness that logic can never hope to grasp. However, regarding the latter topic, mysticism prevalent in the 'great' religions (monotheisms, henotheisms, which are perhaps relatively recent, and which the word 'mysticism' is more recent than,) includes systems of discipline that forbid drugs that damage the body, including the nervous system.

Mysticism (to initiate) is the pursuit of communion with, or conscious awareness of ultimate reality, the divine, spiritual truth, or Deity through direct, personal experience (intuition or insight) rather than rational thought. Mystics speak of the existence of realities behind external perception or intellectual apprehension that are central to being and directly accessible through personal experience. They say that such experience is a genuine and important source of knowledge.

Esotericism is often spiritual (thus religious) but can be non-religious/-spiritual, and it uses intellectual understanding and reasoning, intuition and inspiration (higher noetic and spiritual reasoning,) but not necessarily faith (except often as a virtue,) and it is philosophical in its emphasis on techniques of psycho-spiritual transformation (esoteric cosmology). Esotericism refers to "hidden" knowledge available only to the advanced, privileged, or initiated, as opposed to exoteric knowledge, which is public. All religions are probably somewhat exoteric, but most ones of ancient civilizations such as Yoga of India, and the mystery religions of ancient Egypt, Israel (Kabbalah,) and Greece are examples of ones that are also esoteric.

A sadhu performing namaste in Madurai, India.

Spirituality

Members of an organized religion may not see any significant difference between religion and spirituality. Or they may see a distinction between the mundane, earthly aspects of their religion and its spiritual dimension.

Some individuals draw a strong distinction between religion and spirituality. They may see spirituality as a belief in ideas of religious significance (such as God, the Soul, or Heaven), but not feel bound to the bureaucratic structure and creeds of a particular organized religion. They choose the term spirituality rather than religion to describe their form of belief, perhaps reflecting a disillusionment with organized religion (see Major religious groups), and a movement towards a more "modern" – more tolerant, and more intuitive – form of religion. These individuals may reject organized religion because of historical acts by religious organizations, such as Christian Crusades and Islamic Jihad, the marginalisation and persecution of various minorities or the Spanish Inquisition. The basic precept of the ancient spiritual tradition of India, the Vedas, is the inner reality of existence, which is essentially a spiritual approach to being.

Mythology

The word myth has several meanings.

> A traditional story of ostensibly historical events that serves to unfold part of the world view of a people or explain a practice, belief, or natural phenomenon;
>
> A person or thing having only an imaginary or unverifiable existence; or
>
> A metaphor for the spiritual potentiality in the human being. [21]

Ancient polytheistic religions, such as those of Greece, Rome, and Scandinavia, are usually categorized under the heading of mythology. Religions of pre-industrial peoples, or cultures in development, are similarly called "myths" in the anthropology of religion. The term "myth" can be used pejoratively by both religious and non-religious people. By defining another person's religious stories and beliefs as mythology, one implies that they are less real or true than one's own religious stories and beliefs. Joseph Campbell remarked, "Mythology is often thought of as other people's religions, and religion can be defined as mis-interpreted mythology."[22]

In sociology, however, the term myth has a non-pejorative meaning. There, myth is defined as a story that is important for the group whether or not it is objectively or provably true. Examples include the death and resurrection of Jesus, which, to Christians, explains the means by which they are freed from sin and is also ostensibly a historical event. But from a mythological outlook, whether or not the event actually occurred is unimportant. Instead, the symbolism of the death of an old "life" and the start of a new "life" is what is most significant.

Cosmology

Religious cosmology, Philosophy, Metaphysics, Esotericism, and Mysticism

Spirituality, Mythology, and Philosophy of religion

Humans have many different methods which attempt to answer fundamental questions about the nature of the universe and our place in it (cosmology). Religion is only one of the methods for trying to answer one or more of these questions. Other methods include science, philosophy, metaphysics, astrology, esotericism, mysticism, and forms of shamanism, such as the sacred consumption of ayahuasca among Peruvian Amazonia's Urarina. The Urarina have an elaborate animistic cosmological system,[23] which informs their mythology, religious orientation and daily existence. In many cases, the distinction between these means are not clear. For example, Buddhism and Taoism have been regarded as schools of philosophies as well as religions.

Given the generalized discontents with modernity, consumerism, over-consumption, violence and anomie, many people in the so-called industrial or post-industrial West rely on a number of distinctive religious worldviews. This in turn has given rise to increased religious pluralism, as well as to what are commonly known in the academic literature as new religious movements, which are gaining ground across the globe.

Criticism

Main articles: Criticism of Religion, Antireligion, Secularism, Agnosticism, and Atheism

The Canadian scholar of comparative religion, Wilfred Cantwell Smith argued that religion, rather than being a universally valid category as is generally supposed, is a peculiarly European concept of comparatively recent origin.

Most Western criticism of religious constructs and their social consequences has come, however, from atheists and agnostics. Anti-religious sentiment first gathered force during the 18th century European Enlightenment, although pioneering critics such as Voltaire and his fellow Encyclopedists were for the most part deists. The French Revolution then instituted what later became known as secularism, a constitutional declaration of the separation of church and state.

As well as being adopted by the new French and U.S. republics, secularism soon came to be adopted by a number of nation states, both revolutionary and post-colonial. Marx famously declared religion to be the "opium of the people," a statement the implications of which were applied with an iron fist in social systems inspired by his writings, most notably in the Soviet Union and China and, most notoriously, in Cambodia. The possible implications of the rest of Marx's celebrated sentence - that religion is "the heart of a heartless world" - were left stubbornly unconsidered. Systematic criticism of the philosophical underpinnings of religion had paralleled the upsurge of scientific discourse within industrial society: T.H. Huxley had in 1869 coined the term "agnostic," a baton taken up with alacrity by such figures as Robert Ingersoll and, later, Bertrand Russell, who told the world Why I am not a Christian.

Many contemporary critics consider religion irrational by definition.[24][25][26] Some assert that dogmatic religions are in effect morally deficient, elevating to moral status ancient, arbitrary, and ill-informed rules - taboos on eating pork, for example, as well as dress codes and sexual practices[27] - possibly designed for reasons of hygiene or even mere politics in a bygone era. Some consider religion, as such, as little more than a noble lie.

In North America and Western Europe the social fallout of the 9/11 attacks has fertilized a flurry of secularist tracts with titles such as The God Delusion, The End of Faith and God is not Great: How Religion Poisons Everything. This criticism is mostly focused on the monotheistic Abrahamic traditions.

NOTES AND REFERENCES

1. Jack Goody as cited in "Sacred and Profane - Durkheim's Critics". Retrieved on 2007-07-10.
2. Durkheim 1976, p.36
3. The words "belief system" may not necessarily refer to a religion, though a religion may be referred to as "belief system."
4. Lewis & Short, A Latin Dictionary[1]
5. qui omnia, quae ad cultum deorum pertinerent, diligenter retractarent et tamquam relegerent, sunt dicti religiosi ex relegendo, ut elegantes ex elegendo, tamquam a diligendo diligentes, ex intellegendo intellegentes: his enim in verbis omnibus inest vis legendi eadem, quae in religioso, Cic. N. D. 2, 28, 72
6. George A. Lindbeck, Nature of Doctrine (Louisville: Westminster/John Knox Press, 1984), 33.
7. Religion [First Edition]. Winston King. Encyclopedia of Religion. Ed. Lindsay Jones. Vol. 11. 2nd ed. Detroit: Macmillan Reference USA, 2005. p7692-7701.
8. Penguin Dictionary of Religions (1997) as quoted on "ReligionFacts".
9. Encyclopædia Britannica (2006) as quoted on "ReligionFacts".

Retrieved on 2007-03-17.

10. Religion Explained: The Evolutionary Origins of Religious Thought, Pascal Boyer, Basic Books (2001)

11. Quotation: "The Second Vatican Council affirmed academic freedom for natural science and other secular disciplines". From the essay of Ted Peters about Science and Religion at "Lindsay Jones (editor in chief). Encyclopedia of Religion, Second Edition. Thomson Gale. 2005. p.8185"

12. By Dr Paul Murdin, Lesley Murdin Photographs by Paul New. Supernovae Astronomy Murdin Published 1985, Cambridge UniversityPress Science,256 pages.

13. Godfrey-Smith, Peter. 2003. Theory and reality: an introduction to the philosophy of science. Science and its conceptual foundations. Chicago: University of Chicago Press.. Page 14.

14. Stanley Jaki. Bible and Science, Christendom Press, 1996 (pages 110-111)

15. Spitz, Lewis (1987). (The Rise of modern Europe) The protestant Reformation 1517-1559.. Harper Torchbooks, pp 383. ISBN 0-06-132069-2 The historian of early modern Europe Lewis Spitz says "To set up a 'warfare of science and theology' is an exercise in futility and a reflection of a nineteenth century materialism now happily transcended".

16. Quotation: "The conflict thesis, at least in its simple form, is now widely perceived as a wholly inadequate intellectual framework within which to construct a sensible and realistic historiography of Western science." (p. 7), from the essay by Colin A. Russell "The Conflict Thesis" on "Gary Ferngren (editor). Science & Religion: A Historical Introduction. Baltimore: Johns Hopkins University Press, 2002.

17. Gary Ferngren (editor). Science & Religion: A Historical Introduction. Baltimore: Johns Hopkins University Press, 2002. ISBN 0-8018-7038-0. (Introduction, p. ix)

18. a b Esslemont, J.E. (1980). Bahá'u'lláh and the New Era, 5th ed., Wilmette, Illinois, USA: Bahá'í Publishing Trust.

19. 'Abdu'l-Bahá [1912] (1982). The Promulgation of Universal Peace, Hardcover, Wilmette, Illinois, USA: Bahá'í Publishing Trust. ISBN 0-87743-172-8.

20. Effendi, Shoghi (1938). The World Order of Bahá'u'lláh. Wilmette, Illinois, USA: Bahá'í Publishing Trust. ISBN 0-87743-231-7.

21. Joseph Campbell, The Power of Myth, p. 22 ISBN 0-385-24774-5

22. Joseph Campbell, Thou Art That: Transforming Religious Metaphor. Ed. Eugene Kennedy. New World Library ISBN 1-57731-202-3.

23. Bartholomew Dean 1994 "The Poetics of Creation: Urarina Cosmology and Historical Consciousness." Latin American Indian Literatures Journal (10):22-45

24. Bryan Caplan. "Why Religious Beliefs Are Irrational, and Why Economists Should Care". The article about religion and irrationality.

25. Dawkins, Richard. The God Delusion.

26. Harris, Sam. THE END of FAITH.

27. Nobel Peace Laureate, Muslim and human rights activist Dr Shirin Ebadi has spoken out against undemocratic Islamic countries justifying "oppressive acts" in the name of Islam. Speaking at the Earth Dialogues 2006 conference in Brisbane, Dr Ebadi said her native Iran as well as Saudi Arabia, Kuwait and Yemen "among others" were guilty of human rights violations. "In these countries, Islamic rulers want to solve 21st century issues with laws belonging to 14 centuries ago," she said. "Their views of human rights are exactly the same as it was 1400 years ago."

REFERENCES

Saint Augustine; The Confessions of Saint Augustine (John K. Ryan translator); Image (1960).

Descartes, René; Meditations on First Philosophy; Bobbs-Merril (1960).

Barzilai, Gad; Law and Religion; The International Library of Essays in Law and Society; Ashgate (2007).

Durant, Will (& Ariel (uncredited)); Our Oriental Heritage; MJF Books (1997).

Durant, Will (& Ariel (uncredited)); Caesar and Christ; MJF Books (1994).

Durant, Will (& Ariel (uncredited)); The Age of Faith; Simon & Schuster (1980).

Marija Gimbutas 1989. The Language of the Goddess. Thames and Hudson New York

Gonick, Larry; The Cartoon History of the Universe; Doubleday, vol. 1 (1978), vol. II (1994)

Haisch, Bernard The God Theory: Universes, Zero-point Fields, and What's Behind It All – discussion of science vs. religion (Preface), Red Wheel/Weiser, 2006.

Lao Tzu; Tao Te Ching (Victor H. Mair translator); Bantam (1998).

Marx, Karl; "Introduction to A Contribution to the Critique of Hegel's Philosophy of Right", Deutsch-Französische Jahrbücher, (1844).

Saler, Benson; "Conceptualizing Religion: Immanent Anthropologists, Transcendent Natives, and Unbounded Categories" (1990).

The Holy Bible, King James Version; New American Library

(1974).

The Koran; Penguin (2000).

The Origin of Live & Death, African Creation Myths; Heinemann (1966).

Poems of Heaven and Hell from Ancient Mesopotamia; Penguin (1971).

The World Almanac (annual), World Almanac Books.

The Serotonin System and Spiritual Experiences - American Journal of Psychiatry 160:1965-1969, November 2003.

United States Constitution

Selected Work Marcus Tullius Cicero

The World Almanac (for numbers of adherents of various religions), 2005

Religion [First Edition]. Winston King. Encyclopedia of Religion. Ed. Lindsay Jones. Vol. 11. 2nd ed. Detroit: Macmillan Reference USA, 2005.

World Religions and Social Evolution of the Old World Oikumene Civilizations: A Cross-cultural Perspective by Andrey Korotayev, Lewiston, NY: Edwin Mellen Press, 2004.

On religion definition: The first major study: Durkheim, Emile (1976) The Elementary Forms of the Religious Life. London: George Allen & Unwin (in French 1912, English translation 1915).

Wilfred Cantwell Smith The Meaning and End of Religion (1962) notes that the concept of religion as an ideological community and system of doctrines, developed in the 15th and 16th centuries CE.

A distillation of the Western folk category of religion: Geertz, Clifford. 1993 [1966]. Religion as a cultural system. pp. 87-

125 in Clifford Geertz, The Interpretation of Cultures: Selected Essays. London: Fontana Press.

An operational definition: Wallace, Anthony F. C. 1966. Religion: An Anthropological View. New York: Random House. (p. 62-66)

A recent overview: A Scientific Definition of Religion. By Ph.D. James W. Dow

CHAPTER TWO

Philosophy of Religion

Philosophy of religion is a branch of philosophy that is concerned with the philosophical study of religion, including arguments over the nature and existence of God, religious language, miracles, prayer, the problem of evil, and the relationship between religion and other value-systems such as science and ethics, amongst others.

It is sometimes distinguished from religious philosophy, the philosophical thinking that is inspired and directed by religion, such as Christian Philosophy. Instead, philosophy of religion is the philosophical thinking about religion, which can be carried out dispassionately by a believer and non-believer alike.

Philosophy of religion as a part of metaphysics

Philosophy of religion has classically been regarded as a part of metaphysics. In Aristotle's, Metaphysics, he described first causes as one of the subjects of his investigation. For Aristotle, the first cause was the unmoved mover, which has been read as God, particularly when Aristotle's work became prevalent again in the Medieval West. This first cause argument later came to be called natural theology by rationalist philosophers of the seventeenth and eighteenth centuries. In Aristotle's Metaphysics he also states that the word that comes closest to describing the meaning of the word God is "Understanding".[citation needed] Today, philosophers have adopted the term philosophy of religion for the subject, and typically it is regarded as a separate field of specialization, though it is also still treated by some, particularly Catholic philosophers, as a part of metaphysics.

To understand the historical relationship between metaphysics and philosophy of religion, remember that the traditional objects of religious discussion have been very special sorts of entities (such as gods, angels, supernatural forces, and the like) and events, abilities, or processes (the creation of the universe, the ability to do or know anything, interaction between humans and gods, and so forth). Metaphysicians (and ontologists in particular) are characteristically interested in understanding what it is for something to exist—what it is for something to be an entity, event, ability, process, and so forth. Because many members of religious traditions believe in things that exist in profoundly different ways from more everyday things, objects of religious belief both raise special philosophical problems and, as extreme or limiting cases, invite us to clarify central metaphysical concepts.

However, the philosophy of religion has concerned itself with more than just metaphysical questions. In fact the subject has long involved important questions in areas such as epistemology, philosophy of language, philosophical logic, and moral philosophy. See also world view.

Questions asked in philosophy of religion

One way to understand the tasks at hand for philosophers of religion is to contrast them with theologians. Theologians sometimes consider the existence of God as axiomatic, or self-evident. Most theological treatises seek to justify or support religious claims by two primary epistemic means: rationalization or intuitive metaphors. A philosopher of religion examines and critiques the epistemological, logical, aesthetic and ethical foundations inherent in the claims of a religion. Whereas a theologian could elaborate metaphysically on the nature of God either rationally or experientially, a philosopher of religion is more interested in asking what may be knowable and opinable with regards to religions' claims.

A philosopher of religion does not ask "What is God?", for such is a complex question in that it assumes the existence of God and that God has a knowable nature. Instead, a philosopher of religion asks whether there are sound reasons to think that God does or does not exist.

Still, there are other questions studied in the philosophy of religion. For example: What, if anything, would give us good reason to believe that a miracle has occurred? What is the relationship between faith and reason? What is the relationship between morality and religion? What is the status of religious language? Does petitionary prayer (sometimes still called impetratory prayer) make sense?

What is God?

The question "What is God?" is sometimes also phrased as "What is the meaning of the word God?" Most philosophers expect some sort of definition as an answer to this question, but they are not content simply to describe the way the word is used: they want to know the essence of what it means to be God. Western philosophers typically concern themselves with the God of monotheistic religions (see the nature of God in Western theology), but discussions also concern themselves with other conceptions of the divine.[original research?]

Indeed, before attempting a definition of a term it is essential to know what sense of the term is to be defined. In this case, this is particularly important because there are a number of widely different senses of the word 'God.' So before we try to answer the question "What is God?" by giving a definition, first we must get clear on which conception of God we are trying to define. Since this article is on "philosophy of religion" it is important to keep to the canon of this area of philosophy. For whatever reasons, the Western, monotheistic conception of God (discussed below) has been the primary source of investigation in philosophy of religion. (One likely reason as to why the Western conception of God is dominant in the canon of philosophy of religion is that philosophy of religion is primarily an area of analytic philosophy, which is primarily Western.) Among those people who believe in supernatural beings, some believe there is just one God (monotheism; see also monotheistic religion), while others, such as Hindus, believe in many different deities (polytheism; see also polytheistic religion) while maintaining that all are manifestations of one God. Hindus also have a widely followed monistic philosophy that can be said to be neither monotheistic nor polytheistic (see Advaita Vedanta). Since Buddhism tends to deal less with metaphysics and more with ontological (see Ontology) questions, Buddhists generally do not believe in the existence of a creator God similar to that of the Abrahamic religions, but direct attention to a state called Nirvana (See also Mu).

Within these two broad categories (monotheism and polytheism) there is a wide variety of possible beliefs, although there are relatively few popular ways of believing. For example, among the monotheists there have been those who believe that the one God is like a watchmaker who wound up the universe and now does not intervene in the universe at all; this view is deism. By contrast, the view that God continues to be active in the universe is called theism. (Note that 'theism' is here used as a narrow and rather technical term, not as a broader term as it is below. For full discussion of these distinct meanings, refer to the article Theism.)

Monotheistic definitions

Monotheism is the view that only one God exists (as opposed to multiple gods). In Western (Christian) thought,

God is traditionally described as a being that possesses at least three necessary properties: omniscience (all-knowing), omnipotence (all-powerful), and omnibenevolence (supremely good). In other words, God knows everything, has the power to do anything, and is perfectly good. Many other properties (e.g., omnipresence) have been alleged to be necessary properties of a god; however, these are the three most uncontroversial and dominant in Christian tradition. By contrast, Monism is the view that all is of one essential essence, substance or energy. Monistic theism, a variant of both monism and monotheism, views God as both immanent and transcendent. Both are dominant themes in Hinduism.

Even once the word "God" is defined in a monotheistic sense, there are still many difficult questions to be asked about what this means. For example, what does it mean for something to be created? How can something be "all-powerful"?

Polytheistic definitions

The distinguishing characteristic of polytheism is its belief in more than one god(dess). There can be as few as two (such as a classical Western understanding of Zoroastrian dualism) or an innumerably large amount, as in Hinduism (as the Western world perceives it). There are many varieties of polytheism; they all accept that many gods exist, but differ in their responses to that belief. Henotheists for example, worship only one of the many gods, either because it is held to be more powerful or worthy of worship than the others (some pseudo-Christian sects take this view of the Trinity, holding that only God the Father should be worshipped, Jesus and the Holy Spirit being distinct and lesser gods), or because it is associated with their own group, culture, state, etc. (ancient Judaism is sometimes interpreted in this way). The distinction isn't a clear one, of course, as most people consider their own culture superior to others, and this will also apply to their culture's God. Kathenotheists have similar beliefs, but worship a different god at different times or places. In Kali Yukam all gets unified into Ayya Vaikundar for destroying the Kaliyan.

Pantheistic definitions

Pantheists assert that God is itself the natural universe. The most famous Western pantheist is Baruch Spinoza, though the precise characterization of his particular set of views is complex and is often cited as one of the most internally consistent philosophical systems.

Panentheism holds that the physical universe is part of God, but that God is more than this. While pantheism can be summed up by "God is the world and the world is God", panentheism can be summed up as "The world is in God and God is in the world, but God is more than the world and is not synonymous with the world". However, this might be a result of a misinterpretation of what is meant by world in pantheism, as many pantheists use "universe" rather than "world" and point out the utter vastness of the universe and how much of it (temporal causality, alternate dimensions, superstring theory) remains unknown to humanity. By expressing pantheism in this way and including such elements, rather than limiting it to this particular planet, and specifically limiting it to human experience, the theory is somewhat nearer to the view of panentheists while still maintaining the distinct characteristics of pantheism.[original research?]

Rationality of belief

Positions

The second question, "Do we have any good reason to think that God does (or does not) exist?", is equally important in the philosophy of religion. There are five main positions with regard to the existence of God that one might take:

Theism - the belief in the existence of one or more divinities or deities.

Pantheism - the belief that God is both immanent and transcendent; God is one and all is God.

Deism - the belief that God does exist, but does not interfere with human life and the laws of the universe.

Agnosticism - the belief that the existence or non-existence of deities is currently unknown or unknowable, or that the existence of a God or of gods cannot be proven.

Atheism - the rejection of belief, or absence of belief, in deities.

It is important to note that some of these positions are not mutually exclusive. For example, agnostic theists choose to believe God exists while asserting that knowledge of God's existence is inherently unknowable. Similarly, agnostic atheists lack belief in God or choose to believe God does not exist while also asserting that knowledge of God's existence is inherently unknowable.

Natural theology

The attempt to provide proofs or arguments for the existence of God is one aspect of what is known as natural theology or the natural theistic project. This strand of Natural theology attempts to justify belief in God by independent grounds. There is plenty of philosophical literature on faith (especially fideism) and other subjects generally considered to be outside the realm of natural theology. However, throughout much of philosophy of religion is the assumption of natural theology (i.e., that the existence of God can be justified or otherwise proven on rational grounds from observations about the universe). There has been considerable philosophical and theological debate about the kinds of proofs, justifications and arguments that are appropriate for this discourse.[2]

The philosopher Alvin Plantinga has shifted his focus to justifying belief in God (that is, those who believe in God, for whatever reasons, are rational in doing so) through reformed epistemology, in the context of a theory of warrant and proper function.

Hinduism, Judaism, Christianity, and Islam have all developed religious world views based on, or incorporating, philosophical investigation. There are separate entries on Hindu philosophy, Jewish philosophy, Christian philosophy, and Islamic philosophy.

Major philosophers of religion

Abhinavagupta
Adi Shankara
Avicenna
Ramanuja
Madhva
Marilyn McCord Adams
Robert Adams
William Alston
Anselm of Canterbury
Averroes (also known as Ibn Rushd)
Thomas Aquinas
Augustine of Hippo
Anicius Manlius Severinus Boethius
Giordano Bruno
Joseph Butler
Samuel Clarke
Anne Conway
William Lane Craig
René Descartes
Pseudo-Dionysius
Herman Dooyeweerd

Mircea Eliade
Desiderius Erasmus
Siddartha Gautama
Al Ghazali
Yehuda Halevi
Charles Hartshorne
Heraclitus
John Hick
David Hume
Peter van Inwagen
Allama Iqbal
William James
Immanuel Kant
Søren Kierkegaard
Nishida Kitaro
Ruhollah Khomeini
Nishitani Keiji
Harold Kushner
C. S. Lewis
Gottfried Leibniz
Knud Ejler Løgstrup
J. L. Mackie
Maimonides
Nicolas Malebranche
Jean-Luc Marion
Michael Martin
Herbert McCabe
Alister E. McGrath
Thomas V. Morris
Nagarjuna
Milarepa
Dogen Zenji
Friedrich Nietzsche
William of Ockham
Rudolph Otto
William Paley

Blaise Pascal
D. Z. Phillips
Philo of Alexandria
Alvin Plantinga
Plotinus
Sarvepalli Radhakrishnan
Bertrand Russell
Duns Scotus
Ninian Smart
Abdolkarim Soroush
Baruch Spinoza
Melville Y. Stewart
Richard Swinburne
Denys Turner
Peter Vardy
Vasubandhu
Keith Ward
William Whewell
Nicholas Wolterstorff
Ramakrishna
Vivekananda
René Guénon
Frithjof Schuon
Seyyed Hossein Nasr
F.W.J. Schelling
Paul Tillich
Gordon Clark
Ahmad Rafique
Dr. Zakir Naik

REFERENCES

1. Evans, C. Stephen (1985). Philosophy of Religion: Thinking about Faith. InterVarsity Press, page 16. ISBN 0877843430.

^ see eg Antony Flew, John Polkinghorne, Keith Ward and Richard Swinburne

CHAPTER THREE

Religion Culture in India Accessories Worn by Indian Women

India, the land of spirituality and philosophy considers religion as an integral part of its entire tradition. The worship of various religions and its rituals play a significant role in every aspect of human life in the country.

India is the birthplace of two great religions of the world, namely, Hinduism and Buddhism. It is also the birthplace of one of the oldest religions of the world, Zoroastrianism, and home to an ancient religion, Jainism. Sikhism is another very recognizable religion which began here bringing together the best aspects of Hinduism and Islam. Followers of religions originated in other countries such as Islam, Christianity, Bahaism and Judaism also form a part of the population of secular nation, India.

Hinduism is the dominant faith. According to 2001 Census, 80.5% of the population of the country are designated 'Hindu'. It is one of the ancient religions in the world, which began about 6000 years ago. Besides Hindus, Muslims are the most prominent religious group and are an integral part of Indian society. There are approximately13.4% Muslims (over 100 million), 2.3% Christians (over 20 million), 1.9 %

Sikhs (18 million) and others including Buddhists (6 million), Jains, Parsis (Zoroastrians), Jews, and Bahais, less than 2 percent.

Hindus and Muslims are spread throughout the country. Muslims are found mostly in the states of Uttar Pradesh, Bihar, Maharashtra, West Bengal, Andhra Pradesh, and Kerala. They represent a majority in Jammu and Kashmir and Lakshadweep. Christian concentrations are found in the northeastern states like Nagaland, Mizoram and Meghalaya and the southern states of Kerala, Tamil Nadu, and Goa. Sikhs are a majority in the state of Punjab whereas Buddhists are found in large numbers in Arunachal Pradesh, Ladakh, Bengal and Sikkim. Though a tiny minority, Jains are found all over India. Majority of Jains live in the states of Maharashtra, Rajasthan, Karnataka and Gujarat

Religion Culture India

India is the birthplace of many of the world's religions. Hinduism, Buddhism, Jainism and Sikhism, originated in India. India also has many places of worship and holy sites of Islam, Christianity and the Jewish faith. Religions such Zoroastrianism and the Bahai also have places of worship in India, a land where people of different religions and cultures are free to live in harmony. When in India, you can travel to the holy cities of the different religions and cultures of India. You can witness the celebrations of various festivals in India, where people of different faiths come together in communal harmony.

The message of love and brotherhood is expressed by all the religions and cultures of India. Whether it's the rows of the faithful, bowing in prayer in the courtyard of a mosque, or the rows of lamps that light up houses at Diwali, the good cheer of Christmas or the bonhomie of Baisakhi, the festivals of India are celebrations of shared emotion that bring people together. People from the different religions and cultures of India, unite in a common chord of brotherhood and amity in this fascinating and diverse land. India Profile brings you a complete picture of the Religions and Cultures in India.

Dotting the Line – Accessories Worn by Indian Women

A woman needs no reason to adorn herself but Indian tradition makes it easy for her by giving her some compulsive ones.

Since aeons a woman is known to adorn herself with as many accessories as she could physically manage to carry. If there were bells on her toes, there were rings on her fingers and belts on her waist not to mention the necklaces around her neck. In India there are texts that describe her many adornments in details and even the many ways in which she should make herself up.

No feminist movement has been able to wipe away this penchant for adornment, more so because all of them are couched in beliefs of prosperity and happiness. They are symbols of a secure future.

The most eloquent example of this are the symbols that identify a married woman from the unmarried. A married woman would never he caught without these accessories. She believes the happiness and life of her marriage is embodied in them

You must have seen many women wear the bindi or the dot on the forehead. There are many reasons attributed to why a woman should wear a bindi. Some say its place between the eyes on the forehead is a spirtitual centre, the colour of which is red.

To awaken it and nourish it, a woman wears the red dot on her forehead. Tantrics say that it is the spot by concentrating on which a person can be easily hypnotized.

So a woman wears it as a security against Tantrics.

Extending the argument further is the feeling that when there is a bindi on the forehead, the intensity with which anybody can gaze into the person's eye is reduced. The bindi is believed to distract attention and so it is believed that women will not be hoodwinked by any man.

There are yet others who say that to keep a woman's amorous feelings heightened in a society that is restraining on her, she wears the red mark on her forehead and along the parting of her hair.

If that is one way of looking as it, jewellery designers say in those days when women and men wore a lot of jewellery, women wore a piece on the parting of their hair. This piece fell on to the forehead either as a big pearl or a beautifully designed pendant. When women stopped wearing this piece of jewellery, they started wearing the bindi.

It is for these reasons that a bindi got inextricably involved with the marital status of a woman. Today, however, most urban women have not heard of any such explanations. They wear it as an ornament and it comes in different colours and shapes.

All you have to do is to sick it on to your forehead. In earlier times it was a powder in varying shades of red, one of the main components of which was turmeric powder. Turmeric powder is considered very auspicious and so once again it is associated with fertility, prosperity and good omens.

In South India, the bindi is worn even before marriage, but for an older woman it signifies her marital status. In some northern states and in Bengal, the sindoor is worn all along the parting of the hair. Only a married woman wears it this way. In fact her husband is supposed to fill the parting with sindoor (vermilion) and thus marry her.

Another symbol common to women across the country is the mangal sutra also called the thali. Different communities have fashioned specific chains worn for the first time by a woman at the time of her marriage and she is never to take it off as long as her husband lives.

There are some communities that perform special prayers to the chain while wearing it around their necks. No wonder then that women want this chain to be thick, with large quantities of gold, for ornamentation apart, its strength will, they believe be in direct proportion to the strength of their marriage.

In South India, two chains are worn. One is a golden one and the other a thick thread coated with turmeric. Both of them have a thali woven into them. The thali is a rectangular piece that bears the cast mark. The shape of the thali may, however, change from community to community. In Maharashtra, women wear black beads around their neck as symbols of marriage.

In the western state of Bengal, a red Bengal with gold work and a white bangle made form conch shell are worn together as a sign of marriage. In Rajasthan ivory bangles signify martial status.

In many parts of the country, toe rings are also a sign of a happily married woman. Toe rings are made of silver and gold and they are worn on the first toe. If you catch the vain woman you may see it on all her toes. In a tribe in Arunachal Pradesh, huge anklets of bamboo rings in bright colours used to be worn around women's ankles to signify that they were married.

In another tribe, tattoos signified the marital status of women. In a tribe in central India, the sari itself was worn in a different manner after marriage. This is true even in Tamil Nadu where before marriage the style of draping the sari changed and for this style nine yards were required.

Today, in urban India thalis are worn for decoration rather than sentimental reasons while in rural India, they are being embedded with diamonds purely for sentimental reasons. Toe rings are the ethnic in-things and come in fascinating shapes, sizes and designs, Bindis, ofcourse are in infinite number of colours and there are even some little blocks with the help of which you can stamp a very complicated design on your forehead!

Saraswati - Goddess of Learning and Wisdom

The original concept of Saraswati was that of a feminine water deity. Over a period of time, this riverine goddess came to be associated with all coursing and flowing energies and forces. Today, Saraswati is hailed as the patron goddess for the thought process and all creative arts.

The Hindu religion or Sanatana Dharama, as it is called, recognizes a Supreme Godhead (Paramatma) who is omniscient, omnipresent and omnipotent. This supreme being performs three essential functions of creation (shrishti), sustenance (samrakshana) and annihilation (samhara) in relation to this universe and beyond. In his personalized manifestation, this Godhead assumes the triple forms of Brahma, the Lord of Creation, Vishnu or Narayana, the Lord of sustenance and Rudra or Shiva, the Lord of Annihilation. These three entities comprise the Trimurtis or the Holy Hindu Trinity. Each of these three gods has been associated with a consort or female aspect who provides the requisite support and energy to the respective Godhead in the discharge of his ordained functions. The Vedas which are the most ancient of the Hindu religious scriptures, postulate that Goddess Saraswati is the consort of Creator God Brahma.

The word Saraswati is of Sanskritic origin and etymologically, it denotes a person or being of the feminine gender. This name has different connotations which, in the final analysis, are all related with water bodies such as stream and river (sarit) and lake and pool (saras). In a figurative manner, all things that are fluid or free-flowing in nature have had their associations with Saraswati.

References to a river bearing the name Saraswati could be found in the Vedas and other Hindu scriptures of yore. The Rig Veda says that the River Saraswati originated in the Himalayas, flowed westwards and joined the Arabian Sea. At Prayag—modern day Allahabad—in Uttar Pradesh, the rivers Ganga and Yamuna are believed to be joined by a third river called Saraswati, which is invisible. Hindu faithfuls take the name of Saraswati, in addition to the Ganga and Yamuna, while they take a dip in any river held sacred by them. Thus, it can be inferred that the name Saraswati in itself has a purificatory significance.

As per Vedic lore, Goddess Saraswati manifested herself from the mouth-or tongue to be precise—of Lord Brahma. Having been bewitched by her beauty and grace, and impressed by her divine attributes, the Creator God decreed that Saraswati should become his consort and provide him assistance in his task of creation. Since Brahma was responsible for the creation of Saraswati, he was by logic her father. His act of marrying Goddess Saraswati was, therefore, regarded as a transgression of accepted norms of behavior and so Vishnu and Shiva uttered a curse that henceforth Brahma would cease to be worshipped as a God by faithfuls. Even to this day, this curse seems to be holding true since there are only a few temples dedicated exclusively to Brahma, whereas there are hundreds of thousands of temples and shrines dedicated to Vishnu and Shiva. In this background, Goddess Saraswati traditionally has come to be worshipped in her individual capacity as the patron goddess for all knowledge and wisdom without her being associated with Brahma. Idols of Goddess Saraswati are installed in temples and shrines dedicated to her exclusively or sometimes find a place with other gods and goddesses of the Hindu pantheon in Vishnu, Devi and Shiva temples. Such temples are more in number in the southern and eastern parts of the country.

In the states of Tamil Nadu, Karnataka, Andhra Pradesh, Kerala, Rajasthan, West Bengal, Madhya Pradesh, Uttar Pradesh and the union territory of Pondicherry skilled craftsmen have been making beautiful icons of Saraswati since generations. Around the festival of Durga Puja in October, innumerable craftsmen move out from West Bengal to different parts of the country and display their artistry in making clay images of Saraswati and other deities that are ceremonially installed in the pavilions erected for the celebrations.

Saraswati worship spread during the medieval period from the Indian sub-continent to many south and east Asian countries. Several references to the Goddess can be evidenced in the local traditions and literature of those countries. Even sculptures and graphic representations of Saraswati have been identified in some of those countries, notably in Sri Lanka, Thailand, Cambodia and Indonesia. Hinduism apart, Buddhism and Jainism have also accorded an honoured place to Saraswati. In modern times, wherever Indians have gone, they have carried the Saraswati lore and erected shrines for her worship.

The term Saraswati, besides referring to the goddess also stands as an appellation to the names of sanyasis (religious pontiffs or recluses) of the Advaitic (non-dual) religio-philosophic order. A sect of Hindu Brahmans in the western and northern parts of India go by the name of Saraswat Brahmans. Eminent poets and litterateurs are addressed as Bharatis by virtue of their scholarship, literary accomplishments or poetical ability which are all deemed to be the gifts of the goddess. A state level award instituted for the recognition of excellence in literature, fine arts and writing goes by the name Saraswati Samman. Trophies given to scholars, eminent artistes and craftsmen sometimes have the Saraswati motif or connotation. All in all, Saraswati dominates the entire scholastic, literary, cultural and aesthetic domains.

In the field of Indian classical music, the Carnatic system has accorded due importance to Goddess Saraswati who is the patron deity for music and dance. Innumerable musical compositions dedicated to the goddess can be identified in both Hindustani and Carnatic systems of music. Saraswati Vandana or invocation of the goddess forms an essential part of dance recitals.

Saraswati is generally depicted in sculptures, icons and graphic representations either as seated on an ornate pedestal or standing on a fully blossomed white lotus. She is shown wearing a jeweled crown over her head and bedecked with resplendent pearl ornaments. Her face is said to resemble the full moon with a smile on it. She is fair complexioned and possesses four arms signifying her divine attributes. Her raiment is of white silk. She holds a stringed instrument, the veena, diagonally across her chest. In another arm she holds a palm leaf manuscript—the book of knowledge. Her fourth arm displays a rosary. The goddess radiates feminine beauty, grace and beatitude. Seen near her feet it the white swan which is her mount. In some depictions, instead of the swan, the colourful Indian peacock is shown standing at her feet. Likewise, in some pictorial representations, Saraswati is shown holding a pitcher containing holy water instead of a rosary. These symbols have been explained in esoteric texts as possessing philosophical connotations. The lotus, white swan, pearls and pitcher symbolize association of Saraswati with water. The colour white which predominates her personage alludes to purity, tranquility and equanimity. The manuscript held in her arm is symbolic of knowledge and intellectual excellence.

For the traditional worship of Saraswati elaborate rituals, supported by Vedic incantations, have been prescribed. While these are observed even today, the average householder installs an image, icon or pictorial reproduction of the goddess in a corner of his home and performs the rituals. Generally he recites verses in Sanskrit or in his own mother tongue, makes votive offerings and circumambulating it before the icon. He prays for the atonement of sins and then shares the votive offerings with members of his family. On festive occasions more elaborate worship is done and numerous delicacies are prepared by the housewife. The fare offered and blessed by the deity is partaken of as prasadam (benedictory meal).

Saraswati worship is done round the year. But certain specified periods of the Hindu calendar are regarded as especially propitious for her worship. Basant Panchami which is the fifth day of the fortnight following the new moon occurring during spring (basant), generally in the month of March or late February, is observed as the day dedicated to the goddess. On this day young men and women dressed in yellow attire and adorned with flower garlands congregate and sing verses in praise of the goddess' consecrated idol. The best part of the day is spent in music and dance and exchange of greetings. In West Bengal, the Nobel laureate, Rabindranath Tagore had organized such celebrations at Shantiniketan near Calcutta. The tradition started by him continues to this day. Wherever there are large concentrations of people of Bengali origin, there is bound to be a Basant Panchami celebration. Various cultural and entertainment programmes and competitions of skill are organized on this occasion, which sustain the interest of the young and old alike.

The other occasion on which ritualistic worship of Goddess Saraswati is done is during October every year coinciding with the first 10 days of the fortnight following the new moon (Sharad Ritu) in the autumnal month of Aswina of the Hindu lunar calendar. These 10 days are called Dussehra. In the southern part of India this period is denoted by term Navratri (nine nights) and the tenth day is called Vijaya Dashami (victorious tenth day). From the sixth day (Shashti) to the ninth day (Maha Navami) Saraswati is worshipped. In fact, the ninth day is termed as Saraswati Puja day in south India. On this day students are enjoined to worship the Goddess of Learning and seek her blessings for success in their educational pursuits. Factories and workshops are spruced up and the tools of production are worshipped since Saraswati Puja day is also the ayudha (implements) puja day. Prasadam made to the deity and tools are partaken by the management and staff.

In West Bengal, Saraswati Puja forms part of the Durga Puja celebration. Saraswati in the Bengali tradition is regarded as the daughter of the Mother Goddess Durga or Parvati, the consort of Lord Shiva. In Durga Puja, images of Durga and her children – Lakshmi, Saraswati, Ganesha and Kartik – are installed in the specially built pavilions and celebrations go on for four days, ending with the immersion of the images in the sea of river. Durga Puja is the most important festival for the Bengalis world over and it is not only a religious festival but also an occasion for promotion of fine arts, culture and universal brotherhood.

Goddess Parvati - Feminine Power

Of Goddesses, one stands above all: Parvati. In certain texts she is even called the Goddess of Wealth, Lakshmi, and the Goddess of Learning, Saraswati, in addition to being idolized as the Goddess of power.

The daughter of the snowclad mountains. The consort of Shiva. The one who is incarnation of all energy, she is A Parvati, also called Uma, Gauri, Durga, Kali and so on.

As a deity Parvati has the unique distinction of being thought of as the only goddess. All other goddesses are referred to as incarnations or manifestations of Parvati. As a woman Parvati has the distinction of one who had the most devoted husband and as a form of energy, Parvati, also called Shakti, is the embodiment of the total energy in the universe. As a mother, Parvati is looked upon as the mother, Parvati is looked upon as the mother of all creation; the Mother Goddess.

She, Sati, Parvati, Gauri is the consort of the magnificent Shiva. She, Kali, is also the consort of Time, as Shiva himself is the embodiment of time in his form as Mahakal.

For a deity with such a profile, Parvati is rather unassuming. Of course as Durga or Kali she is portrayed as ferocious, but therein too lies a story painted in the live colours of the indignation of the wronged.

A long, long time ago, Brahma created a beautiful maiden called Sati who was born to a king called Daksha. Siva married her. Years of conjugal bliss followed. One day, however, Sati heard that a major religious function was being celebrated in her father's house. She was a little upset that her parents had not invited her or her husband. After tossing and turning in bed for many a night, one morning she decided she would go even if she were uninvited.

After all it was only to her father's house, Siva, however, cautioned her. He did not want her to go uninvited. Sati thought a while, but eventually left because she just wanted to go to her parents. There, as Siva had predicted, Sati was insulted. She jumped into the sacred fire burning for the ceremony for she could not bear to go back and tell her husband her parents had insulted her.

Siva was enraged. He was deeply grieved. He just could not bear the loss. As he carried her body across the country, different parts of her body are believed to have fallen off in many places and even today these places are sacred in Hindu mythology.

The Gods were, however, anguished. Siva had been mourning too long and his grief and wrath was almost harming the people. So Sati was reincarnated as Parvati and born to the King of the Himalayas, Himavat.

As Parvati grew into a young woman, her subconscious guided her towards penance. She had to reunite with Siva. Years and years of penance finally brought Siva before her one day, just for a second. Parvati was only more besotten afterwards. Very soon afterwards, Siva came to Parvati in the guise of an old man and asked why a beautiful woman such as her should waste her time dreaming of a man who wore leopard skin and smeared his body with ashes. Surely there are more handsome men in the world!

Was Parvati offended! She blew up the old man for saying such things about her beloved. Her objection convinced Siva of her love for him and he showed her his true form.

A happy marriage lasted many years, and guess where the problem came when it did? Siva and Parvati were playing around when Siva called her, "Kali, Kali". Now Kali means black and Parvati was very dark complexioned. Brahma had in fact made a deliberate decision to make her so because he did not want the world to know that Sati was being reincarnated. Now Parvati was deeply offended that her husband should think of the colour of her skin to hail her with. He could have called her any number of endearing words instead.

So she told him that she was going. That she would not meet him again till she was fair complexioned. Bewildered Siva was left ruing his tongue while Parvati went into the forests to do severe penance.

Another thousand years of penance, and Brahma appeared before Parvati. She asked for golden coloured skin. Brahma granted her the boon. Thereon Parvati came to be called Gauri or the one with skin the colour of gold.

Of Durga and her ferocious form, the story is told as this:

Once upon a time there was a demon called Mahishasura. He was troubling the people on earth. No God could subdue him. All the gods came together and their energies together formed the goddess called Durga. The Gods then empowered her with their weapons which epitomized their strength. Thus armed and blessed, Durga went to tackle Mahishasura. She vanquished him and thereupon came to be called Mahishasura mardini or the killer of Mahisha the demon.

This month, all over India, Dusshera is being celebrated. Dusshera celebrates this story of how Durga conquered Mahishasura. In the eastern part of the country, Dusshera is called Durga puja or praying to Durga.

Janni Shikar - When the Women Go to War

Every 12 years, the women of Chota Nagpur sharpen their weapons, dress in male attire and set out on a hunt. Thought the exact origins of the tradition are unknown, the many legends point to this festival symbolizing the quality of men and women.

Like the Mahakumbh, Janni shikar, a festival of tribal women of Chhota Nagpur region in Bihar, is celebrated every 12 years. Also known as Era Sendra, the celebrations of this festival continue for a month during the months of March and April. The literal meaning of Janni Shikar is, hunt by women.

Much before the actual period of the festival, the women start sharpening their weapons and getting the male clothing together. On the first day of the month long festival, they set out from their homes in male attire, with their weapons in the hand and hunt for cocks, goats, pigs etc. and cook them at night for their meal.

There is no precise evidence to indicate exactly how this festival originated. A number of different legends have grown around this festival due to lack of sufficient research and non-availability of literature on the subject and it is difficult to pinpoint the one authentic legend with any degree of certainty. We talked to many elderly tribesmen of both Munda and Oraon origin and were able to separate three significant historical legends which are most likely to explain the origins of the festival.

According to one, this festival commemorates an event which occurred in ancient times. The Munda tribesmen believe that when they were in the Indus valley near Mohenjo-daro, they were attacked by the Aryans. When the womenfolk saw their men beating a hasty retreat, they donned male attire, took weapons in their hands and successfully drove away the Aryan invaders. The tribal women celebrate their victory as Janni Shikar.

The Oraons, however, trace this event to the battle of Rohtas, a district in western Bihar. In medieval times they were invaded by Turks who forced them to take shelter in what is today Chhota Nagpur. But the women of the tribe had a significant part to play in the legendary battle.

The menfolk were either drunk, tired or simply not available at the time. So the women took up the challenge, changed into male attire, fought the invaders and repulsed them. The day reminds the tribal women that they are not inferior to the men and can give good account of themselves in an activity considered exclusive to men.

The close cultural, historical and geographical links of the Mundas and the Oraons with the region of ancient

Kalinga (present Orissa) also leads to the speculation that the Janni Shikar may have some connection with the bloody Kalinga war, fought between Ashoka and the Kalinga kingdom. This battle, it may be recalled took a heavy toll of male soldiers and when Kalinga was on the brink of defeat, the women come to the fore, took arms and were ready for the battle. It is possible that Janni Shikar is celebrated to commemorate this event.

Whatever be the legend behind this festival, it has now become the most important festival of the tribal women. As it is celebrated after a gap of 12 years, the women wait for it with great eagerness. During the festival one can see hordes of tribal women, many of them from neighbouring villages, in male dress with traditional tribal weapons in their hands, looking for small animals. By convention, each family must send at least one member for the shikar, else they will be fined by the elders collectively.

Some of the elders in the tribe feel that today the ritual hunting has been perverted in many ways. While tradition strictly prohibits men from joining in the hunt, young men are seen to accompany the women. As in some Hindu festivals, the participants have now started collecting money from passing vehicles. There are also accusations that the women hunters are often scantily dressed.

There are many instances in Indian history where heroines like Chand Bibi and Rani Laxmi Bai have led men to fight against their foes. Janni Shikar celebrates a communal effort and symbolizes the equality of men and women.

CHAPTER FOUR

Women and Religion: General Comparative Interfaith Views

Information on women and religion: either general information across faith lines, comparing views in several faiths, or looking at women with an interfaith perspective.

A British religious thinker addresses the 1893 Parliament of the World's Religions on the subject of unity beneath religions.

"The Unvarnished Truth About Religion, Christianity and Spirituality in 2008"

Seven great myths of organized religion: A closer look

Over the centuries, billions of people have fallen prey to religion run amok. How many Jews and Gypsies suffered in Nazi concentration camps while churches in Germany turned their heads? How many people were murdered in the Crusades during the middle ages—in the name of God?

Some religious leaders seem to tell us that we're not smart enough or good enough to discover God on our own. Who says?

If God is good and perfect, why is there so much evil and suffering in the world?

How can anyone rely on the Bible for answers, if it's just a loose translation of ancient myths anyway?

How can we trust a religion that has advocated slavery and the subjugation of women throughout history?

These are serious questions-hot potatoes that nobody wants to touch. So I wrote a 7-day course called "The Seven Great Lies of Organized Religion."

In this course we're going to dissect the most common lies – and illuminate the fault line that separates genuine spirituality from empty religious dogma.

To sign up, just fill in the spaces and click on the button. I promise not to spam you—that only creates hard feelings anyway—and you can un-subscribe at any time.

The course starts today, and the first installment will show up in your email box within the next few minutes.

How to Convert to Islam and Become a Muslim

The word "Muslim" means one who submits to the will of God, regardless of their race, nationality or ethnic background. Becoming a Muslim is a simple and easy process that requires no pre-requisites. One may convert alone in privacy, or he/she may do so in the presence of others.

If anyone has a real desire to be a Muslim and has full conviction and strong belief that Islam is the true religion of God, then, all one needs to do is pronounce the "Shahada", the testimony of faith, without further delay. The "Shahada" is the first and most important of the five pillars of Islam.

With the pronunciation of this testimony, or "Shahada", with sincere belief and conviction, one enters the fold of Islam.

Upon entering the fold of Islam purely for the Pleasure of God, all of one's previous sins are forgiven, and one starts a new life of piety and righteousness. The Prophet said to a person who had placed the condition upon the Prophet in accepting Islam that God would forgive his sins:

"Do you not know that accepting Islam destroys all sins which come before it?" (Saheeh Muslim)

When one accepts Islam, they in essence repent from the ways and beliefs of their previous life. One need not be overburdened by sins committed before their acceptance. The person's record is clean, and it is as if he was just born from his mother's womb. One should try as much as possible to keep his records clean and strive to do as many good deeds as possible.

The Holy Quran and Hadeeth (prophetic sayings) both stress the importance of following Islam. God states:

"...The only religion in the sight of God is Islam..." (Quran 3:19)

In another verse of the Holy Quran, God states:

"If anyone desires a religion other than Islam, never will it be accepted of him; and in the Hereafter, he will be in the ranks of those who have lost (their selves in the Hellfire)." (Quran 3:85)

In another saying, Muhammad, the Prophet of God, said:

"Whoever testifies that there in none worthy of being worshipped but God, Who has no partner, and that Muhammad is His slave and Prophet, and that Jesus is the Slave of God, His Prophet, and His word[1] which He bestowed in Mary and a spirit created from Him; and that Paradise (Heaven) is true, and that the Hellfire is true, God will eventually admit him into Paradise, according to his deeds." (Saheeh Al-Bukhari)

The Prophet of God, may the blessing and mercy of

God be upon him, also reported:

"Indeed God has forbidden to reside eternally in Hell the person who says: "I testify that none has the right to worship except Allah (God),' seeking thereby the Face of God." (Saheeh Al-Bukhari)

The Declaration of the Testimony (Shahada)

To convert to Islam and become a Muslim a person needs to pronounce the below testimony with conviction and understanding its meaning:

I testify "La ilah illa Allah, Muhammad rasoolu Allah."

The translation of which is:

"I testify that there is no true god (deity) but God (Allah), and that Muhammad is a Messenger (Prophet) of God."

To hear it click here or click on "Live Help" above for assistance by chat.

When someone pronounces the testimony with conviction, then he/she has become a Muslim. It can be done alone, but it is much better to be done with an adviser through the "Live Help" at top, so we may help you in pronouncing it right and to provide you with important resources for new Muslims.

The first part of the testimony consists of the most important truth that God revealed to mankind: that there is nothing divine or worthy of being worshipped except for Almighty God. God states in the Holy Quran:

"We did not send the Messenger before you without revealing to him: 'none has the right to be worshipped except I, therefore worship Me.'" (Quran 21:25)

This conveys that all forms of worship, whether it be

praying, fasting, invoking, seeking refuge in, and offering an animal as sacrifice, must be directed to God and to God alone. Directing any form of worship to other than God (whether it be an angel, a messenger, Jesus, Muhammad, a saint, an idol, the sun, the moon, a tree) is seen as a contradiction to the fundamental message of Islam, and it is an unforgivable sin unless it is repented from before one dies. All forms of worship must be directed to God only.

Worship means the performance of deeds and sayings that please God, things which He commanded or encouraged to be performed, either by direct textual proof or by analogy. Thus, worship is not restricted to the implementation of the five pillars of Islam, but also includes every aspect of life. Providing food for one's family, and saying something pleasant to cheer a person up are also considered acts of worship, if such is done with the intention of pleasing God. This means that, to be accepted, all acts of worship must be carried out sincerely for the Sake of God alone.

The second part of the testimony means that Prophet Muhammad is the servant and chosen messenger of God. This implies that one obeys and follows the commands of the Prophet. One must believe in what he has said, practice his teachings and avoid what he has forbidden. One must therefore worship God only according to his teaching alone, for all the teachings of the Prophet were in fact revelations and inspirations conveyed to him by God.

One must try to mold their lives and character and emulate the Prophet, as he was a living example for humans to follow. God says:

"And indeed you are upon a high standard of moral character." (Quran 68:4)

God also said:

"And in deed you have a good and upright example

in the Messenger of God, for those who hope in the meeting of God and the Hereafter, and mentions God much." (Quran 33:21)

He was sent in order to practically implement the Quran, in his saying, deeds, legislation as well as all other facets of life. Aisha, the wife of the Prophet, when asked about the character of the Prophet, replied:

"His character was that of the Quran." (As-Suyooti)

To truly adhere to the second part of the Shahada is to follow his example in all walks of life. God says:

"Say (O Muhammad to mankind): 'If you (really) love God, then follow me.'" (Quran 3:31)

It also means that Muhammad is the Final Prophet and Messenger of God, and that no (true) Prophet can come after him.

"Muhammad is not the father of any man among you but he is the Messenger of God and the last (end) of the Prophets and God is Ever All-Aware of everything." (Quran 33:40)

All who claim to be prophets or receive revelation after Muhammad are imposters, and to acknowledge them would be tantamount to disbelief.

We welcome you to Islam, congratulate you for your decision, and will try to help you in any way we can.

The Bible says, "God so loved the world that He gave His one and only Son, that whoever believes in Him shall not perish, but have eternal life"

The problem is that . . .

2. All of us have done, said or thought things that are wrong. This is called sin, and our sins have separated us from God.

The Bible says "All have sinned and fall short of the glory of God." God is perfect and holy, and our sins separate us from God forever. The Bible says "The wages of sin is death."

The good news is that, about 2,000 years ago,

3. God sent His only Son Jesus Christ to die for our sins.

Jesus is the Son of God. He lived a sinless life and then died on the cross to pay the penalty for our sins. "God demonstrates His own love for us in that while we were yet sinners Christ died for us."

Jesus rose from the dead and now He lives in heaven with God His Father. He offers us the gift of eternal life – of living forever with Him in heaven if we accept Him as our Lord and Savior. Jesus said "I am the way, the truth, and the life. No one comes to the Father except by Me."

God reaches out in love to you and wants you to be His child. "As many as received Him, to them He gave the right to become children of God, even to those who believe on His name." You can choose to ask Jesus Christ to forgive your sins and come in to your life as your Lord and Savior.

4. If you want to accept Christ as Savior and turn from your sins, you can ask Him to be your Savior and Lord by praying a prayer like this:

"Lord Jesus, I believe you are the Son of God. Thank you for dying on the cross for my sins. Please forgive my sins and give me the gift of eternal life. I ask you in to my life and heart to be my Lord and Savior. I want to serve you always."

Women and religion in Bangladesh: new paths

Islam's rising public profile in Bangladesh also offers

opportunities for young urban women to make more of their own lives, finds a research project headed by Firdous Azim.

In south Asia as elsewhere in the world, religion has come to play an increasing role in shaping and reshaping women's lives. This process is a particular challenge to people like myself, a feminist who "grew up" intellectually and politically via involvement in the women's movement of the 1980s in Bangladesh. The activism of that period was explicitly secular; its main priorities were the issues of rights, inequalities and violence prevalent in a young state which had achieved independence only in 1971.

Firdous Azim is professor in the department of English and the humanities at BRAC University, Dhaka, BangladeshAt that time, the idea of religion - specifically, in Bangladesh, Islam - as a site in which women might find or exercise "empowerment" was unthinkable to us. A generation later, however, the whole area of religion - the application of its foundational beliefs, its public presence, its social and cultural practices - has acquired different meanings. The new ways that women are engaging with these aspects of religion form the basis of a research project I and my colleagues are conducting, as part of the international "pathways to women's empowerment" initiative. This article describes how the focus of our work is evolving to take account of the growing influence of religion in women's lives.

A generation's journey

Also in open Democracy:

Andrea Cornwall, "Pathways to women's empowerment" (27 July 2007)

Srilatha Batliwala, "Putting power back into empowerment" (27 July 2007)

Mulki Al-Sharmani, "Egypt's family courts: route to empowerment?" (7 September 2007)

Cecilia Sardenberg, "The right to abortion: briefing from Brazil" (26 October 2007)

These articles are part of a collaboration between openDemocracy and the research consortium Pathways of Women's Empowerment, project of the Institute of Development Studies, University of Sussex.

This explores ideas, projects and initiatives from around the world - Brazil to Egypt, Sierra Leone to Bangladesh - which aims to understand what enables women to empower themselves and sustain changes in gendered power relationsMany women from secular or only mildly religious backgrounds have - in Bangladesh as elsewhere - viewed Islam very often as a regressive force. Today, however, such views are challenged by the undoubted influence of modernising tendencies in Islam. The projection of a new, public face via numerous television channels dedicated to Islam is but one example. This face is often more militant, assertive, and dominating than in earlier generations; but this too is where its modernity lies.

The impact of such trends on women is striking. In the women's movement of the 1980s, religion was seen as a personal issue: a private segment of a traditional way of life, and nothing to do with the "movement". In many ways, the modernising currents of Islam create the potential for women to move into the emerging public space - but within an Islamic framework. The result is a connection between the private and the public that did not exist before.

When we sought to develop a women's movement in the 1980s, our main themes were grounded in a certain idea of the "woman" our efforts were dedicated to nurturing: she was the citizen of a newly independent country, where the tools of citizenship could be used to establish her identity, her rights, her social and political position. That kind of women's movement had a real and important effect in many countries, Bangladesh included; when it was combined with the energies of NGOs and development agencies - especially those focused on women's empowerment (and specifically women's economic emancipation) - the results were dynamic. Together, the partnership between local, national and international strands coalesced into the worldwide movement of women that culminated in the Beijing conference of 1995.

Today, the architects of the 1980s movement remain feminists, but we are addressing a different set of issues - and a different "woman". After all, a generation has passed since those pioneering days. The questions of citizenship, rights, identity and social and political place with which we began have either been transformed or are understood very differently from twenty or thirty years ago. The women who set out on this journey have also changed along the way.

A matter of practice

In light of these considerations, and in seeking to identify the influences on the "new" women around us, our research team felt that religion - particularly Islam - needed to be understood through a fresh set of lenses. In making this choice, however, we were torn between two ways that religion "works". The first is in relation to the wider cultural sphere: how religion addresses women, gives women certain rights, separates women along communal lines (which lends force to the great effort of the women's movement in breaking down these religious dividing-lines and talking about women as citizens). The second is in relation to women's own experience: how they are taking on religious roles for themselves, such as starting classes to study the Qur'an (which suggests the need for researchers to be more actively involved in studying women's religious practice).

The choice of the second path has led us in our research to try to understand religion as everyday, active experience - something that women live and engage with, rather than as doctrine or politics. In Bangladesh, after all, religion is not doctrinal or dogmatic. When Islam entered this region, no one could read Arabic; the first preachers didn't recite the Qur'an, they took up the stories, the myths, and the religious beliefs that were already here and mixed them up with the stories of Islam to preach a religion and an ideology of equality in and liberation from a caste-divided society.

Also in open Democracy about women in Bangladesh:

Naila Kabeer, "The cost of good intentions: 'solidarity' in Bangladesh" (23 June 2004)

Farida Khan, "Getting real about globalisation in Bangladesh" (14 April 2004)

Santi Rozario, "The dark side of micro-credit" (10 December 2007)

In the focus-group discussions that have resulted from this approach, we have talked about women's identification as Muslims, but we have also brought in other issues such as attitudes towards sex and marriage, and then looked at how religion influences our ideas and behaviour. We have yet to do a systematic analysis of the findings from this research, but initial anecdotal evidence suggests that women negotiate their relationship with religion in a very fluid, creative manner. Islam is often used in a practical way, as "the religion for us and what we need to do"; when it is not needed it is ignored, and other factors are allowed to come into play. Islam, however, does play a crucial role in the way women negotiate their personal lives and as such is of both strategic and real importance in their lives.

The heart of change

This research is urban-based, as we're looking at young urban women to provide us with a picture of change and transformation. The activity and public role of these women are key: they are working women and young students who embody and illuminate issues of sexuality, marriage and paid employment (rather than motherhood, children and housework). The challenge for us is to "read" these discussions in a way that brings out the empowering factors in young women's testimonies, to look at how they are reframing the cultural contours that surround them.

These women's negotiation of the new spaces that religion has created can be empowering, but the nature of these spaces remains defined by patriarchy. This element is not being contested or denied; rather, what women seem to be doing is negotiating for greater rights within patriarchal structures.

The research group's focus on urban women has a particular relevance in today's Bangladesh. This is a country where ideas of women's empowerment have almost always been seen in relation to rural women. But there is increasing movement from rural to urban areas, and this is just one aspect of a society where migration is becoming the defining principle. In this increasingly dynamic and fluid society, the most fertile spaces are urban slums - which are often, quite literally, here today and gone tomorrow. A generation of women has grown up and then moved out of them, to be replaced by new arrivals. These energetic, mobile, and unsettled spaces are also the environment where where new female identities - including those which use religion in creative and practical ways - are being formed.

What makes change happen in women's lives?

Photo/Sheikh Rajibul Islam

Pathways of Women's Empowerment is a DFID funded

research and communications programme which will link with academics, activists and practitioners to find out what works to enhance women's empowerment. We want to identify where women are achieving real gains and discover the positive and negative factors which have influenced their journey.

Our aim is to make these pathways of change visible and to build on them to inspire a radical shift in policy and practice. By involving policy actors and practitioners directly in our research and learning, we hope our work will be in itself a catalyst for change.

Latest

Representations of Women in Popular Culture - Upcoming Workshop

On Wednesday 30 July, the West Africa Hub will be holding a reflection workshop with popular artistes in Accra, Ghana. Participants will include various sections of the music industry as well as the listening public who will come together to reflect on the content of song lyrics and what impact they may have on the representation of women...see more details on the events page.

International Day for Sharing Life Stories

Photo/Gary Edwards

On Friday 16 May, Pathways of Women's Empowerment joined with the Centre for Life History and Life Writing Research at the University of Sussex to celebrate the inaugural annual International Day for Sharing Life Stories. The event showcased the life history work being done at the University and invited people to find out more about telling their lives in a variety of ways.

Parallel events to share and gather life stories took place in Africa, Australia, Europe, India and in North and

South America. More than 200 individuals and organisations, including the British Oral History Society and Studs Terkel, have endorsed the establishment of the International Day for Sharing Life Stories. See Sussex University Bulletin and Centre for Life History and Life Writing Research.

Women Treading the Corridors of Corporate Power

Globalisation is transforming the lives of women workers. Large numbers of women are being drawn into waged employment in global production, often in poor working conditions. Women are an increasingly important consumer force. Yet women's perspectives and voices rarely inform the commercial processes that shape the global economy. Stephanie Barrientos' research for the Global Hub looks at examples of where women's concerns have been given some voice in mainstream commercial corridors of power. See Global Hub Research.

Ghana Photography Workshop

From the 25-27 April 2008, the Ghana Team held a workshop where they learnt photography and video techniques, facilitated by Tessa Lewin, the RPC Communications and Learning Officer and Anna Kari and Guilhem Alandry of Documentography. See the West Africa Hub project news page for images and outputs from this meeting.

Also see http://www.pathwaysghana.blogspot.com/ for more images and news from the West Africa Hub.

Changing Narratives of Sexuality

Members of the Changing Narratives of Sexuality Theme used the opportunity of the Sexuality and the Development Industry workshop to get together at IDS from 7-9 April for an update and planning session on the theme. We used the chance to interview some of the researchers on their projects

- listen to the podcasts on the Changing Narratives Theme page.

Sexuality and the Development Industry

Pathways of Women's Empowerment jointly convened a workshop, together with the IDS Sexuality and Development Programme, on Sexuality and the Development Industry from 3-5 April 2008. Around 70 participants met to examine how sexuality is framed and influenced by international aid and the development industry and to look for more creative and constructive means of engagement.

See IDS Webpage, Siyanda Discussion Board and the IDS Sexuality and Development Programme webpage

The cost of good intentions: 'solidarity' in Bangladesh

Naila Kabeer

How can the lives and conditions of women garment workers in Bangladesh be improved? Naila Kabeer questions whether the workers themselves benefit from the campaigning approach of Anita Roddick and the National Labor Committee.24 - 06 - 2004

Anita Roddick writes on openDemocracy with passionate anger about the conditions of women workers in the export garment sector based on testimonies of workers she met on her visit to Bangladesh. Her account is supported by the United States-based National Labor Committee (NLC) which has been active in the country on this issue.

Farida Khan, citing the World Bank country director in Bangladesh, offers a different perspective on the garment industry's importance in the national economy and to Bangladeshi workers, one that partly counters Anita Roddick's and the NLC's views.

Naila Kabeer is responding to three openDemocracy

articles:

Anita Roddick, "If shirts could speak and 'we the people' would listen" (April 2004)

Farida Khan, "Getting real about globalisation in Bangladesh" (April 2004)

National Labor Committee, "Defending Bangladeshi workers: a response to Farida Khan" (May 2004)

I have been engaged in research on different aspects of gender equality in Bangladesh, including the economic, for many years now; I have been particularly interested in how women themselves view their choices and life options. In contributing to this discussion, I will emphasise the issues that seem to me to be especially important in assessing the experience of women garment workers in Bangladesh, and where the best possibilities for improvement in their conditions might lie.

Bangladesh in transformation

Bangladesh, like much of south Asia, has always been a strongly patriarchal country. There are strict restrictions on women's ability to participate in the public domain - whether to earn an income, attend school, or take part in politics. It remains one of the world's poorer countries, classified by the United Nations as among its forty-eight least-developed economies.

However, Bangladesh is also undergoing major social transformation. Poverty has been declining slowly but consistently over the past decade. The country moved, after several years of military dictatorship, to a fragile democracy in 1990. There have also been important positive changes in the area of gender equality, something which would not have been possible if Islamic fundamentalists had the kind of presence that Farida Khan suggests.

In this period, successive governments have played an active role in improving girls' educational prospects. The gender gap in education has been eliminated at primary level and reduced at secondary level. A very active NGO sector, working largely with women from poorer households, has promoted self-employment opportunities for women in the countryside through the provision of microcredit, as well as greater awareness of their rights.

There has been a high voter turnout by women at recent national and local elections - between 75% and 85% - and increasing numbers of women are standing as candidates in local elections.

Poverty remains a major problem in Bangladesh and many people still go hungry. No amount of effort by NGOs can solve the problem of unemployment in a country where, despite declining rates of population growth, there are a million new entrants to the labour force each year.

Women from poorer households who need paid work in order to survive face particular problems. Returns to women's enterprise are low and social barriers to women's participation in paid work outside the home remain strong, particularly in rural areas. Those women who do find wage work earn wages far below those of men.

It is in this context that the million or so jobs generated for women by the export-oriented garment industry have to be assessed. As Farida Khan points out, the participation of women in factory work is a relatively new phenomenon in a country where women were almost invisible in public space. In the Bangladeshi context, this is not a "novelty": it is a social revolution. Nor is it necessary to have any illusions about employers' motivations in "preferring" female labour in a globally competitive industry to appreciate what these jobs have meant to women workers in Bangladesh.

Thus, Farida Khan's contribution, though it portrays

a picture of Bangladesh which underestimates the possibilities for change, at least balances a recognition of the exploitative aspects of work in the garment industry with attention to its more positive implications. By contrast, Anita Roddick's article does not.

Between slavery and freedom

The anger that impels Anita Roddick makes it clear that she draws from Bangladeshis' experience the view that garment workers there are treated little better than "slaves". She relates stories of workers being kicked and beaten, locked up by police at employers' instigation, and roped together by their legs like cattle. Whether these are routine or exceptional incidents in the industry – and my own view is that they are not typical – they are indeed shocking and should be acted upon. The courts in Bangladesh work slowly and imperfectly, but they can and should be made to work in the interests of justice.

But in making this point, we should also remember that these women are not "slaves" – however terrible their situation may appear to Anita Roddick. They are a group of workers who are exploited by their employers because of their social vulnerability and their limited choices, but they have exercised considerable strength of will and independent agency in making their way to these jobs.

Most of them have migrated from the countryside, often on their own, explicitly in search of garment employment. It is true that they are partly "pushed" into this sector by the lack of employment opportunities in the countryside and the low wages they are able to earn there. But they are also "pulled" into the industry by what they view as its more positive characteristics: regularity of income, and at higher levels than women with equivalent levels of education can earn in other sectors.

Moreover, it is difficult to reconcile the unrelentingly harsh portrait painted by Anita Roddick with some of the evidence from research on garment workers. Consultations with urban poor households carried out by one of the largest NGOs in Bangladesh found that, of all the formal institutions that they had contact with, the poor identified the garment industry (alongside NGOs themselves) as the most positive.

More micro-level research, including my own, suggests that women have many complaints about their jobs in the garment industry – but there is also much that they value. These jobs have allowed them an opportunity to earn their own living, to get out of the house, to exercise some independent purchasing power, to postpone marriage or marry someone of their own choice, to save and send money back to their families at home. Above all, these women value the opportunity these jobs provide to be economically self-reliant, rather than a burden on their families.

The contradictions of activism

Anita Roddick and the NLC miss these significant dimensions of women garment workers' experience. The campaigning proposals that flow from their selective approach are equally problematic.

They pledge to engage in an international campaign to "name and shame" those multinational companies that do business with Bangladeshi employers who do not respect women workers' rights. Farida Khan, while rightly emphasising the importance of guaranteeing international mobility of labour and increased access of Bangladeshi products to international markets as ways of improving conditions in the country, also suggests that campaigners might focus instead on the buying houses that deal directly with the employers.

But these are the same companies and the same buying

houses that have been reducing the prices they offer local employers – often at the same time as they pressurise them to improve labour standards. "Naming and shaming" may indeed galvanise multinationals into action, but what will that action be? Offer higher prices per unit so that employers can pay for maternity leave – the "win-win" outcome? Deal only with those employers who can afford to pay for maternity leave and let the rest go out of business? Or simply move to a location where living standards and working conditions meet the requirements of global campaigners?

It is important to ask: why do women workers not themselves organise to protest against what they consider to be the unacceptable aspects of their working conditions? The brutal tactics used by some of the employers that Anita Roddick describes are only part of the story. More important is their fear of losing their jobs when they know that there are many thousands of women ready to replace them.

What workers need is to know that it is possible to protest without the fear of immediate dismissal. There is a law to that effect in Bangladesh but it is observed mainly in the breach. Yet this is a fundamental precondition for the right to organise. I would suggest that if the goal is to improve women's capacity to speak for and organise themselves, then high-profile campaigns targeting individual companies are not the best way to achieve it.

International solidarity would have more positive and lasting effects if it were focused on providing human rights and other organisations in Bangladesh with the support and resources they need to publicise workers' rights and to take employers to court when these rights are violated.

I have no doubt that Anita Roddick and the National Labor Committee have the interests of Bangladeshi women workers at heart. But good intentions implemented without due regard for their likely outcomes carry the danger of doing more harm than good to those they seek to benefit.

Bangladesh Homeworkers Women Association (BHWA) is an NGO working with women homebased workers in the country since 1986 towards improving their socio-economic status. Our activities encompass all aspects of developmental work related to women homeworkers in our country. Along with our fight for worker rights issues, we also work towards increased awareness and financial independence for women homeworkers in collaboration with like-minded international agencies (Home Net South Asia, UNIFEM etc.)

Ms. Dilruba Anguri, General Secretary, BHWA, has been working in this sector for a long time. A homeworker is the first to arise in the morning and the last to go to sleep at night. During the day, she has to finish all the duties involved in running a household as well as do other homebased work that will give her some additional income. A home worker's contribution to the social and economic development of the nation cannot be overlooked. Her hard work is not given due recognition and value. Homeworkers are a neglected group in Bangladesh.

Many organizations including the ITGLWF and its member trade union organizations have been supporting us in our effort towards getting due recognition for the homeworker by requesting the government to include homebased women workers in it's new *Labour Code* and adopt a *National Policy* (based on the *ILO Homework Convention* 1996) on home based workers to ensure better justice and representation to their cause. Unfortunately, government support and recognition has not been forthcoming in spite of the immense potential of this sector in terms of export earnings.

Homeworkers are a neglected group in Bangladesh. BHWA has repeatedly presented statistics to show that though individual homeworker contributions might be negligible, the vast numbers of homeworkers make the total contribution to the national economy quite substantial.

Given the poor financial and economic status of the majority population in our country, women are increasingly looking towards some alternate source of income to supplement the wages that the male earning member brings in. However, they cannot afford to overlook their primary responsibility of managing the household and the children. So, working from home provides them with the best of both worlds, allowing them to utilize their skills to earn money and keep an eye on the household at the same time. They can also allocate time to all the duties at their convenience. Creating various handicrafts from a wide range of raw materials available locally, these hard working women also need to look for appropriate outlets for their products. Whatever they earn from their work is very often instrumental in giving their children a better education than they had or for family medical expenses. Thus their children will hopefully be physically and mentally better equipped to improve their living standards.

In the current economic scenario, globalization has meant that many big business houses and factories have been shut down because they were unable to cope with the various difficulties arising from globalization. BHWA firmly believes that their motto, *"My Home, My Workplace"* is an idea that will help combat the future labour and economic problems faced by the country. If the government can equip and fund every home as a workplace, then unemployment caused by closure of factories can be dealt with effectively. And, as a result, the country's economic downslide can be prevented

Vision

The vision of Steps Towards Development is a democratic society that: provides equal opportunities and benefits to men and women; is characterized by good governance, justice and respect for women's human rights; eliminates discrimination and patriarchy; is educated and poverty free, and preserves social and human values.

Mission

Steps's mission is to enhance gender equality, to improve the condition and position of women, to protect the human rights of women and girls, and to increase women's participation in decision-making and governance at all levels.

Values and Priciples

Steps Towards Development wants to be an institution and a nationwide platform that builds up capacity to promote and respect gender equality and women's human rights, and that sets an example through its basic values and principles in the organisation: justice, transparency and accountability, linking and learning, equality and equity, trust mutual respect, shared vision.

Objectives

- Increase in women's participation in decision-making and governance

  The promotion and protection of women's human rights - Increase birth registration and marriage registration - Reduce early marriage and combat violence against women

- Increase responsiveness of urban and rural governance (Community Service Delivery Institutions/ committees)§ Increase gender sensitive development organization§ Steps continues to develop as equitable, action and outcome-oriented organization that is strategic, coordinated, sustainable and evidence-based.

Domains of Intervention

- Network development and support to local initiatives for women's rights.
- Training and capacity building of support groups
- Institutionalization of gender equality and women's human rights
- Advocacy and campaign
- Research and documentation, print and audio-visual materials Organizational development of Steps

History

In 1993, a group of social activists went to work on an initiative, inspired by the belief that the gender inequalities prevalent in this country could only be addressed by working together. That initiative led to the establishment of Steps Towards Development (Steps). With its formation, Steps developed its organisational set-up. The following year, SIDA accepted to finance a project that allowed Steps, among others, to develop an audio-visual unit. The project provided basic video facilities and the collection of still photographs on specific issues. That same year, 1994, Steps Towards Development was officially registered at the NGO BNureau of the Government of Bangladesh. Over the next three years, Steps strengthened the organisation. It created a Central Management Team which was the decision making body of the organisation. In 1997, Steps developed its Human Resource Policy manual, and Account Management manual.

During this first phase of the organisation, Steps worked at developing its Network, Training and Materials Development components. Steps started to network with NGOs at the local level and to develop and disseminate different types of information materials. Training modules and Bengali IEC materials on gender were produced in both print and multi-media forms. Through training, Steps created Local Trainer Groups and identified Social Entrepreneurs, the National Trainers Core Group and Gender Change Activists. Meanwhile the Audio-Visual component continued to move ahead. It managed to broadcast a monthly production on television, and received awards for documentaries: "Rokeya," at the first international video festival in Bangladesh (1998), and "Black House," as the best documentary award at the International Film Festival in Iran (2001).

In addition, Steps developed a book describing the existing gender policies in Bangladesh, and a resource manual on gender trainers in Bangladesh. With these feats, Steps gained recognition in both the local and national levels. Steps Towards Development has created the image as a gender-promoting organisation.

Steps Towards Development continues to develop as an equitable, action and outcome-oriented organisation that is strategic, coordinated, sustainable and evidence-based.

By 2003, as Steps entered its second phase, the Materials Development component became two separate components: Gender and Development Communication Component (GDCC) and Gender and Development Resource Component (GDRC). This came about in response to the expanding responsibilities of Steps as a gender organisation. In 2004, the components were renamed Centres, in a move towards the autonomy of each. The Organisational Development component, which used to be with the office of the Director, was renamed Advocacy and Research Centre. Meanwhile the Finance and Administration team provides technical support on staff and finance related matters. Steps Towards Development is now a well-established NGO with competent staff and good office facilities. A General Body rules the organisation and is composed of representatives from civil society and stakeholders. From the GB, a 7 - member Executive

Committee is elected, which is the final policy and decision-making body. At the operations level, there is the Core Management Team, composed of the Executive Director, five directors and two three consultants. The CMT is the planning, monitoring and decision-making body for all programme related issues. Presently, Steps Towards Development has 54 staff, 31 of which are males, and 23 are females.

Steps Towards Development continues to develop as an equitable actiion and outcome-oriented organisation that is strategic, coordinated sustainable and evidence-based.

Firdous Azim

CHAPTER FIVE

Women's Liberation

Over the past three decades of second-wave feminism, particular kinds of feminist mainstream have come into being, emanating, in the main, from Britain. France, and America. The last decade has produced a number of criti-ques of this hegemonic feminism issuing from groups of women who, for a variety of reasons, have found themselves marginalised even in this movement which purports to deal with and attempt to change women', oppression everywhere. As Hazel Carby puts it, anonymity and the tendency to generalize into meaninglessness, the oppression of an amorphous category called 'Third World women', are symptomatic of the ways in which the specificity of our experiences and oppression are subsumed under inapplicable concepts and theories.'

In 1985 the British feminists Michele carrett and Mary McIntosh published an article dealing with the unacknowledged ethnocentrism within the white women's movement.' In a later issue, Caroline Ramazanoglu argued that it was not simply a matter of ethnocentrism, 'but of a crushing, institutionalized racism'.' Increasingly, there has grown an awareness within all areas of the women's movement t hat we too are not free of the tendency to universalize and thereby to construct an exclusionary norm. As women within the left-wing movement had to [earn, an emancipatory politics does not in itself necessarily and inevitably serve their particular needs. The women's movement has tended to treat race and class as subservient in ways that the left-wing movement saw gender as being of secondary importance.

Within Australia, the specific needs of Aboriginal women have only recently surfaced and, in the first reading, Jackie Huggins takes up the point that in its current constitution, the Australian women's movement is irrelevant to Aboriginal women since white women are still unable to confront their own racism. That particular painful battle is finally on the feminist agenda in Australia as it IS in Britain and America. Huggins continues that white women have also not concentrated on the specific effects of sexism as regards black women. She also emphasizes the fact that class differences must be kept in mind since Aborigines in general are economically discriminated against within the workforce. One dis-turbing element she identifies is the increasing incidence of black male chauvinism, which has eroded Aboriginal women's traditional rights and powers within their own communities.

Diane Bell starts from the proposition that only certain privileged whites are in a position to delineate the niceties of whether class, or race, or gender are of primary significance. Bell carefully differentiates the position from which these categories are defined for white feminists and for Aboriginal women. Her central contention is that these terms arc not necessarily as separate as they may appear and that for Aboriginal women racism too is gendered. She then focuses on the different experience of Aboriginal women's so-called separatism. It is necessary to view this in the larger context of Aboriginal society where the equal but different relationships between the sexes prevails. Whereas white feminists are concerned with infiltrating dominant male power structures. Aboriginal women have always maintained their separate spheres. She goes on to summarize points made by black women activists concerning the differences between black and white women's experiences. She cites Roberta Sykes' thesis that, in a way not recognized by white women, Australian culture was predicated on the rape of black women and that their struggle centres on the right to say no to sex at a time when white feminists were to some degree fighting for the right to attain a certain kind of sexual initiative. The black activist Pat O'Shane's emphasis has been on the primary need for Aboriginal women to co-operate with Aboriginal men to combat racism in general, similar to Higgins' point in the previous reading. Marcia Langton argues that black women, from their different experiences, 'mock and satirize' white women, but that their strategy is not yet coherent.

Bell herself makes the point that Aboriginal women's traditional strategy of retreat *Uiliml)* differs in several important respects from a variety of such moves by white women. These differences need to be understood so that Aboriginal women are not excluded from current important decisions being made between blacks and whites here in Australia. Because Aboriginal women's sexuality is not intertwined with their economic status, *jilimi* does not constitute a retreat from hetero-sexuality in ways that are associated with a radical feminist position. Women-only groups have always posed a threat in (le past when men are denied sexual access to women, as in the medieval nunneries, and this has been compounded when the women also enjoyed economic indepen-dence, as did the *beguines.* Bell argues that, unlike white separatists, Aboriginal women do not operate with the notion of battlelines between the sexes and that their emphasis is rather on dialogue: between men and women on the one hand, and with white women on the other. *As* well, the paper examines the responsibility white' feminists have to engage with issues relating to Aboriginal women and to cross-cultural women III general.

In the third reading, Bell Hooks (Glona Watkins) contends

that rather than pretend t hat I here is no conflict among women, we need lawai k through racism in order to move beyond it. She identifies the model for sisterhood created by white women as one based on shared victimizat ion and that such a model did not encourage the visibility of class and race as analytical categories as well as excluding the concept of women's strength and strategies of resistance. It encouraged women not to confront their own sexism as displayed in violence against other women. She points out, furthermore, that the women's movement is not owned by white women to the extent that they can decide whether and when to invite other women to participate and on what terms. After the recogni-tion that racism exists, the next step is to transform it by actively translating culture-specific codes of behaviour across all groups. Only this, in conjunction with the redistribution of wealth, will transform society.

Black Women and Women's Liberation

Black women have yet to see even their menfolk attain positions of power and influence in the mainstream culture. It is understandable then, that in terms of priorities, black women seek to raise the life chances of the whole group. They view disadvantages of race and class before disadvantages of sex.'

This paper focuses on the women's liberation movement and its proven irrelevance to Aboriginal women, the role of Aboriginal women and men with a strong theme of women's 'independence' prevailing, and the multitude of social problems faced by Aborigines. I argue that Abori-ginal men and women both are fighting for the same things, regardless of gender differences. The overall scenario is that, in such a deprived and oppressed culture, it would seem ludicrous to suggest that either sex could be a victor.

Although the women's liberation movement was first activated in the 1960s from such movements as the anti-war and civil rights groups in America, the contemporary women's movement has a' much longer history. It dates back to at least the nineteenth century with struggles over universal suffrage, the exploitation of women's labour, unionization of women, and the temperance movements. However, several black American critics insist that blacks are always left to fight their own battles: 'Women's Liberation won't be any different. White women won the right to vote but black people, including black women, didn't get it for another hundred years. ,2 There is also a commonly voiced suspicion that the women's liberation movement has 'attached' itself to the black movement in order to take advantage, for its own interests, of the momentum and attention that the blacks have recently achieved.

Historically, the women's liberation movement in Australia began some-eighteen years ago and, in that time, it has developed a size and diversity which has made it a nebulous and rather elusive body, with feminists having had different priorities in their agendas for change. These divergences have led also to different tactics and strategies, and to competing ideologies and world views.

As the movement grew, some feminists saw that class and race differ-ences meant that women experienced different forms and degrees of oppression. However, if the white women who organized the contem-porary movement towards feminism were at all aware of racial Policies in Australian history, they would have known that overcoming barrier\ that separate women from one another would entail confronting the reality of racism; not just racism as a general evil in society, but the race hatred they might harbour in their own psyches. Despite the predomin-ance of patriarchal rule in Australian society, Australia was colonized on a racially imperialistic base and not on a sexually imperialistic base. No degree of patriarchal bonding between white male colonizers and Abori-ginal men overshadowed white racial imperialism.' In fact, white racial imperialism granted to all white women, however victimized by sexist oppression, the right to assume the role of oppressor in relationship to black women and black men.

White liberation leaders are also fond of pointing to the analogy between blacks and women as second-class citizens in a white, male chauvinist society. One of the clearest points of similarity between the situation of blacks and women is that they have both been brainwashed into the same 'low self-image'; they are not supposed to use their minds, they are incapable of making decisions. They are both second-class members of the society who should be kept in their place.

If white women in the women's movement needed to make use of a black experience to emphasize women's oppression, it would only seem logical that they focus on the black female experience - but they have not. Had white women desired to bond with black women on the basis of common oppression, they could have done so by demonstrating an awareness of the impact of sexism on the status of black women. Unfor-tunately, despite all the rhetoric about sisterhood and bonding, white women are not sincerely committed to bonding with black women to fight sexism. They are primarily interested in drawing attention to the oppression they consider they experience as white upper- or middle-class women.

The further notion that all women as a sex have more in common than do members of the same class is false. Upper-class women are not simply bed mates of their wealthy husbands. As a rule, they have more compell-ing ties that bind them together. They are economic, social, and political bedmates united in defence of private property, profiteering, militarism, racism - and the exploitation of other women. It would be quite another matter to expect any large number of wealthy women to endorse or support a revolutionary struggle which threatened their capitalist interests and privileges. Will the wives of bankers, generals, corporation lawyers, and big industrialists be firmer allies of women fighting for liberation than working-class men, black and white, who are fighting for theirs'."

The ruling powers breed and benefit from all forms of discrimination and oppression. Therefore, for a middle-class white woman to compare her environmental situation with that of a black is totally naive. While white women are fighting to get out of the kitchen, black women are fighting to get into it.

For these reasons, many black women do not see the women's move-ment as relevant to their own situation. Black women, who have worked from necessity are apt to view women's liberation as a white middle-class battle irrelevant to their own, often bitter, struggle for survival. As Ida Lewis commented: 'The women's liberation movement is basically a family quarrel between white women and white men." Similarly, Abori-ginal women are aware of the divisiveness of feminism in terms of their own black movement. Women's liberation has meant very little to both black American women and Aboriginal women who believe that the black woman has always been placed in a position of asserting herself.

The patriarchal nature of contemporary society means that Aboriginal women were subject to further specific oppression by both Aboriginal and white men. They have been typecast as capable only of roles and deserving only of treatment deemed unworthy or undesirable for that more highly valued, rarer 'commodity' - the white woman. Male dominance was, and is, a major ingredient in the culture Europeans brought with them to Australia. The message came through to Abori-gines, directly or indirectly, in words and deeds, in almost all their contacts with Europeans.

Black women have never been interested in being jockeyed into the position of fighting their own men. Women must support their every effort for equality and to emerge as a valuable force in this society: it is a time for uniting, not dividing. 'We should stand behind our men, not against them' is a popular militant battle-cry. There are, none the less, black women who question just how far behind that is. The black militants' idea of a submissive female, walking silently five paces to the rear, is a little more than many independent black women can stomach. Black men today are not necessarily innocent of the chauvinist attitudes charged against white men by white women's liberationists. Black male chauvinism is creeping into Aboriginal society, particularly with the advent of more visible and vocal Aboriginal and Islander women's groups. When once Aboriginal women were encouraged to enter the workforce, they are now being pulled down by their own black males. Pat O'Shane exemplifies this: 'It's not easy being a black woman at the top of a white bureaucracy. The hardest part has been dealing with chauvinist males (mostly black) who are threatened by a woman having this much power. Black men may perhaps be more inclined to be comfortable with men in power rather than women. Today, black men, as well as white men, are finding an assertive woman a threat.

In some ways Aboriginal women have suffered less trauma than their menfolk. It is often observed in culture-contact situations that the men of the culture that is disrupted by a more dominant culture have in a sense further to fall and, hence, suffer a worse shock and dislocation ill terms of identity than the women. The men had controlled the society, had been the chief sacred and political figures. Now I hey found men of an alien culture controlling the parameters of their existence. Women were accustomed to taking direction ill some areas, and could transfer autonomy less painfully. Their roles in the family did at least continue, even if carried out under drastically changed circumstances, which gave their lives greater continuity.

Today, women's status has been changing, their prestige and opportunities increasing more rapidly than men's. Aboriginal women have continued important work-roles. But, of course, to add to the disadvantage of sex and class, black women carried the additional burden of racism. Women have been prominent as workers, office-bearers, and spokespersons in Aboriginal lobby groups and pressure groups arousing public awareness of Aboriginal needs. Women have also participated in the various state and Commonwealth consultative bodies, II along with many men.

Black liberation for men and women seems a more important goal to many black women than women's liberation. What is holding black men back is the same thing that holds back their black mates: the white power structure. In other words, the main oppressor is a class society.

For instance, the occupational distribution of Australian males shows that Aborigines are virtually absent from the white-collar world. Only 2 per cent of Aboriginal males occupy the top seven occupation groups, which ye the most responsible, least onerous physically, and best rewarded materially, compared with 35 per cent of non-Aboriginal workers. A large percentage of the Aboriginal workforce is locked into the least rewarded and least promising occupational spheres, and experienced in jobs with little or no transfer value to dynamic parts of the economy. Aborigines are not only highly concentrated in the poorest-paid jobs, in some areas they monopolize them.

Aborigines have also been easy to ignore till now because they have been geographical, political, and social outcasts. They are non-European, with few technologically useful skills; they are often unemployed; they suffer from malnutrition and sickness to such a degree that, by the age of forty, many are unemployable; they figure prominently in crime statistics and have a low reputation in the larger society.

The position of black Australians compared with white Australians is daily eroding, in relative- and absolute terms - relative because the life-chances for the white majority improve at a faster rate, and absolute because the rate of population growth is much higher among black

Australians: any change in the position of Aborigines, for better or worse, affects a continuously. expanding population. While the formal legal and political barriers to full citizenship have been removed, the barriers that remain are social; the legacy of generations of training in dependency, poverty, and isolation from the mainstream of the national life. In a highly urbanized nation, Aborigines are the least urban element, in a rich nation they are the poorest, in a well-educated nation they are the least educated. In the Australian capitalist economy they participate as an under-class, moving from unemployment into unskilled labouring jobs or into invalidity.

Aborigines do not have the training to take advantage of opportunities in expanding industries, and there is every evidence that, as a conse-quence of their weak educational backgrounds, their occupational dis-advantages will persist. At 45 and above, one-half to three-quarters of the Aboriginal population report no formal education and are presump-tively illiterate. Even among ages 25-9, nearly one-quarter of Aborigines have not been to school, and at ages 15-19 the fraction is one-tenth. By comparison, in the non-Aboriginal population, even among those aged 50 or older, only I or 2 per cent have no formal schooling. While white capitalist education leaves much to be desired, the basic skills it provides are necessary for employment or, sometimes, even for survival within the system.

Health, housing, and education make up a complex of interrelated factors that mutually reinforce one another. Poor health is often caused by poor housing, and poor health retards future growth. Moreover, whatever happens in the schools is likely to be wasted, unless a parallel effort is directed -;0 improving the home environment. Educational performance is a faction not only of innate intelligence and educational exposure, but also of the reinforcement that a child gets from the home. To make effective gains in health, housing, or education, inputs are needed in all three areas simultaneously.

Like health, decent housing is recognized as an elementary right.

Aborigines are among the worst-housed people in the world. The poor housing conditions of Aboriginal Australians reflect their past low earn-ing power, and their status in Australian society as economic drop-outs and cast-offs. The structures in which they live are made of the most fragile materials. They are the most segregated group, they have least access to community facilities such as schools, sewerage, rubbish removal, reticulated water, or adequate or clean water of any kind.

Jobs and income come last in the chain of causation that maintains Aborigines in a depressed status. In the absence of good health, jobs are uncertain. In the absence of education, unskilled and poorly paid work is the only realistic expectation. In the absence of a living wage, housing will be poor, overcrowded, and in sanitary. Poorer health follows as a consequence. And so the chain of causation continues. J Unless Aborigines are to remain social and political outcasts, they must be able to participate on an equal footing in the central institutions of the society. To do that, they must be able to achieve educational levels that permit them to manipulate the symbol system and the legal. bureaucratic system. Aboriginal women particularly are aware of this factor, and are striving to instil into their young children the importance of education.

If enough effort is applied, the vicious circle of poor education, poor jobs, low income, and poverty could be broken at anyone of several points, or several points simultaneously. For many Aboriginal people, the 1982 election was designated 'the election of hope', and was seen as producing major changes in economic, political, and social development programmes.

However, in fact, what has occurred (nothing) has been a disaster for our people. The present Labor Party's backdown on land rights has opened and festered the old wounds of the deprivation and dispossession of our people. Neither has the Bicentennial convinced Aboriginal people of their welcomed participation (in a genuine way that will focus on 'the true history of this country and the sufferings Aboriginal people have endured), or that they will receive their rightful place in Australian society. Without question, it is easier for a black woman to consider herself first a human being, second an Aborigine, and only third a member of the female sex. As Hilary Saunders eloquently sums up the feelings of many black women: We must not let this awareness as women go too far. We are a race of people who have suffered many injustices, we are fighting for self-determination.

CHAPTER SIX

The Women's Liberation and Spiritual Movement

Having been turned off by institutional religion they choose to leave it behind and forget it, except when it really shows muscle - as in the struggle over abortion laws. Some, on the other hand, have opted to continue their relationship with church or synagogue in the hope of changing sexist beliefs, laws, and customs in those institutions. Women who are committed to achieving liberation and equality often turn away from organised religion, seeing it either as irrelevant or as a stubborn and powerful enemy, placing obstacles to all they seek to attain.

The second choice is based upon a conviction that there are important values transmitted through these institutions that make it worth the pain and effort of staying in and fighting the system. These are personal choices and no one can set down hard-and-fast rules for everyone to follows.

However, it is important that women be aware of the issue of religion. First of all, it is necessary to understand institutional religion's role in the oppression of women, which it continues to exercise in this culture whether they personally relate to it or not. Second, women should be sensitive to the fact that the movement itself s a deeply spiritual event which has the potential to awaken a new and post-patriarchal spiritual consciousness.

The Judaic-Christian tradition has been patriarchal down through the millennia, although sometimes this has been modified or disguised.[1] The Bible reflected the oppressed condition of women in ancient times. In the Decalogue of the Old Testament a man's wife is listed among his possessions, along with his ox and his ass. The biblical story of Eve's birth which has been called the hoax of the ages, fixed women's place in the universe. The story of the Fall of Adam and Eve perpetuated the myth of feminine evil, giving a powerful image of women as temptress – a dominant theme in western culture for thousands of years. In the New Testament, the Apostle Paul put women in their place; veiled, silent, and subordinate. In the early centuries of Christianity the Fathers of the Church classified women as fickle, shallow, garrulous, weak, and unstable.

In the Middle Ages, Thomas Aquinas decreed that they are misbegotten males, and theologians dutifully taught this for centuries. In the modern period popes and theologians greeted the first wave of feminism with the double-talk of the feminine mystique: women should be equal but subordinate. On childbirth, Pope Pius XII pontificated; 'Sheloves it [the child] the more, the more pain it has cost her.' Today, some liberal Catholic and Protestant theologians admit that sexism exists in the churches but show little inclination to do anything about it. All of this, of course, is in blatant contradiction to Christian teaching about the worth and dignity of every human person.

Although there have been outstanding 'exceptional women' in every period of Christian history, their existence has had almost no effect upon the official ideology and policies of the churches. This fact can be understood when it is realized that the Judaic-Christian tradition has functioned to legitimate male dominated society. The image of God as exlcusively a father and no t a mother, for example, was spawned by the human imagination under the conditions of patriarchal society and sustained as plausible by patriarchy. Then, in turn, the image has served to perpetuate this kind of society by making its mechanisms for the oppression of women appear right and fitting. If god is 'his' heaven is a father ruling his people. Then it is in the 'nature' of things and according to divine plan and the order of the universe that society should be male-dominated. Within this context a mystification of roles takes place: the husband dominating his wife can feel that he represents God himself. A theologian such as Karl Barth could feel justified in writing that women is 'ontologically' subordinate to man. It might seem that intelligent people do not really think of God as an old man with a beard, but it is quite possible for the mind to function on two different and even contradictory levels at the same time.

For example, many speak of God as spirit and at the same time, on the imaginative level, envisage 'him' as male. The widespread concept of the Supreme Being has been a not very subtle mask of the divine father figure, and it is not too surprising that it has been used to justify oppression, especially that of women, which is said to be 'God's plan'.

Doctrines about Jesus also have often reflected a kind of phallic obsession. Some theologians have agued that since Jesus was male and called only males to become apostles, women should not be ordained. The doctrine of a unique 'incarnation' in Jesus reinforced the fixed idea of patriarchal religion that God is male ad male is God. So also did the image of the Virgin kneeling in adoration before her own Son.

The mechanism that can be seen in all of this is the

familiar vicious circle in which the patterns of a particular kind of society are projected into the realm of religious beliefs ad these in turn justify society as it is. The belief system becomes hardened and functions to resist social change, which would rob it of its plausibility. (In a matriarchal or a diarchal society, what credibility would the image of a divine patriarch have?) Patriarchal religion tends to be authoritarian. Given the fact that the vicious circle is not foolproof, there is always the possibility that beliefs may lose their credibility. For this reason they are often buttressed by notions of 'faith' that leave no room for dissent.

For example, the believer is often commanded to assent blindly to doctrines handed down by authority (all male). The inculcation of anxieties and guilt feelings over 'heresy' and 'losing the faith' has been a powerful method used by institutional religion to immunize itself from criticism. Women especially have been victimized by this. Traditional Christian ethics also have been to a great extent the product and support of sexist bias. Much of the theory of Christian virtue appears to be the product of reactions on the part of men - probably guilt reactions - to the behavioural excesses of the stereotypic male. There has been theoretical emphasis upto charity, meekness, obedience, humility, self-abnegation, sacrifice, service.

Part of the problem with this moral ideology is that it became generally accepted not by men but by women, who have hardly been helped by an ethic which reinforced their abject situation. This emphasis upon the passive virtues, of course, has not challenged exploitativeness, but supported it. Part of the whole syndrome has been the reduction of hope to passive expectation of a reward from the divine Father for following the rules. Love or charity has been interpreted to mean that people should turn the other cheek to their oppressors. Within the perspective of such a privatized morality, 'sin' often become sand offence against those in power, or against 'God' – the two being more or less equated.

The structures of oppression are not seen as sinful. It is consistent with all of this that the traditional Christian moral consciousness has been fixated on the problems of reproductive activity to a degree totally disproportionate to its feeble concern of or existing human life. The deformity of perspective was summed up several years ago in Archbishop Robers' remark that 'if contraceptives had been dropped over Japan instead of bombs which merely killed, maimed, and shriveled up thousands alive, there would have been a squeal of outraged protest from the Vatican to the remotest mass center in Asia.' Pertinent also is Simone de Behavior's remark that the church has reserved its uncompromising humanitarianism for a man in the foetal condition although both of these remarks are directed at the Catholic Church, the same attitudes are widespread in Protestantiam. Many theologians today do, of course, acknowledge that this passive and privatized morality has failed to cope with structures of oppression. However, few seriously face the possibility that the roots of this distortion re deeply buried in the fundmental and all-pervasive sexual alienation which the women's movement is seeking to overcome.

The Spiritual Potential of the Movement

As the women's revolution begins to have an effect upon the fabric of society, beginning to transform it form patriarchy into something that never existed before – into a diarchal situation that is radically new – it will, I think, become the greatest single challenge to Christianity to rid itself of its oppressive tendencies or go out of business. Beliefs and values that have held sway for thousands of years will be questioned as never before.

The movement, if it is true to its most authentic and prophetic dimensions, is possibly also the greatest single hope for the survival and development of authentic spiritual consciousness over against the manipulative and exploitative power of technocracy. The caricature of a human being which is presented by the masculine stereotype depends for its existence upon the acceptance by women of the role assigned to them – the eternal feminine. By becoming whole persons women can generate a counterforce to the polarization of human beings into these stereotypes, forcing men o re-examine their own self-definition.

This movement towards the becoming of whole human beings, to the degree that it succeeds, will transform the values and symbols of our society, including religious symbols. The women's liberation movement is a spiritual movement because it aims at humanization of women and therefore of the species. At its core it is spiritualized in the deepest sense of the word, because it means the self-actualization of creative human potential in the struggle against oppression. Since the projections of patriarchal religion serve to block the dynamics of creativity, self-actualization, and authentic community by enforcing reduction of people to stereotyped roles, the challenge to patriarchy which is now in its initial stages is a sign of hope for the emergence of more genuine religious consciousness. The becoming of women may not be only the doorway to deliverance from the omnipotent Father in all of his disguises, but, to many also a doorway to something, namely, to a more authentic search for transcendence, that is, for God. Women's liberation is an event that can challenge authoritarian, exclusivist, and non-existential ideas of faith and revelation, since women have been extra-environmentals, that is, since we have not been part of the authority structure which uses 'faith' and 'revealation' to reinforce the mechanisms of alienation, our emergence can unmask the idolatry often hidden behind these ideas.

There could result form this becoming of women a

remythologizing of western religion. If the need for parental symbols of God persists, something like the Father-Mother God of Mary baker Eddy will be more acceptable to the new woman and the new man than the Father God of the past. A symbolization for incarnation of the divine presence in human beings may continue to be needed in the future, but it is highly unlikely that women or men will find plausible that symbolism which is epitomized in the Christ-Mary image. Perhaps this will be replaced by a bisexual imagery which is non-hierarchical.

The becoming of women can bring about a trasvaluation of values. Faith can come to be understood in a non-authoritarian and universalist sense. Hope, rather than being restricted to expectation of regards for conformity, can come to be experienced and understood as creative political, and revolutionary. Love will mean uniting to overcome oppression. It will be understood that the most loving thing one can do for the oppressor is to fight the oppressive situation that destroys both the oppressor and the oppressed. Suffering, which has been so highly esteemed in Christianity, will be seen as acceptable not when abjectly and submissively endured, but when experienced in the struggle for liberation. The ethic emerging in the struggle has as its main theme not prudence but existential courage. This is the courage to risk economic and social security for the sake of liberation. It means not only risking the loss of jobs, friends, and social approval, but also facing the nameless anxieties encountered in new and uncharted territory. There is the anxiety of meaninglessness that can be overwhelming at times when the old simple meanings, role definitions, and life expectations have been rooted out and rejected openly, and a woman emerges into a world without models. There is also the anxiety of guilt over refusing to do what society demands, an anxiety that can still hold a woman in its grip long after he guilt has been recognized as false. To affirm oneself and one's sisters in the face of all this requires courage.

Such courage expresses itself in sisterhood, which is not at all merely the female counterpart of brotherhood. Sisterhood is a revolutionary fact. It is the bond in of those who have never bonded before, for the purpose of overcoming sexism and its effects, both internal and external. It is the coming together of those who are oppressed by sexual definition. The Christian churches have been fond of preaching the 'brotherhood of man, which included women incidentally, as baggage. However, the concept his never been realized because brotherhood in patriarchy, despite frequent attempts to universalize the term, is exclusive and divisive. 'Brother' means us versus them. It begins by excluding women as 'the other' and continues its divisiveness from there, cutting off 'he other' by familial, tribal racial, national, economic and ideological categories.

Women are learning to be aware that brotherhood, even when it attempts to be universal, means a male universalism. The churches, the peace movement, the New Left, for the most part fail to notice the need for change in the situation of the more than 50 per cent female membership of the groups to which they would extend their brotherhood.

The 'sisterhoods' of patriarchal society have really been mini-brotherhoods, following male models and serving male purposes. The religious sisterhoods within the catholic church, for example, have been male-dominated according to canon law. These communities, though they have offered an alternative to marriage and attracted some gifted women, have used the word 'sister' in an elitist and divisive sense and have supported the ideology of sexism.

The sisterhood of women's liberation involves a strategic polarization for the sake of women's internal wholeness or oneness, because as in the case of all oppressed groups, women suffer from a duality of consciousness. We have internalized the image that the oppressor has or us and are therefore divided against ourselves and against each other by self-hatred. We can only overcome this by bonding with each other. Sisterhood implies polarization also for the sake of political oneness, to achieve liberation. However, its essential dynamic is directed to overcoming the stereotypes that reduce people to the role of 'the 'other'. That is, it points towards a unity deeper than most theologians are capable of envisaging, despite the great amount of ink that has been spilled on the subject of 'the bonds of charity.'

Sisterhood is an event that is new under the sun. It is healing, revolutionary, and revelatory – which is what Christian brotherhood was claimed to be but failed to be. It is at war with the idols of patriarchal religion, but it is in harmony with what is authentic in the ideals of the religious traditions. In this sense, the movement in its deepest dimensions is itself both anti-church and Church.

The Visionary Task

Synopsis

The essential feminist tension is dual-vision, i.e., living in the world as men have fabricated it while creating the world as women imagine it could be. Dissociation from, assimilation to, and victimism in the world are three different forms of worldlessness to which women have been subject. All three militate against a vision of female friendship, which locates women in the world. The author argues for a hopeful vision and reality of female friendship that avoids a misplaced optimism, shallow sentimentionalism, and disillusioned pessimism about the possibilities of friendship among women.

The possibilities of female friendship are founded on vision. Today, vision is all the more important to task about when the fabric of friendship among women seems often rent by disagreements, disruptions, and dissensions.

There are many ways to speak about vision. Every meaning of vision, however, is possessed of a certain tension. This tension is linguistically present in its dual dictionary definition, but it is also experienced in any attempt to live out a vision. At one and the same time, vision is 'the exercise of the ordinary faculty of sigh' and 'something which is apparently seen otherwise than by ordinary sight'. Another way of phrasing this is to ask how indeed it is possible to se with the ordinary faculty of sight, that is, to maintain a necessary realism about the conditions of existence, and to see beyond thee conditions that is, to overleap reality. Or, how do women live in the world as men have defined it while creating the world as women imagine it could be?

An undivided vision is based on two sights-seeing – near – and far-sightendness. In my opinion, this dual vision is the essential tension of feminism. Feminists must learn to live in and with that tension. This means not being crushed by the contrast between what the world is and the way it ought to be.

The state of female atrocity, or all of the ways in which women have been oppressed, abused, and rendered invisible under patriarchy presents one view of women. The state of female friendship resents another. If women do not have a vision of female friendship, if women do not come to realise how profound the possibilities are of being for each other, as well as how buried these possibilities have been for us, I believe there is no true realism about the possibilities of feminism itself.

Dual vision poses a tension but not a contradiction. Realism about the conditions of man-made existence must be illuminated by a vision of feminist imagination. And the feminist visionary task must root itself in the real world else, like an electrical charge hat has no ground, its energy becomes diffuse and dispersed in all directions (Hynes, 1981).

Hannah Arendt wrote

Humanity in the form of fraternity invariably appears historically among persecuted peoples and enslaved groups... it is often accompanied by so radical a loss of the world, accompanied by so radical a loss of the world, so fearful an atrophy of all the organs with which we orient ourselves in a world common to our-selves and others and going on the sense of beauty or taste, with which we love the world. (Arendt, 1968, p.13)

Using the example of sisterhood instead of fraternity, we can apply these words to the situation of women under patriarchy. Feminist literature, theory, and action have emphasized the ideal of sisterhood as a collective response women's oppression. Different schools of feminism have stressed the political nature of feminism and the necessity to build a strong solidarity of sisterhood.

Indeed sisterhood is powerful, but perhaps not powerful enough when it comes to the visionary task of which I speak. To resist the state of atrocity that men have perpetrated against women may generate sisterly solidarity, but it may not provide anything beyond the communion of resistance. It may not provide, as Arendt says, 'a world common to ourselves and others and going on the sense of beauty or state, with which we love the world', and I would add, 'are happy in it'.

At the same time that feminism is a political reality, it is also a way of life full of struggle, risk, and promise, the promise of happiness in this world, Organised sisterhood against the conditions of female oppression and the feminist struggle against all states of female atrocities serve as a powerful bulwark against the forces and structures of patriarchy. But a purely political feminism accentuating only conflict and resistance bears too similar a resemblance to religious eschatologies which would have women believe that true happiness is achievable only in the life to come.

Women must reject the sentimentality and false vision of patriarchal romanticism precisely because men have dreams for women. This does not mean that women should reject vision. It does not mean that women will shape our own vision so that we will not only enable our freedom but create the conditions of female friendship.

In order to move beyond oppression and the struggle and conflict that inescapably accompany resistance to oppression, there must be a vision of 'moreness'. Let it not be misunderstood that in advocating a movement 'beyond' struggle, I mean one that leaves the struggle behind. Rather one revivifies that struggle hopefully by a moreness that enriches female life and living. Friendship invigorates the reality of feminist resistance with this moreness. It augments sisterhood with spirit, thereby infusing feminist solidarity with an energy or vital force of affection.

Affection is a carefully chosen word in my discussion of vision and female friendship. The more commonly understood meaning of affection is a feeling, emotion, fondness, attachment, and love for another. There is another meaning of affection, however, that conveys more than personal movement of person to person. Affection in this sense means the state of influencing, acting upon, moving, and impressing, and of being influenced, acted upon, moved, and impressed. I maintain that women who affect other women stimulate response and action; brain about a change in living; stir and arouse emotion, ideas, and activities that defy dichotomies between the personal and political aspects of affection.

Elsewhere, I have suggested a new word Gyn/affection, to describe this personal and political movement of women towards each other (Raymond, 1982). I define Gyn/affection as synonym for female friendship, but it has a district meaning context of its own. The basic meaning of Gyn/affection is that women affect, stir and arouse each other to full power through friendship. One task of feminism has been to show that 'the personal is political'. Female friendship gives integrity to that claim. The world Gyn/affection is meant to reunite the political and personal aspect of friendship.[1]

Sisterhood signals the kind of political community that is and has to be possible among women who are not necessarily friends. None of us is beyond sisterhood because feminist resistance to all forms of female oppression is ongoing. However, sisterhood and friendship have a richer meaning when they are brought together that is when political sisterhood proceeds from a shared affection, vision, and spirit, and when friendship has a more expansive political effect. We need to create a feminist politics base don friendship, and we need a philosophy of friendship that is realized in personal and socio-economic power for women. A genuine friendship goes beyond the self's relations wit other Selves to the society in which the female self is allowed to grow. Thus the active and dynamic expression of female friendship involves more than feeling. It means the sharing of a common life and participation in a common world.

Worldliness and friendship must be intimately linked in the lives of women today who live with the basic tension that feminism presents – that of acting in a world that men have fabricated while yearning to go beyond it. Alice Walker has eloquently described the lucidity she experienced hen her daughter told her that 'there's a world in you eye' (Waker, 1983, p. 393).[2] There must be a world in each of our eyes.

More than most philosophers, Hannah Arendth has discussed the concept of worldliness. Arendt's notion of worldliness, originally analysed in the context of the history of the Jews and of Judaism, has much pertiness for feminist worldliness.[3] Because women have been the eternal victims of male cruelty and injustice; because survival has been the key focus of female existence and feminist political thought; because women have almost everywhere lacked involvement in and control over the political world in which we have lived; and because the world is man-made, many women have developed a worldlessness by dissociation from he world. Women in general have assumed this woldlessness almost by default, that is, by virtue of the passive positions mot women have been forced into throughout history and in almost every culture. Other women, such as some feminist separatists, have made dissociation from the world a political ideal and reality. The difficulty in both cases is that when women make dissociation the basis for survival or for affinity, many come to conceive of their existence as independent from the rest of the world. Philosophically, this can make women very narrow in vision; politically it can make them very vulnerable. Even radical and voluntary dissociation from the world, originally undertaken as a necessary and daring political stance, can culminate in women developing a worm's-eye view of the world and being more exposed to attack than ever before. The more women dissociate from the world, the further removed are women from a definite share of what should be a common world. This is the condition of any group within any diaspora, whether scattered voluntarily o forcibly. A Gyn/affective friendship cannot exist under these conditions of worldlessness.

On the other hand, the dissociation from the world that is not chosen for consciously defined feminist reasons – in other words, that experienced by women in general whose apprehension of the world is derivative from husbands or other men – is reinforced by these women's lack of knowledge that women are a common people. In contrast to other oppressed groups, women do not possess the past of a cohesive and self-conscious community with its own political traditions, philosophical vitality, and history. Or should I say that this past is one that most women know little about? The rootlessness of women in their own group identity contributes more than anything to the worldless, unrealistic, and unpolitical perception that many women have.

Female friendship - not just any kind of friendship - but the Gyn/affection of which I have spoken, is one way to rootedness, to the grasp of reality that women need, and to the experience of our own history. Female friendship, of this nature, orients women to the world, not as persons but as women. To paraphrase Arendt, when one is oppressed as a woman, one must respond as a woman. Female friendship cannot arise in a context where women have 'the great privilege of being unburdened by care for the world' (Arendt, 1978, p. 27), because Gyn/affection is a political virtual with a political effect.

Any strong and vital reality of female friendship cannot be created within a dissociated enclave of women who have little knowledge of or interest in the wider world. Female friendship is strongest and most effective when it takes shape within on enclave of women who are located in the world by virtue of their thinking and action and who do not dissociate from the world or from each other. The feminist task of 'reconstituting the world', to use Adrienne Rich's phrase (1978), can only come about in a worldly context and in struggle against the forces that threaten us. Reconstituting the world means reconstituting our lost bonds with our Gyn/affective Selves and with others like our Selves. Strong friendships wit strong women share the world as women imagine it could be, while permitting women to move with worldly integrity in the world men have made.

The opposite of dissociation is assimilation to the world. This is another posture that many women have assumed as a location in the world. Assimilation is the sance of a woman who desires to succeed in the world of men and who forgets, or constantly tries to ignore, the fact of her femaleness. The assimilation is strives to lose her female identity, or to go beyond it, or to be regarded as a person in a world that grants the status of persons only to men. Realism, survival, worldliness are all acquired by assimilation to the male dominant world on its own term.

Assimilation spells the end of any strong reality of female friendship even before it begins. For the assimilationist, men and/or male-defined structures are what counts. As women assimilate, they are reluctantly accepted into the ranks of male society mainly as exceptions and only in so far as they do not interfere with the homo-relational bonds[4] that men have established. In order to become part of the male dominant society, women have to believe (or pretend) that they are both persons and women, in the ways that men have defined both for women. What is demanded of assimilationist women by the male dominant world is that they behave in ways that distinguish them from ordinary women, e.g., they are encouraged to be bright, articulate, upwardly mobile professionals, but, at the same time, they must exhibit acceptable manners and modes of man-made feminity, e.g. charming behaviour, warning feminine clothing or make-up. The complicated psychology learned well by the assimilationist woman is how t be and not be a woman, or how to be the woman that men still recognize as their own creation while avoiding the women who recognizes her Self and other women who are Self-defined.

Assimilation fosters private solutions. Everything is reduced to personal self-propulsion. It is a forward self-propulsion that does not depend on authentic self-definition, Self-movement, and certainly not on Gyn/affection. Thus it locates women in an isolated sphere of action that is built upon a pseudo-individualism. For the assimilation is, the world becomes anywhere that is accessible to any 'rational' person without questioning the boundaries of the terrain or one's location within them. This world becomes an inauthentic one for women not by virtue of the fact that it is man-made but because that fact is not doubted and defied.

In a society that is not only hostile to women, but pervaded by what Andrea Dworkin has named woman-hating (1974), it is possible to assimilate only by assimilation to anti-feminism also. Explicitly or implicitly, assimilationists disidentify with other women, whether they are in the company of men or women, or both. Their only of this is that both men and women will always perceive them first and foremost as women. It is unfortunate that assimilationists do not recognize, or ignore, this basic fact, wishing I will go away, when it never will.

The road to assimilation is the road to conformism: a conformism very often creating new stereotypes that assume shape under the guise of liberation and 'new woman' rhetoric, but conformism none the less. Thus what we witnesses a brand of assimilationisms that often displays the verbiage and outward lifestyle of liberation. Assimilationists frequently view their freedom as an emancipation from the world of traditional women, as well as from the world of feminist women. Sometimes, they exaggerate declarations that they are not feminists, or they take pains to proclaim that they have moved beyond feminism. In the latter case, many women have taken the term post-feminist as a badge of maturity. The irony of such disidentifications with feminism is that often assimilationist women engage in quite extraordinary activities that are feminist in the sense that these endeavours require unconventional capabilities, courage, determination, and persistence. One also thinks of women scientists, truck drivers, welders, and presidents of colleges who are not only very excellent at what they do, b very often more astute and humans than men in the same fields. However, many of these women, hen asked, would deny any kind of woman-identification in a strong sense of the phrase. Assimilationist women want no social roots in any community of women. Hetero-relations become their guiding ethic.[5] their emancipation is their assimilation. Hence assimilation, like dissociation, leads to a worldlessness that constricts rather than constructs female friendship.

In addition to assimilation and dissociation, *victimism* is a third posture that women have assumed towards the world. I use the word to describe women whose primary female or feminist identity seems to be grounded in women's shared state of having been victimized by men. In relationships with each other, such women emphasize their heritage of shared pain, although the ways in which various women have been victimized differs by age, class, race, and other factors.

I am not trying to minimize the pain of women's victimisation by men in a patriarchal culture. It is extremely important that women understand and act n the full picture of female oppression. However, one dimensional emphasis the state of atrocity can have the unintended effect of stressing that what women have in common is only, or mostly, our shared pain. Such as perspective, as reflected in women's relationships, in women's sharing of experiences, and in feminist literature and activism, can also create the impression that because women have been historically bound to and by men, that woman is for man, no matter how she might have to be forced to do his bidding.

Victimism drives women further away from strong female friendships by obscuring the historical reality that women have been and can be for women in other than sisterly suffering ways. Among many feminists, the emphasis on victimism bolsters the conviction that female friendship can only arise negatively, that is, because men are so bad, and/or in reaction to the atrocities promoted by a woman-hating culture. Here female friendship seems spawned by the results of the oppression of women. Thus in a better world, presumably one in which men were good, female friendship might not be necessary.

It is obvious that feminist analysis and action has to be well acquainted with the varieties of male terrorism perpetrated against women. It should be as obvious that a vision of Gyn/affection is a vital counterpart of the reality of women as abused, battered, and killed. Sustained and one-dimensional emphasis on victimism, however, reduces the history of women to an eternal state of atrocity over which women have never exerted any counter-control. While it is necessary for women to recognize the prevalence and the longevity of anti-feminism across historical ages and cultural lines, the imperative for such recognition should not lead women to the conclusion that the force of anti-feminism is almost a natural and without end - so overwhelming that any will to feminist action is lost.

Ultimately what victimism does is negate Self-definition and Self-responsibility in the world. When women do not define themselves beyond the role of sufferer, then women will set the for the word as men have made it. Victimism means annihilation by the world. It makes women world-sufferers rater than world-makers. It establishes women in he world negatively. Women's commonality is reduced to our shared oppression. There is the unstated, and hopefully unintended, premise that feminists might lose their feminist identity if anti-feminism disappeared from the world.

Women have indeed been broken by men. Yet men would make the case that it is they who have been damaged by women. For example, they blame mothers who gave them too much or too little attention, or wives who dominate or are too dependent. Men have always claimed the wounded role. The overcoming of brokenness by women, as well as the rejection of men as broken creatures in need of women's restorative power, is necessary to the process of female friendship.

Women, as a people, cannot be held together nor move in the world linked primarily by a common enemy or by a negative identity of oppression. Only within the framework of female friendship can a woman live as a woman, working for a reconstituted world, without exhausting herself in the struggle against woman-hating, and without despairing at the enormity of the task.

This issue has been entitled 'rethinking Sisterhood: Unity in Diversity.'* Much emphasis in recent years of feminist writing and activity has been on the necessity to recognize and accept the diversity of women's lies and life experiences. Race, class, age, sexuality have all been in the forefront of this focus. Sometimes diversity of women's lies and life experiences. Race, class, age, sexuality have all been in the forefront of this focus. Sometimes diversity has turned divisive. My work is meant to convey a sense of hope about the possibilities of friendship among women. It is not a naïve hope, but one that has been tempered by a diversity that has often turned divisive, as well as by a myriad of other obstacles to Gyn/affection that women have experienced in the 'maturity' of feminist movement. All of us, in our relationships with omen have met with a host of stumbling-blocks; unfulfilled expectations, betrayal, lack of real caring, and the wall of entrenched differences between friends that becomes insurmountable. Dissociation, assimilation, and victimism have worked in their own ways to erase female friendship While it is not my intention to romanticize the subject of female friendship, I am called for the regaining of hope about the present and future of friendship. This hope is grounded in several things: the reality of friendship that lives in my Self and in other women; the fact that women have been each other's best friends, relatives, faithful companions, emotional and economic supporters, and faithful lovers in all times and places; the continuity and consistency of these woman-to-woman affinities that veritably have formed historical and cultural traditions of female friendship in all epochs and cultures.

Hope is not necessary when things go smoothly, when there is a euphoria about the possibilities of women together as there was in the first stages of this particular wave of feminism. Many women have come through the feminism of the 1960s and early 1970s jaded, 'turned off'. Or disillusioned by other women. Women who 'should have been different' turned out to be 'just as bad, if not wore than men'. Both hope and friendship are easy when things proceed well. Hope is hard to hold but is no less called for when things are not as good s we expected them to be, when sisterhood does not seem as powerful as it once was, or as once we felt it to be. Yet the failures of friendship can never destroy the presence of its past in our lives, and certainly not its possibilities.

A hopeful vision of female friendship is not based on some ontological essence of female energy and vitality that women naturally possess by virtue of a more refined capability for over, caring, and respect for others. Rather it is anchored in the historical and cultural facts of what women have created for our Serves in spite of the state of female atrocity. The obstacles to female friendship and the divisiveness that often attends diversity serve as correctives to a shallow sentimentalism about women's affinities with women. Such difficulties remind us that to ground Gyn/affection in an ontological capability of women to bond with each other is a false optimism that will betray itself.

Misplaced optimism and shallow sentimentalism are two sides of a similar coin. Another position to be avoided is pessimism about women's ability to originate and sustain Gyn/affection. Relationships disintegrate. Violence against women issues in horizontal violence among women. Even something like the defeat of the ERA (for the moment) may dull the spirit of women working together to achieve simple and concrete goals for their selves and other women. In the maturity' of feminist life and living, old direction are questioned.

A feminist vision realistically accepts these facts of worldly existence. Seeing with 'the ordinary faculty of sight', or being in the world as men have created it, is to know that the possession of vision will not make such facts disappear. Yet the same vision when it sees 'something which is apparently seen otherwise that by ordinary sight' knows that such realism is not the whole perspective. Simultaneously two sight-seeing is needed. Vision, near-and far-sightedness, is neither false optimism nor disillusioned pessimism. But vision is imperative to build Gyn/affection. Female friendship alone cannot vanquish the oppression of women nor can it guarantee that friendship lasts forever. But it can create and sustain hope in the midst of all the factors that militate against Gyn/affection.

NOTES AND REFERENCES

1. The classical Greek philosophical tradition on friendship taught that friendship had a public nature. It was, in fact, the basis of the polis. Aristotile, for example, held that friendship fastened the moral and political fibres of the state together, and that friendship and justice coalesce. Of course, the citizens of this polis were all male. Women had no civil status, and therefore friendship and politics were affairs between men.

2. In her essay, 'Beauty: When the other dancer is the self', Walker tells the story of her eye, wounded in early girlhood y a copper pellet from her brother's 'BB' gun, She trenchantly portrays years of feeling shame and ugliness, and the changes such feelings produced in a young life against the backdrop of her mother's and sister's refrain, 'You did not change'. Only when her almost thee-year-old daughter declares 'Mommy, there's a world in your eye' much later in Walker's life does the latter make peace with both her outer and inner vision. Rebecca's insight is no mere metaphor. It has significance for the visionary takes of all women. It succinctly states the tension between the near – and far-sightedness with which

my essay is concerned.

3. I am enormously indebted to Arendt's development of the typologies of dissociation and assimilation, and have drawn on many of her ideas in this section.

4. The fact, prevalence, and power of male homo-relations is disguised by such man-to-man rapport being institutionalized in every aspect of an apparently hetero-relational culture. It is women who bear the burden of living out the hetero-relational culture. It is women who bear the burden of living out the hetero-relational imperative. In truth, this is a male homo-relational society that is built on male-male relations, transactions, and bonding at all levels, See again, Raymond (1982).

5. I use the word hetero-relations to express the wide range of affective, social, political, and economic relations that are ordained between men and women by men. The literature, history, philosophy, and science of patriarchy have reinforced the supposedly mythic and primordial relationships of woman for man (Raymond, 1982).

Arendt, Hannah, *Men in Dark Times* (New York: Harcourt, Brace & World, 1968).

Arendt, Hannah, *The Jew as Pariah; Jewish Identity and Politics in the Modern Age*, Feldman, Ron (ed.) (New York: Grove Press, 1978).

Dworkin, Andrea, *Woman Hating* (New York: E.P. Dutton, 1974). Hynes, H. Patricia, conversation (Mass.: Montague, 1981).

Raymond, Janice G., 'A genealogy of female friendship', *Trivia: A Journal of Ideas*, I (I) (1982), pp. 5-26.

Rich, Adrienne, "Natural resources', in *The Dream of a Common Language*, Poems, 1974-1, (New York: Norton, 1978).

Walker, Alice, In *Search of Our Mother's Gardens* (New York: Harcourt Brace Jovanovich, 1983).

CHAPTER SEVEN

Lords of Creation: Marxism, Feminism, and 'Utopia' Socialism

Exactly a century ago Engels consigned the ideas and hopes of the first British socialists, the Owenites, to a utopian prehistory of scientific socialism, a period of 'crude theories' and 'grand fantasies' which had to be superseded by historical materialism before the communist struggle could be waged on a sound, scientific basis. Here I want to suggest that it is time this evaluation was assessed, and that an important beginning point for this reassessment is one aspect of Owenite policy on which they sharply differed from they Marxist successors: the issue of women's emancipation.

The Owenites' commitment to feminism was part of the general humanist outlook which Engels later identified as a key feature of all utopian thought: the 'claim to emancipate…all humanity at once' rather than 'a particular class to begin with'. The goals were spelled out in detail; with the establishment of a worldwide network of Communities of Mutual Association, all institutional and ideological impediments to sexual equality would disappear including oppressive marriage laws, privatized households, and private ownership of wealth. The nuclear family (which was held to be responsible not only for the direct subordination of women to men but also for the inculcation of 'competitive' ideology) would be abolished and replaced by communal homes and collective child-rearing. This transformation in living conditions would allow a new sexual division of labour to be introduced: housework ('domestic drudgery') would be performed on a rotational basis (either by men or be children of both sexes) with 'the most scientific methods available', leaving women time to participate in all other aspects of community life, from manufacturing and agricultural labour to government, office, and educational and cultural activities. With childcare collectivized and all economic pressures removed, marriage would become a matter of 'romantic affection' only to be entered into by mutual agreement and dissolved by mutual choice. Or as one leading socialist feminist told an Owenite congress in 1841, 'when all should labour for each, and each be expected to labour for the whole, then would woman be placed in a positioning which she would not sell her liberties and her finest feelings...'

Alongside these revolutionary hopes went a whole series of lesser reform proposals, including demands for immediate changes in the marriage laws to allow civil marriage and divorce, support for the female franchise (the Owenites frequently criticized the Chartists for excluding women from the suffrage demands), and campaigns to extend education for women and girls. Many of the women who agitated for these reforms were lower-middle class, but as the popular base of the movement expanded they were jointed by a small number of working-class feminists, particularly during the general union phase of Owenism in 1833-4, when a number of women's trade unions were formed.

These unions sometimes became centres of lively feminist discussion, encouraged by the owenite newspaper, The *Pioneer*, which opened a 'Woman's Page' to carry letters from female trade unionists on subjects like equal pay and the right to equal employment. The problem of sex prejudice within the radical working class itself was a common theme. 'The working men complain that that masters exercise authority over them; and they maintain their right to associate, and prescribe laws for their own protection', ran one 'Woman's Page' editorial at the height of the trade union agitation, 'but speak of any project which will diminish the authority of the male, or give him an equal, where once he found an inferior, and then he spirit of Toryism awakes...' when it comes to women, another woman wrote, all men are aristocrats, whatever their class. 'Can it be right, can it be just...that woman should be thus trampled on and despised by those who style themselves the lords of creation?' she demanded, going one to add that in her view:

> Nothing short of a total revolution in all present modes of acting and thinking among all mankind, will be productive of the great change so loudly called for by [women'] miserable state; and there is certainly no system so...likely...as that proposed the benevolent Owen, of community property and equality of persons, in which all are free and equal. ... Indeed, I am confident that if women really understood the principles and practice of Socialism, there would not be one who would not become a devoted Socialist.

These were indeed, as Engels later said of the utopian outlook as a whole, 'stupendously grand thoughts'; but were they only that? Before going on to consider this question in greater detail, it is worth reminding ourselves that what he and later Marxists offered instead was a wholly different account of gender/class relations, one in which sexism was reduced to a bourgeois property relations, and thereby evacuated from the working-class struggle. The Owenite emphasis on the universal, trans-class character of 'male supremacy' (their own term) disappeared, to be replaced with dogmatic assertions of sexual equality within the proletariat, calls for sex unity in the face of the common class enemy, and a repudiation of organized feminism as bourgeois liberal deviationism. The vision of a reorganized sexual and family existence which had been so central to owenite thinking was increasingly pushed to the far side of the socialist agenda whose major focus became an economic revolution which would automatically liberate the whole of the working class. This is something of caricature, since so many staunch sexual egalitarians were to be found in the ranks of later Marxist organizations, but even the bravest of them rarely flouted an orthodoxy in which the woman Question was subsumed under the Class Question. "It is not women's petty interests of the moment that we should put in the foreground,' Clara Zetkin told a cheering audience of fellow Social Democrats in 1896, 'our task must be to enroll the modern proletarian woman in the class struggle.'

There was more separating these two ways of thinking about women's oppression than merely the alleged gap between an immature, voluntarist utopianism and a mature, scientific socialism. The movement from Owenism to Marxism meant the epudiation of an independent feminist platform within socialist politics. Why was the struggle against sexual oppression an integral part of the early socialist strategy?

For the owenites, unlike later Marxist theorists, capitalism was not simply an economic order dominated by a single, class-based division, but an arena of multiple antagonisms and contradictions, each of them living in the hearts and minds of woman and men as well as in their material circumstances. The very term which they used to describe this society – 'the competitive system' – indicated the style of their critique, which moved freely between an economic analysis of workers' exploitation, a moral condemnation of selfish individualism and a psychological account of the 'dissocial impulses' which were being bred no only in factories and workshops, but in schools, churches, and – above all – in the home where, in the words of William Thompson, the uniform injustice...practised by man towards woman, confounds all notions of right and wrong...'

Every family is a centre of absolute despotism where of course intelligence and persuasion are quite superfluous to him who has only to command to be obeyed: from these centres, in the midst of which all mankind are now trained, spreads the contagion of selfishness and the love of domination through all human transactions...

The psychological underpinnings of the competitive system, in other words, were habits of domination and subordination formed within the most intimate areas of human life. The enslavement of women by men deformed human character and strangled human potential to the point where social hierarchy became generally accepted as both natural and inevitable. Having been trained to mastery within the family, men took this self-seeking mode into public life as well: homo economic us, atomized, competitive individual at the centre of bourgeois culture, was the product of a patriarchal system of psychosexual relations.

Building an alternative to this crippling style of social existence would involve not merely the transfer of economic power from one class to another, but a wholesale transformation of personal life in which all 'artificial' division of wealth and power would be supplanted by the organic bonds of communal fellowship. Within each co-operation community women and men would learn new ways of living and living together. This project, which seemed so 'phantastical' to later Marxists, was absolutely central to the early socialist strategy. For how could 'social sentiment' defeat the 'competitive spirit' unless competition was uprooted form the most intimate areas of life? 'Where does freedom begin, unless in the heart?' For the Owenites, like the earlier Puritan reformers and all the Romantics of the period, it was the establishment of a correct order in sexual relations which was the key to general moral reorganization. Communism found its first and foremost expression in the liberated male-female relation. Feminism was therefore not merely an ancillary feature of the socialist project, but one of its key motivating impulses.

Why did Owenism develop in this way? If, as I have suggested, later Marxist thinkers took a different view of the Woman question, how and why did all this difference arise?

Owenism developed in a period of rapid social transition, when both class and gender relations were being sharply transformed by new patterns of work and family life. Most early socialists were craft workers or small trades people for whom the 0s and 1840s represented a period of extended economic and social crisis: the crisis which produced a modern working class. At the most general level, early socialism represented a systematic struggle against these critical developments, and an attempt to reroute them in a new, progressive direction. Unlike later socialist movements in which working people organized as proletarians, the Owenites were organizing against the process of proletarianization, believing that through economic co-operation and the remoulding of human character they could effectively short-circuit capitalist social relations.

But if in the 1830s plans to establish a new world outside the range of capitalist control still seemed viable option, by the 1880s, when the second phase of British socialism began, there was far less 'outside' to go to, and working-class organisations which developed within the boundaries of their proletarian status had their ability to see past those boundaries correspondingly reduced. The experience of living within capitalism wore down the socialist imagination, and the effects of this erosion were felt at the theoretical level as well. 'At any point after 1850,' Edward

Thompson has written, 'Scientific Socialism had no more need for Utopias (and doctrinal authority for suspecting them). Speculation as to the society of the future was repressed, and displaced by attention to strategy' (Postscript to William Morris,1976, p. 787). The result for British revolutionary Marxists was a systematic denial of the necessary visionary element within socialist consciousness, ending all too often in what William Morris described as a 'sham, Utilitarian Socialism' divested of any genuine libertarian aims, or what his twentieth-century disciple, Thompson, has characterized as:

> The whole problem of the subordination of the imaginative utopian faculties within the late Marxist tradition: its lack of moral self conscisouness or even a vocabulary of desire, its inability to project any images of the future or even its tendency to fall back in lieu of these upon the utilitarian's early paradise – the maximization of the economic growth. (ibid., p. 797).

The decline of a genuine feminist vision within British revolutionary movements was one measure of this loss. As the older dream of emancipating 'all humanity at one's was displaced by the economic struggle of a single class, so women and women's interests were pushed to one side. This occurred in two ways.

First, the strategic shift way from the struggle against proletarianization to the proletarian struggle meant the political marginalization of all those who were not, scientifically speaking, proletarians. If the Owenites had cast their net too wide in hoping o attract 'all classes of all nations' to the co-operative cause, Marxism, with its insistence that there was only one route to communism and only one group who would walk it – organized productive workers – tightened the net to the point where only a minority of women were drawn into it, even on a class basis. When combined with a low level of female employment in the mot highly organized industrial sectors, this made the fight for socialism seem pretty much a masculine affair. Women Marxist who challenged this situation did so not on the grounds that there was a separate women's cause to be fought alongside and within the class movement, but that women (at lest working women) had a right to stand alongside their men folk in the common cause. The Woman question which displaced earlier socialist-feminism within late nineteenth-century Marxism was concerned not with the question of how to make a revolution which would free women as a sex, but how to shape women for the class revolution. 'What do women have to do?' Eleanor Marx demanded in 1892, 'we will organize – not as 'women' but as proletarians...for us there is nothing but the working-class movement.'

Second, this contraction of the socialist struggle pushed a whole range of issues beyond the boundaries o revolutionary politics. Since it was no longer the total reformation of women and men which was at stake, but simply the reorganisation of productive relations, all questions connected to reproduction, marriage, or personal existence became converted from central problems of strategy to merely private matters. "I have been told that at the meetings arranged for reading and discussing with working women, sex and marriage problems come first,' Lenin scolded Cara Zetkinin their famous dialogue. 'I could not believe my ears when heard that. The first state of proletarian dictatorship is battling with the counter-revolutionaries of the whole world...and active communist women are busy discussing sex problems. 'Not all British revolutionaries, even Leninist ones, shared this attitude, but those who held out against I tended to be a beleguered minority, particularly in this century. It is thus not surprising to find that when socialist-feminists began to organize in the 1970s, it was with the slogan 'the personal is political' that they mounted their first challenge to the male-dominated Left. The issues had never disappeared it was jut that the voices which could raise them had been long suppressed.

The present must always condescend to the past, and from our vantage point there is indeed a great deal in the thinking of the pre-Marxian socialist which seems theoretically naive and strategically implausible. It is not necessary to deny this, however, in order to suggest that the wholesale dismissal of utopian socialism by later Marxist socialists revealed certain limitations in their own thinking as well: a narrowing of both means and ends which has had serious consequences for the libertarian cause in general and for the liberation of women in particular. Socialist-feminists look back to the Owen its, then, not our of nostalgia for a transition long past, but as a way of tracing the beginnings of a democratic-communist project which is still very much our own, and with which we are still struggling to redefine the ends of modern Marxist movements. For, after all, what count as utopian answers depends on who is raising the questions.

Marxism and Feminism

The task of selecting a representative collection of socialist feminist theorizing is an impossible one. the task of collecting a few statements that exemplify a set of arguments is, however, more feasible. The arguments to be developed her use two extracts; Barbara Taylor (1980). 'Lords of creation: Marxism, Feminism and "utopian"socialism' and Mia Campioniand Elizabeth Grosz [Gross] (1983) 'Love's labours lost: Marxism and feminism'. East is designed to complement a more extensive commentary on socialist feminist theoretical interventions in the companion volume feminist Knowledge: Critique and Construct.

The arguments revolve around the nature of the Marxist tradition, which socialist feminists inhabit, critique, and reconstruct. The British socialism as producing a set of ideas and practices which had women's oppression as a central focus. This was a focus displaced by the ascendancy of Marxism as the dominant socialist orthodoxy – an orthodoxy that rendered 'The Woman Quesiton'[2] peripheral. As someone still within – if critical of – the subsequent Marxist tradition, Taylor interprets this shifts in terms of its historical context. But as a socialist and a feminist, her criteria for evaluating this tradition are based on how those within it consider or marginalize the position of women. On these grounds Marxism is found wanting, but not rejected. The character and consequences of this legacy from the emergent phase of the Marxist tradition is explored in more detail by the Australian philosophers, Mia Campioni and Elizabeth Grosz.[3] In this examination, their position is less as loyal adherents to Marxism and more as feminists reconsidering that tradition. It is from this perspective that they evaluate recent socialist history and theoretical statements on 'The Woman question'. Marxism is seen as the only radical alternative to capitalism both practically and theoretically. As such, they argue, Marxists share many phallocentric assumptions with bourgeois theory. Begin the primary oppositional discourse but sharing many assumptions with patriarchal theorizing, means they Marxism both dominates over and arbitrates within the theoretical field. Marxism sets the rules for radical political practice in such a way as to delegitimize the theoretical and pragmatic claims of feminism. Socialist feminism 'remains locked in a paradox as feminist position unless it can somehow develop a radically woman-entred version of 'socialism" which entails "seeing women first"' (p.357). The vehicle for moving beyond Marxism involves seizing the principle of historical materialism and moving its foundations from economic ones to those of the sexually differentiated body. It is from a recognition of the lied oppressions and autonomy of women's bodies that further theoretical critiques and reconceptualizations can be built.

New socialist feminisms thereby emerge, not form further interventions into Marxist theory, but form an historical materialism built on women bodies and lived realities. The move is from critique, to reformulation, to massive recoceptualisaiton.4

In the rest of this introduction, the selected readings will be used to illustrate further the boundary transgressons which are reconstructing socialist feminist interventions in which Marxism itself is redefined, as is the socialist feminism loyal to it. These traditions are also used to affirm new possibilities for the future. The argument proceeds in there parts:

1 The assumption of hegemony by Marxism;
2 The theoretical problems of such dominance for socialist feminism;
3 New possibilities for socialist feminism.

Marxist Hegemony

The socialist tradition predates Marxism and, for Barbara Taylor, utopian socialism is the beginning of the 'democratic communist project' (p. 355) to liberate women and men from oppressions. She sees in the theory and practices of owenism a major concern for the place of patriarchy is sustaining capitalism. Capitalism for utopian socialists was not an 'economic order dominated by as single, class-based division, but an arena of multiple antagonisms and contradictions...living in the hearts and minds of women and men as well as in their material circumstances' (p. 352). The atomized, economistic, competitive individual at the centre of bourgeois culture – and some later Marxist analyses of it – for the Owenities: 'was the product of a patriarchal system of psycho-sexual relations. Building an alternative...would involve not merely the transfer of economic power from one class to another, but a wholesale transformation of personal life' (p. 353). Robert Owen's utopian socialism, designated as 'unscientific' by Marx and Engels, is supplanted by their 'scientific socialism'. With this shift, for Taylor, the centrality of women's oppression to the theorization of capitalist social relations by socialists, disappears.

> The owenite emphasis on the universal, trans-class character of 'male supremacy'...disappeared, to be replaced with dogmatic assertions of sexual equality within he proletariat, calls for sex unity in the face of the common class enemy, and a repudiation of organized feminism as bourgeois liberal deviationism. (pp. 351-2).

Marxism thereby subsumes 'The Woman Question' under the Class question. Why this occurs and comes to be the dominant version of socialism which feminists confront in the 1960s is explained by Taylor in terms of historical context. In the early years of industrialisation, she argues, it was easier to envisage a very different world and to fight the very process of proletarianization. In contrast, by the 1850s, working people were a dominant reality and it was as proletarians that they were to be organized. Campioni and Grosze offer a different interpretation, seeing in the triumph of Marxism the reassertion of male political and theoretical authority. Borne by masculinist theoreticians, revolutionary party members, trade unionists, and academics, Marxist theoretical dominance was assured by means of their power. For Campioni and Grosz, another element in maintaining Marxist hegemony was the adoption of common assumptions on the nature of truth, reality, and reason and a sharing of organizational forms such as planned, effective social organization and respect of or law and order with the very bourgeois order it condemned.

Consequences of Marxian Hegemony for Socialist Feminism

As the dominant oppositional discourse with a great

deal of power, Marxism becomes the standard against which all other revolutionary discourses are compared and found wanting. All other forms of political struggle or theorization are thereby incorporated as variants; as a part of the Marxist project (the classic example being the domestic labout debate); or seen as impurities and therefore unworthy; or counter-revolutionary, to be condemned and discarded. Marxism as the arbiter dismisses claims of an autonomous feminist position and political practice.

Such a dismissal also follows from a strict definition of the legitimate discursive field of socialist feminism by Marxist theory. With concepts such as 'class', 'labour', and 'alienation' based on productive wage-labour, women become theoretically and politically relevant only when they inhabit the male word of paid work. Since the revolutionary objective is defined as the reorganisation of productive relations, issues of male power in reproduction, sexuality, or the family, became private matters and explicable solely in terms of the interests 'capital' has in maintaining them.

It was against such practical and theoretical marginalization that socialist feminism emerged in the 1970s. And in their theorizations of reproduction, women's domestic and paid work, the family and the state, Marxism was critiqued and the reformulation begun. But for campioni and Grosz these contributions were primarily to Marxism. As a result socialist feminist innovations tended to strengthen rather than fundamentally challenge Marxism's 'globalizing and reductionist tendencies' (p.362). They continue: 'The potential explanatory power of the conceptual tools feminisms may possess as an *alternative,* not a complement to Marxism are effectively denied in order that Marxism's hegemony may be salvaged' (p. 362). Theoretical unity is achieved through domination and incorporation. It is therefore in elation to Marxism that socialist feminisms are defined and given a coherent history. Fragmentary and non-unified theoretical and practical struggles are deplored as weaknesses, while the imposed and accepted taxonomy limits the possibilities of what socialist feminism can be and is.

Socialist Feminist Possibilities

Despite the power of feminist critiques of Marxism, the tradition remains present, if only as something from which socialist feminism is differentiated. Historically, it was from within the ranks and theorizations of the tradition that socialist feminism emerged and proceeded to pose new challenges to Marxists and to Marxism by prioritizing feminist over Marxist concerns.

One of the decisive moments in contemporary socialist feminism is the critical scruting of Marxism itself-its epistemological and ontological premises, as well as its status as a discourse whose practioners hold power, gendered and therefore interested positions. All of these components of Marxism are thereby opened to re-evaluation and elements are taken only when they are of use to feminist concerns. Thus historical materialism, the importance of contradiction, and utopianism, are all seized as analytical tools.

The fundamental break with the Marxist tradition then becomes the assumption of a women-centered position. It is from this perspective that all of Marxism is to be critically reconsidered. If socialist or socialist feminist concepts or analysis are unable to centralize sexual difference, then they become highly suspect and are to be rejected. As to how any further analysis is to proceed, Marxism and its obverse - bourgeois ideologies - remain the touchstones stones. But they no longer have the status of the subject, but of the object in the dichotomous, value-loaded logic of A/ not A, male/not male (female), Marxism/not Marxism. For now the logic is feminist/not feminist or, more accurately and radically, *feminisms/phallocentrism*. Within this conceptually separatist realm, rights to autonomy, difference, plurality, fluidity, and specificity are affirmed. Alliances and affinities are effected to seize, analyse, and transform the various bodily and imaginative spaces inhabited by women in the integrated circuit of contemporary patriarchal capitalism.

The selected readings are vehicles for the elaboration – but also a questioning – of this argument. Two very different statements from different cultures in addressing divergent topics do not, indeed cannot, 'represent' socialist feminism. They are not presented here to do so, but rather to offer observations and challenges and new possibilities for the further critical evaluation of socialist feminist discursive interventions.

Love's Labours Lost : Marxism and Feminism

Marxism and feminism ears a difficult relation to one another. The relation has been conceptualized as union, a marriage – however shaky, a mutually supportive intermingling of theories and modes of practice. Feminism, it was argued, stood to offer Marxism an account of sexual oppression while Marxism, in turn, purported to offer feminism a theory of political struggle and change. More recently, however, strains between thee two political movements have moved discussion away from the ideal of a happy union towards a debate between potentially anatonistic participants. A debate between Marxism and feminism has emerged manifested within feminism as a debate between socialist feminism and other feminisms. The question is which position is politically and theoretically adequate, or which provides the most exhaustive explanations of women's social relations in modern western cultures; and hence which position is more radical and effective in presenting strategies for political change.

Socialist feminists have argued against what they label as 'radical feminism' on philosophical as well as political grounds. Theories that take women, their bodies, sexualities, and consciousness as primary, or which regard patriarchy

– the systematic domination of men over women – as the foundation of all social power are variously declared individualist, subjectivist, humanist, functionalist, essentialist, naturalist, and reductionist from a Marxist or socialist perspective. These feminists' positions are supposed to neglect the primacy of the historico-political determination of women's oppression in favor of such 'natural' or a historical concepts/ categories as 'men' and 'women'. Yet rarely if every has the socialist/Marxist perspective been scrutinized in terms of its epistemological and ontological premises. The impact of historical materialist and scientific socialist presumptions on feminism, including socialist feminism has so far remained outside of debate.

Our aim in this paper is to examine some of the central philosophical and theoretical presuppositions Marxism makes – about the subject, abut the nature of reality and knowledge in so far as these have direct even if unrecognized consequences for the development and growth of feminist theories. We will not be directing our critical analysis at any particular version of Marxism but at a number of shared presuppositions that any form of Marxism typically adopts. While it is clear that no single version or variant of Marxism necessarily maintains ever presupposition we discuss, nevertheless we claim that every version maintains at lest some of these theoretical allegiances. Although there are many Marxisms and socialisms, our aim here is not a detailed textual analysis of one or several positions but a general analysis of Marxism's broad presuppositions and some of the political effects these presuppositions lead to in relation to feminist theory.

Our position is that Marxist concepts of the subject, reality, and reasons are phallocentric.1 This phallocentrism is not eradicated or removed simply by admitting to charges of 'sex-blindness', by adding women's oppression to a whole set of other oppressions. Rather, it needs to be located at the very epistemological and ontological foundations of the

Marxist position. As a consequence, we believe that socialist feminism remains locked in a paradox as a feminist position unless it can somehow develop a radically *woman-centred* version of 'socialism' which entails 'seeing women first', conceptualizing a space which allows women to be considered autonomous shapers and creators of meaning.[2] Whether it is at all possible to realign the Marxist battery of concepts o accommodate sexual difference is a problem that socialist feminism must work out for itself.

This article assesses some of the philosophical assumptions upon which Marxism, as a Master-knowledge of history and society bases itself. In doing so it addresses no just the theoretical principles involved but also some of the political strategies to which these principles give rise. The discussion divides into three parts. The first examines Marxism's dominance of the left intellectual and political field. The second identifies some of the traditional philosophical assumptions it shares in common with 'bourgeois' theory, particularly the uses made of notions of reason, the subject-object relation, reality and truth, and the relationship between theory and practice. The find part offers analysis of some of the effects of Marxism's philosophical adherences and closures on other modes of radical thought, drawing mainly on the case of feminism. This entails scrutiny of the adequacy of Marxist concepts of subjectivity, and its positions on power and the sexually differentiated body, the struggles for equality versus the right to difference in feminisms.

In addressing ourselves broadly to Marxism or Marxist feminism, we wish to counter two common a strategies adopted by Marxists to evade criticism. The first is to separate out 'Marxism' from 'socialism'. While many criticisms of Marxisms are justified, so it is argued, they do not apply to this (i.e. socialist) version. This tactic accommodates criticism by indefinitely altering and reworking secondary hypotheses, Marxism's 'outer shell', such as centralism and the unity of organisation, the primary position of the proletariat, definitions of classes, functions of the state; meanwhile, more primary hypotheses, its 'central core', like the primacy of material production/reproduction, the concept of class, the capitalist state as the locus f power and, more importantly, the unitary goal of Socialist Revolution, are left intact. The second tactic sees a standard mode or reply to criticisms posed to Marxist theory by the existence of so-called socialist systems. (USSR, Eastern Europe, China, Cuba, etc.), which has been to produce or invent another Marxism, which is always elsewhere. This form is immune to criticism because it always posits a different form of state or social organisation, one not yet in existence, one always other to the view that is criticized.

Marxism and the Political Field

In its position as the radical political theory, Marxism maintains a position of power which remains largely unrecognized and which negatively affects its relations to other left political positions. This kind of dominance within left-wing politics is the result of its usually unacknowledged connections to existing institutions ad bodies of authority as well as to its modes operation within left circles. Its strategies seem dual. On the one hand, they can be regarded as institutional and based on acquiring recognition and status from institutional bodies and established agencies of power. On the other hand, they are defensive/offensive in relation to other forms of left politics. This involves the controlling, labeling, and classification of theoretical positions other than Marxism. In defending itself, Marxism criticizes other theories which are then discarded as unworthy or incorporated as part of its project.

At the level of theory, politics, and organisation, Marxism shares many characteristics with the very system it claims to challenge. Rather than being radically 'other', Marxism is virtually the alter-ego, the inversion around a shared axis of its capitalist counterpart. Capitalism and socialism are perhaps two sides of the same coin. This is evident in the way in which Marxism shares with the bourgeois order it condemns, a belief in certain essential values for effective social organisation. These shared values include: respect for law and order, planned organisation, the need for accurate prediction, policy-making, and planning, the need for enlightened leadership, full development of productive capacities, the need for social unity, belief in progress and evolution. As well, it shares: an ideal of society as a unitary totality, a concept of universal (equal) subjectivity, the idea that global explanations are superior to particularized or local explanations, a unitary view of truth, reason, reality, and causality as ultimate neutral and objective principles in knowledge. Where Marxism is indeed a radical opposite of burgeois thought is in its methods – as well as its prescription for how to define or express these values, and for whom.

The first form of institutional support for Marxism thus comes from holding a set of values and interests in common with traditional modes of thought. Second, within existing institutions of power and authority, the position of Marxism can be characterized as one with considerable recognition. Its place in institutions of learning, in the circuits of publications, in trade unions, political parties and movements, and in various cultural and political organisations suggests it has an 'honourable' place within capitalism as an acknowledged, even if not admired adversary. Within the university structure, Marxism has a position comparable to the official trade union movement. It is acknowledged as the 'official enemy' of capitalism occupying a position that is representative of all radical politics. This has the effect of reducing all other forms of struggle for change to variants, impurities, or counter-revolutionary positions within a primary political schema, thereby keeping them in check. Marxism may be critized, but it is also engaged with as a worthy adversary to burgeois theory. The extent to which Marxism has become respectable and recognized in universities as the rival scientific knowledge to bourgeois forms of thought is also indicated by the number of senior academics who are Marxists, the number of courses in Marxist and Marxist-related areas, the recommended reading lists in areas of Marxist expertise in the humanities - particularly in education, law, psychology, sociology, urban studies, history, geography, and languages. Third, apart from its network of institutional supports, Marxism, as a conceptual system, shares another common history with conventional though, and even the understanding provided by common sense. Importantly, in relation to our arguments here, Marxism shares with bourgeois thought a universal representation of humanity that is in fact masculine. It is phallocentric and ignores sexual specificity because of its complicity in a shared set of assumptions that mark all socio-political thought hitherto: that the norm of humanity is best represented by 'man'. Marxism shares with bourgeois thought the strategy of defining women only in relation to male norms. Given this common set of assumptions and methods, it is not surprising that the superiority of Marxism over feminism can be asserted as a natural fact, since for most women it is extremely difficult to articulate ourselves as the norm of judgments and values - to develop a woman-centred concept of ourselves and our world. It is largely because of this shared mode of dominant thinking that Marxism has been unable to claim itself indispensable to feminism. In reinterpreting and redirecting feminist thought and practice according to its priori framework, it simply reflects and reproduces already customary ways of conceptualizing women as incomplete, lacking.

Women are considered only in elation to men, hence there is an emphasis on issues reflecting this assumption in Marxist theory: reproduction, the family, women and work, sexuality. The question of the relationship between Marxism and feminism implies a symmetry between competing but equal politico-theoretical frameworks, but n fact Marxism more often relates to feminism as a form of Master-knowledge, a form of theoretical domination that creates subjugated/ subjected knowledge and perpetuates the silence that has robbed women of their history and culture. In establishing its position as the leader of radical politics, Marxism series for itself a substantial technique fro control – the power of definition. It assumes both the power of self-definition and the power of definition over the whole political field, including other forms of left-wing politics. In this way, Marxism reduces the specificity, aims, and struggles of different groups so that they are commensurate with Marxist criteria and therefore able to be judged by them. This tendency abounds in the fields of women's struggles, anti-raism, anti-heterosexism. It redues these struges so that they are all instanes of one struggle- the one Marxism guides. For example, attempts are made to redue abortion, hildbirth,rape, arposition, andpornography to class issues orto capitalist financial interests, sexuality, and male domination to the bourgeois family, marriage, monogamy, private property, andstate control. All issues raised by the power rlaitons between men and women are claimed to be ultimately explicable in trms of the interests capital has in upholding hem. Capitalism isultimately shwn to bear an intrinsic and essential reltion to patriarchy,and henceits overthrow is supposed to rob the latter of its crucial material base. Ith respectto the 'issue' of heterosexism, thatinstitutuon employed to ensure mens continual access to women, thisis only ever acknowledged if, once again, it can be argued that compulsory heterosexuality service capitalism, not allmen. In thiscontext, we need to examine more closely the continual dismissal by Marxists of attempts to theorize the origins of patriarchy by reference to myths, religion, prehistoric artifacts, modes of symbolic exchange, and kinship categories. Similarly, questions about an inherent ethnocentrism of western culture with its paranoid adherence to materialism and anti-spiritualism, as well as its naïve believe in a scientific progress synonymous with control over nature, are more often than not rephrased in terms of greedy commercial interests. In this way, the evils of white society are reduced to results of imperialism, which has the effect of implying that Marxists are natural anti-racists. These are just a few example of the globalizing/ reductionist tendency in Marxism that enables it to subsume many different struggle and aims a under its umbrella. Marxism is thus able to in tall itself as a Master-knowledge of the left, relegating other forms of knowledge and struggle to a secondary or auxiliary position. Marxism is nevertheless able to utilize the 'inputs' of such knowledge very ably to expand its grip on the political field. By adding 'women's issues,' antiracism, anti-heterosexism to its agenda in the manner we have outlined, it is able to cover an ever wider terrain.

In this way, Marxism exerts a power over other radical struggles that seems only marginally better than the oppressive situations it purports to challenge. Instead of Marxism assuming a position of support and recognition vis-à-vis other radical struggles, it declares a partnership in which it decrees the conditions of interaction. It utilizes a poertodirect 'autonomous' struggles along its path. In any partnership, Marxism is in fact prioritied and taken as the position from which one can ultimately evaluate the other partner, and the partnership as a whole. In this relation, the' junior partner' has to a vow its own *insufficiency* to be accorded a place, marginal' movements are put into the position of having to prove their radical credentials – their 'faith' or 'belief' in radical social change as determined by Marxism. On the other hand, they are also required to admit their ignorance and other need to embrace a more comprehensive and challenging theory. Without Marxist guidance, other theories are regarded as confuse, inconsistent, a historical, romantic, or naive; as lacking objectives and 'adequate explanatory tools', hence co-optable.

In acting as Master-knowledge, Marxism takes the position of the subject, the knower, and its radical 'partner', such as feminism, is assigned the role of object of knowledge. Marxism, in other words, delegates to itself the right of definition and analysis. It establishes grades of judgment, imposes dichotomous categories over a field of differences, defines key concepts and issues, and determines the criteria of intelligibility by which it can reduce its partner to one of two positions. Either the other valiantly tries to insert her. If, her struggles, her knowledges with the master paradigm, expending all energy in the process: or, alternatively, finds herself relegated to the status of heretic, playing the role of hysterical other to the cool of Marxist reason, thereby apt to be ridiculed, or simply refused a hearing.

The debate between Marxism and other radical movements has thus been a one-sided communication of directives and truths. In refusing to acknowledge the self-sufficiency, the difference of other theories and struggles which a may fall outside its paradigm, Marxism effectively acts as a form of control on those movements. By prioritizing Marxist principles which assume the right to decide which issues, goals, and modes of action are appropriate, the very autonomy of other struggles is absorbed an transformed into a form accommodating Marxism.

What is conveniently overlooked is that all of these concepts and principles may prove to mean quite different things from a feminist perspective; that is to say, one that takes women's social relations qua women as primary. Moreover these criticisms and evaluations only gain a status within Marxist discourse, yet this discourse is not open to serious questioning when confronted with the theoretical innovations and developments feminisms have to offer. The potential explanatory power of the conceptual tools feminisms my possess as an alternative, not a complement to Marxism are effectively denied in order that Marxism's hegemony may be salvaged. We would not want to detract from the importance of contributions made by Marxist-feminists in extending Marxism's scope to analyses of women's oppression under capitalism, particularly in areas that Marxism has previously ignored or under-developed such as the family, women, and labour, and women's relation to the state. We would argue, however, that these contributions are also continually fuelling Marxist systems of interpretation, strengthening their globalizing and reductionist tendencies. Moreover, it prevents a thorough examination of the presumed ability of Marxism indefinitely to extend itself beyond the parameters of its original paradigm and of its investments in exerting power over fields of feminist thinking and action. The right t intervene and dominate in this field is simply asserted by pointing to Marxism as the more complete theory of society with an established tradition in political thinking. That this more complete theory of society reflects primarily masculine views and interests defining women with respect to their place in male world and in accordance with how they complement men, is underestimated in favour of pointing out links with capitalist interests.

The effect of this paradigm on the field of women's struggle sin that priorities and evaluations imported from Marxism are imposed on diverse and complex variants of feminism, reducing them to terms oppositional to Marxism. The many differences between and within feminisms are often written off by homogenizing them into net units of 'otherness' such as 'radical feminism', 'bourgeois feminism,' or 'lesbian separatism'. This often services to relegate those outside the Marist framework to the role of adversary to true, social, revolutionary change and, by extension, to that of objective supporter of capitalism and thus of continued oppression and exploitation. This binary logic, the logic of either/or (if you are not for us you must be against us) imputes that not to be a Marxist implies not being able to achieve one's own aim – the liberation of women from male dominion - let alone being in capable of explaining the 'larger, more important' issues of social power.

This practice of transforming difference into dichotomous opposition is significant political strategy. By representing itself simply as a neutral mode of dividing and distinguishing differences as natural opposites. Marxism denies any complicity in the very construction of the dichotomy, let alone its investment in the primacy of one of the terms of the dichotomy a the expense of the other. Dichotomies divide a disparate field according to one value and judge initially non-comparable others on the basis of that value. Male/female becomes male/non-male. The logical form A/not A, the general form of a philosophically dichotomous structure, demonstrates clearly the primacy accorded to A as the positive, affirmative term, and characteristic value governing the field of the dichotomy.

This practice of privileging one of the two trms, defining the second as an absence of the first, is also a faouritemode of descrition of Marxism, for example, such opposites as public/private, political/psychological, objective/subjective, economic/ideological,production/reproduction, class/sex all implicitly proritizethe leftterm at the expense of the right. This tactic establishes a veneer of objectiveity and naturalness which serves to disguise the political values which the dichotomy actualywields. In general them, dichotomous thinking redues multiplicity and plurality of levels and positions to a single oppositional norm. The claim for the appropriateness of this mode of dividing up the world lies in the belief in a singular explanatory paradigm and a universal homogenized politics to combat all the particular expressions of a oppressive social system by giving them an underlying or central cause such as the exploitation of the proletariat by capital.

One of the major effects f Marxism's institutional position

and its modes of definition of itself and others, is an insidious politics of representation. In presenting itself as a form of knowledge, Marxism claims to be able to explain the real conditions of existence beyond lives experience. What is to be considered real is defined as that which is outside of experience, independent of one's perceived place in the social formation and beyond the surface manifestations of everyday life. Knowledge of these real conditions which is considered a prerequisite to viable and effective political action – is possible only if one submits oneself to the central tenets of the Marxist understanding of reality. Marxism articulates what the worker oor the oppressed cannot know or say. It speaks on behalf of those who cannot speak because they lack the capacity for synthesizing particularities into a systematic whole. It is never made clear, however, why this need for totalizing is a need of the oppressed; rather, it seems to functions as a need for the intellectual (who is usually white, middle-class, and male) to think in terms of universals and totalities. The fact that their 'real interests' are not always directly perceived as such by the oppressed, is explained by terms, like 'political apathy', 'false consciousness', 'self-interest (!)', 'ideology', or more recently and rather inappropriately, 'the unconscious'. There is, however, no a priori correspondence between those represented and their representatives, between the objects and the subjects of knowledge, although this is what Marxism assumes when it judges itself to be the true representative of the masses (whoever is included in this category).

It is a reduction of difference and specify to sameness by means of its implicit concepts of truth, reality, and rationality that allows Marxism to intervene, impose its judgements, and claim to represent all other struggles. One of the ways in which Marxism attempts this reduction is in this representation of a common enemy: the macrolithic system of capitalism. While this common enemy may well exist for all such groups it is unwarranted to conclude that its operations and effects are all the same for all groups. To posit patriarchy as 'the enemy' as feminism does offers Marxism a change to co-opt or appropriate its aims and goals by making patriarchy the inevitable double of capitalism.

Marxism suggests not only a common enemy, it also involves a commonness of interests and a shared stake in struggles These positions become subsumed under Marxism's primacy and their particularity, specificity, and appropriateness in context is ignored. All positions are leveled with respect to each other, they all become variations or trends of the same thing, different struggles against a common enemy. These other struggles are seen to e tinged with features of the very system they challenge and are seen as incapable of adequately formulting an understanding of, or programme for social change alone. In this way all other positions are transformed from difference to opposition: non-Marxists become anti-Marxists. They become examples of liberalism, reformism, leftism, irrationalism, functionalism, and pluralism: all degrees of bourgeois complicity. Marxism is able to represent all radical movements as variations, and inadequate ones at that, of a true (socialist) revolutionary theory and practice. In this way, these movements become objects of analysis for Marxism within Marxist theory and are subjected to a logic of reinterpretation and representation.

Given the institutional power of Marxism and its domination of the left political field, it becomes extremely difficult to combat this reduction and to insist on a multiplicity of aims, practices, and theories directed towards revolutionary social change. This may be illustrated in the Marxist search for Feminist theory and a Unified Movement, where differences between women in feminism are seen as fragmented, subjective, or based on confused ideas about political organisation. If Marxism speaks of the need for an autonomous women's movement it actually means a homogeneous entity capable of taking care of or rather keeping in check the struggles over women's issues, those which the theory of capital has not yet managed to allot a place within the ambit of its core principles. The fragmentary, non-unified theoretical perspectives and practices of feminist struggles are deplored as a weakness rather than applauded as a strength. Feminism is seen as being in need of unification, tighter organisation, and a more comprehensive programme that will include all women, somehow, under a single banner. Marxism's claim to one movement with one (true) theory and a singular Marxism's claim to one movement with one (true) theory and a singular programme is simply transposed onto feminism as if fragmentation and regionality were a problem instead of a mode of self-determination. Feminism is judged by Marxist criteria which seem to have little appreciation of the issues and struggles faced by *women as women.*

Marxism and the Theoretical Domain

The so-called 'crisis in Marxism' is no simply a political crisis, a crisis in effectivity organisation, or popular appeal. The crisis Marxism faces is also a theoretical crisis, a crisis at the level of its adherence to problematic concepts of Knowledge, Truth, Reason, and Power which it holds in common with the mainstream of western philosophical thought. This crisis affects not only is place as revolutionary vanguard, it also raises questions about the very politics of scientificity -the *political* function of knowledge, truth, and representation. Questions about the relation between power and knowledge have until recently been discussed with Marxism only in relation to the 'ruling class' or the state. The claim to truth, the will to knowledge, the primacy of reason, are rarely examined in their relation to power, and are taken as somehow pure and neutral values.

Marxism's adherence to these philosophical assumptions is central to its functions of representing all other political groups and its operations as a system of thought. These adherences include: the claim for a universal totalizing theory, capable of explaining various conflicts and disturbances at all levels of the social formation with a concept of (dialectical) causality and a belief in *telos,* in an immanent singular meaning to social event sin their diversity. It is these which lead to a desire for programmes and prescriptions to direct practice towards the realization of reason, to a need to construct a system of social order, and so on.

Marxism, contrary to its own assertions, ahs a great deal invested in traditional philosophical concepts of knowledge truth, reason, and the universal rational intellect, which a have precise political effects. In the face of a world that increasingly finds itself confronted with regional, marginal, and minority groups which revolt against the denial of their claims to a unique irreducible difference, a commitment to concepts of universality may prove historically inappropriate and politically oppressive. A few primary points of interaction between Marxist theory and traditional philosophy serve to indicate Marxism's ensnarement in phallocentric and logocentric assumptions.

The Primacy of Reason

The concept of reason that Marxism shares in common with burgeois thought has an illustrious genealogy in the history of philosophy which dates from Plato. This concept presupposes a unified mind, unhampered by any internal contradictions which may result from its relations to a lived body. Reason is not simply based on a psychical unity, it is also the principle that organized reality. Reasons is the link, the mediating connection between the unitary mind and a singular reality. Reason provides a double guarantee: it ensures that the mind comes progressively to approximate reality (making knowledge, truth, and science the major embodiments of reason); and that reality is grasped in if fullness by the mind, as may be illustrated from effective intervention in practical reason. This double guarantee can be stressed in various ways: by stressing the mind's capacity to make the world understandable, the ideal it position is developed; by privileging the world as having a determinate reason which the mind adequately grasps when it is rational, we are led to materialism. What is perhaps ironic about Marxism's epistemology is that, while claiming to overthrow idealism, it simply takes the opposite side, remaining locked into its underlying assumptions and values.

In common with its historical and philosophical heritage, Marxism does not characterize reason positively, in its own terms but defines it dichotomously, Reason as a privileged value (or value of the privileged) must be contrasted with what it defines as not reason. In this way, reason establishes a positive value and content for itself by creating oppositions, 'others' that serve to locate and implicitly define reason. Thee 'others' of reason give up their independent content to define the ground on which something else can be called rational becoming the completely negative task of illustrating what reason is not. A whole 'anatomy of otherness' is established if the list of all the dichotomies that serve to anchor reason is added together. Taken together, these are constituted as an infinite, homogeneous other leveled to an amorphous category of 'the irrational'. Among the relevant oppositions that serve to define reason are: reason/madness, reason/passions, reason/emotions, reason/sense, reason/experience, reason (mind)/body, reason/spontancism, reason/barbarism, and reason/anarchy.

Moreover, reason is not simply in opposition to various 'others'; its primacy depends on a transcendence, and overcoming or avoiding the dangers this other witness poses. In order to attain the status of reason, the knower must disengage from lived experience, the body, senses, emotions, and so on, putting them on one side, as it were. In separating these 'other' from reason, philosophical tradition must neglect their place, operation, and effects. Only procedures based on reason are acceptable and valuable theoretical contributions – reflection, analysis, synthesis, logical arguments, the dialectic, clear and straightforward expression. Marxism, as their to this tradition, is able thereby to claim a power and appeal as a rational theory and method of change, guiding and informing other political groups who are in some way 'less rational'.

Our point here is not that there are systems of thought which are so naïve as to believe in reason; nor, on the other hand, do we wish to claim a positive value to 'the irrational' as a category. For this would amount to accepting the dichotomy while attempting to reverse its value. Our criticism has to do with the political investments in this process of separating the rational from their rational. Our criticism is not that Marxism uses a concept of reason, but with the particular conception that it uses – a hierarchical, transcendent, and unitary one. Reason is not defined by its incidental properties or qualities, but by its capacity to stand over and above particularities and specificites. Reason, in shedding itself of all particularity, not only leaves behind its own history, it becomes the yardstick or mesure for all the forms that it constitutes as irrational. The unified, singular. Global form of reason, reason, presents a political and historical understanding of the dichotomous mode of characterizing reason. This model of rationality cannot accord a place to other forms of rationality derived form different concrete contexts. This position, however, must not b equated with reletivion. There is nothing relative about politics or power unless for those who presume themselves to be outside of it in some universal position of knowledge. Marxism retains the belief that there can be no thought which remains specific, local, particular, and yet theoretically justified. Thinking and under standing can only attain the position of Knowledge or truth if it attains the universal.

The Subject/object Relation

Marxism also inherits the subject/object dichotomy. This presents a non-reversible hierarchy in which the subject of knowledge has a privileged status in relation to the object of knowledge. The use of this dichotomy has two related consequences; a radical distinction between the subject of knowledge, on the one hand, and the object of knowledge, on the other; and a bifurctation between 'subjective' and 'objective' nteres in knowledge. These have important implications for the Marxist concept of knowledge, of the knower or intellectual and of the relation between these and those who are ignorant.

While Marxism insists that material conditions of existence shape the subject's consciousness, when it comes to the subject of knowledge the concept of a disembodied, rational, or universal consciousness is posited instead. This subject, the subject that produces truthful knowledges, is not implicated in such 'subjective' ensnarements as political, economic or personal interests, for the subject is not a living, experiencing subject at all, but a rational, knowing subject. This rational subject is a neutral subject, a disinterested knower who my be committed or involved with political struggle, but whose commitment does not interfere with the objectivity of the theoretical work that is engaged in. This subject is unhinged form lived experience and the particularity of a position in the world. This is perhaps what explains the table absence of self-critical awareness of the privileged social position of the Marxist intellectual or academic.

Marxist social science divides the politico-social field into objects or potential objects of knowledge – oppressed workers, women, blacks and also capitalists. These 'object' of knowledge do not, at least in crude versions, produce knowledge themselves, but ideology and self-interested rationalisation. They can be known, but not themselves knowers. Their existence as potential objects of knowledge is given. What is significant about this opposition between subject and object of knowledge is that the knowing subject, the agent of the theory's truth never becomes the object of the other's gaze, never gets analysed in turn. Knowledge mediates between the subject and the object in one direction only.

Knowledge produced by a rational subject using the appropriate methods willfully manipulated in he behind so propagandists or advertisers yields a knowledge that is objective, true in all circumstances, for all subjects. Objective knowledge is objective because it is not relative to space and time, because it is independent of all 'subjective' particularities, and because it is politically neutral. All knowledge that does not attain this position is thereby deemed subjective and demoted to the status of opinion or belief. The particular, the experiential, what is variable, the question or viewpoint or perspective are considered subjective, and thus not suitable for the kind of generation that structures objectivity. The politics of knowledge-production and the position and function of those who produce knowledge remains untouched on this conception of knowledge. As a neutral object, the subject of knowledge is not considered to be implicated in the structure or content of knowledge. It is only when the relations of power between the knower and the known are openly discussed that the question of the power of the knowing subject over the object of knowledge can be challenged or overthrown altogether.

Reality and Truth

Marxism's reliance on a traditional concept of rationality is, as we have already suggested, directly connected to a particular conception of reality. Reality and reason are somehow mirror-images of each other, for reality is in principle rational in its underlying structure. It is presumed that reality is governed by particular causal laws which are determinable and understandable, that it is a reality amenable to scientific understanding.

The idea that tee is no meaning or reason in the world other than that which is contributed to it by human thought is unacceptable for Marxism. Indeterminacy, change, discontinuity, event, or accident are only ever acknowledged as operating in reality hen it is understood that these are only apparent occurrences without meaning, which can be given their real explanation by attributing specific causes to them by uncovering their real determination. Adequate or true knowledge is then a knowledge which grasps the underlying structure and totality of reality. Reality is in essence whole, a given object of thought, even if it can be Reality is in essence whole, a given object of thought, even if it can be admitted that reality is perceived differently from different perspectives. This is why, for Marxism, 'lived experience' is a second-order phenomenon which requires knowledge of what structures it so that it may be seen as first-order relation. It is precisely Marxism which can provide this knowledge of the real relations which structure phenomena, because it grasps reality properly in its underlying totality.

The adherence to the concept of a unified and singular reality has led Marxism to conceptualize the relation between this given reality and the processes of signification that present us with knowledge of its as one of correspondence. While two or more theories ma signify this reality in quite different ways, underneath or beyond these representations is a reality to which they may or may not correspond, and which exists quite independently of their representations, incommensurable positions are regarded as forms of interpretation of one and the same underlying reality. S interpretations they are mere embellishments, or acts of consciousness, reflecting a reality other than their own. Interpretations it may e conceded, are the products of differences that are explicable in terms of interests or politics (ideological adherences), but their referent, the real, is outside this areas, free from ideology. It is this neutral reality that determines the true objectivity of competing statements.

We do not want to suggest that there is no reality or that the material world does not exist. Such a traditional form of opposition to realism is hardly a useful concept, politically speaking. But to admit that the world exists does not commit us to a singular truthful mode for accounting for it. Marxism seems to assume an implicit parallelism between the totality of the world (reality) and the totality of knowledges (truth) as well as the function of reason in grasping this totality. A singular reality requires a singular true theory and a singular form of reason to formulate or know it. No place can be accorded to other modes of conceptualization, other forms of experience, and other knowledges. The complexity and multiplicity of the world is reduced to the manifestation of a singular underlying reality which can be used to explain the apparent plurality of the perceived world.

The essential and material unity of reality is what is shred among all human beings. It is thus n surprise that Marxism insists on the need for unitary action. The struggles of women, blacks gays, or youth can, as result, be tabelled directionless, unorganized, unrealistic, but most of all, particularized and thus incapable of grasping the real in its totality and thus of even their own real interests.

In accordance with its conception of a singular form of reality and a singular mode of rationality, Marxism relies on an absolutist and singular concept of truth. Truth is conceived, as in traditional philosophy, as a relation of correspondence between a proposition or discourse and hat part of the word that it depicts. The image or representation of reality, and the reality it represents have a certain isomorphism such that tone could say the image is a true representation of reality. Truth in other words is established by the process of reference. From its commitment to a singular and independent reality already, as it were loaded with meaning and from its adherence to a rather naïve materialism, language as a medium of truth is seen as a passive, reflective second-order phenomenon. Language is capable of being a neutral tool of description and analysis, clearly and simply referring to a reality outside and beyond discourse. Truth is a form of bridge between these two distinct systems, the form in which discourse a grasps reality.

In so far as a proposition is true it is regarded as neutral, objective, universal, and a historical - true under all conditions at all times. It is only in so far as a body of true propositions is organized by systematic rules or laws that it ca aspire to the status of science. Marxism becomes a science from the moment its knowledge is no longer dependent on political or sectarian interests. It becomes scientific when internal interests to knowledge itself become primary. Such knowledge is not the partial or continent discourses of workers oppressed groups, or even intellectuals, but a knowledge directed at and based upon an understanding of the totality and underlying reality of society. The separation of truth from all investments in power relations is based in the belief that the truth condition is established merely by the correspondence of discourse and reality. As representation, is a more or less transparent phenomenon that can be nevertheless capable of being used neutrally, disengaged from power.

Since it is presumed that power lies with political interests or that true knowledges derive from a situation outside of power, Marxism relives itself of the need for self-examination or questioning of its desire for truth as a desire for power.

Marxism, it seems cannot accept the relativity of scientific discourses - a relativity not only with respect to history different cultures, or individuals, but relativity with respect to power.

Marxism is able to justify itself as a truthful and objective theory in two quite different ways. First, as we have jut outlined, Marxism presents itself as a true representation of reality. This marks its aspirations as a social science. Second, Marxism presents itself as a true representative of a universal proletariat, as a the position that most ably or truly represents that interests of the working class. It is able to represent those who need the truth. Both these positions amount to a refusal to see that science, whether 'proletarian science or 'universal science' and the formations of true knowledges are already deeply implicated in power relations. Marxists have spent considerable time and effort connecting the operations and functioning of false or ideological discourses to power (e.g. to the interests of particular groups); but they refuse to acknowlege the 'stakes' of knowledge and science production are just as high as those of ideology, the political investments just as great.

Marxism,as a result, does not need to scrutinize itself or allow other competigntheories an existence as adequate or true accounts of particular historical realities. Sicne, as we have argued, reality is singular and unified for Marxism it is a reality flattened of depth and diversity. Particular experiences, positions, and forms of oppression are relevant only n so far as they relate to this common, universal reality, the mode of production as the 'arche' of all societies, past, present, and future. Direct experience and true knowledge seem, on the Marist conception, to be mutually exclusive - experience mitigates the globality, objectivity, and universality of true knowledge, while presenting experience to the grid of truth somehow mitigates its subjective, experiential nature.

It must be noted here that our claim is not that Marxism includes some phenomena and not others in a highly selective manner. The inclusion of some and the exclusion of other objects of analysis, the existence of criteria which constitute them as appropriate objects, and the establishment of criteria and rules of adequacy all mark the operations of any discourse or theoretical systems. The point however is what is that is included and excluded and the political effects of this selection process. In other words, the openness of objects methods and the closure to other systems of thought marks an unacknowledged set of political investments that belief the claim to neutrality and objectivity made by scientific or true systems.

Marxism can be seen to be waging a battle on two fronts on the battleground of truth. First, it struggles against so-called bourgeois knowledges, particularly those that claim some scientific status in social, political and economic theory. It is claim here is that these social theories are developed and maintained in order to justify the social order – they are bourgeois in so far as they represent burgeois interests and hence are false and ideological. Second, it uses it claims to scientificity and truth to combat, suppress, or supersede there knowledge, based on concrete experiences of exploitation and oppression, analyzing, explaining, and representing these knowledges in its true discourse. A strategy that evolves out of this double-barrelled investment in truth is an attempt to reduce the latter to version of the former. Out of this results a dominance over the field of left politics that cannot be questioned – as a truth able to point out the 'ideological investments' both bourgeois and some radical theories share in common, Marxism stands outside and beyond them.

The significant question that needs to be posed here – one which Marxism cannot ask as soon as it presents itself as a science or true discourse – is at the level of the desire for totality, unity, synthesis, reductive singularity, and what power is invested in it, all of which effects theoretical closures. Why is it necessary to unify/solidity what may be fluid, diverse, and changing, if no tin order to block or control it? Diverse, changeable, strategic knowledges pose a potential thereat that must be minimised- that of the incapacity of theory, of any theory to capture reality in its entire or in its essence. To invoke truth in the way that Marxism does as a singular, universal, absolute, and exhaustive meta-principle is to prevent the question being asked: who poses truth, from where, to whom, and for what purpose?

The theory/practice relation

Marxism's investment in truth and rationalityleads it to a rather paradoxical and circular conception of th ereltion between theory and practice. Admittedly, it is within Marxist discourse that the necessity of theory beign ited to action, and of action beign infused with theory is developed. But the establishment of a dichotomous concept of the relations between theory and practice almotin spite of itself privileges one of the terms of th edichtomy (theory) and reduces the other (practice) to mor ean object of rather thana complement to theory. This dichotomy is represented in the old distinction between mental and manual labour which Marxism has never successfully been able to exorcise other than by attributing its existence to the evils of capitalism. A bifurcation between theory and practice is, in fact a corollary Of Marxism's adherence to a traditional concept of reason; for theory to be reliable and effective, it must be produced elsewhere than practice.

Within Marxism there is a implicit assumption about what constitutes theory and what counts as practice. They must be distinct for a dialectical relation between them to be possible. Theory is presume do be what is written in books in the quiet reflection before lead after action. Remote from polemic or politics; while practice consists in the energies of bodies of individuals and groups in concrete struggles. While this radical separation is to some extent a caricature (it is a firm belief that theory is always at least implicit in effective struggle), nevertheless the two remain quite distinct and in need of mediation. Theory I supposed to provide a rational guide to practice, directing, controlling, interrogating, and analyzing it; while practice informs, reforms, corrects, and is reflected in theory. Practice without theory (if such a thing were possible) would be without aims or objectives, blind in its direction, chaotic or haphazard in its effects. It would be irrational, without sense. Theory, on the other hand, cut off from practice becomes stale, idealist, irrelevant, and unstead. A dialectical relationship between these two terms is necessary to provide an adequate context for each and to account for their inter-relationships. Whichever side is privileged depends on the strategy necessary in a given conjuncture: theory can be invoked when the masses start to define their own practice (Althusser); practice can be invoked when the masses have to be wooed (Mao).

Under scrutiny, this dialectical relation between the terms is not an equal or reciprocal one, for theory always retains a primacy with respect to practice. While theoretical interventions, or more pertinently, interventions by theorists, academics, and party officials representingly, interventions by theorist is, academics, and party officials representing the truth have an enormous power in relation to struggles and political practice (witness the role of the PCF in Paris, 1968), practice changes or directs theory only in its outer protective shell, but does not touch its core. Indeed, it is not from the position of the core that practices, including Marxism's own, and all other theories are evaluated. No possible practice could every undermine its fundamental axioms. The core is a priori confirmed by any possible struggles, successes, or even failures.

This is not to say that internal debates about the

explanatory power of the core principle do not take place. In fact, they do, quite regularly. However, these take place by forcing the reality of successes and failures into the straitjacket of the theory, which can endlessly expand its definitions of basis basic principles by reinterpreting the sacred texts but never questioning their relevance or adequacy. Marxism has an immutable centre beyond debate, analysis, experience, or practice and is thus not regarded as a tool whose usefulness must be tested on the job at hand. The appropriateness of the theory is never in question, only the effectivity of struggles, practices, and strategies can be doubted.

Theory and practice, presented as if they were dialectical partners in revolutionary struggle, are in fact judged and assessed only by theoretical criteria. It is theory that judges the effects of theory on practice and practice on theory. To speak of practice in Marxist terms can only be done in terms of what practice means to Marxist theory. So, even if it is seen as a complement or supplement to theory, practice remains secondary, undirected. Practice is judged by a theory of practice as good/bad, relevant/irrelevant, etc., but theory itself is generally not subjected to practical criticism.

This emphasis on the guiding role of theory in relation to practice is supposedly what distinguishes Marxist politics from other forms of political struggle. Because theory is considered either absent, problematic, or non-directive in other struggles, these struggles are considered irrational, confused, chaotic, unfounded. Marxism, in contrast, derives from a close relation between theory and practice, mediated by the theory in the figure of the theorist/intellectual who claims to master knowledge and thus be capable of representing the other. The subject/object relation in knowledge is reinforced by a mental/manual split that characterized the relations between they and practice. Those that act in concrete struggles are generally considered no to be those who produce theory; they can become so if they conduct their struggles according to the theoretical directives laid down by Marxism.

Beyond Marxism

Marxism, in uncritically adopting traditional concepts of subjectivity and the body, presents an inherently phallocentric or masculinity characterization of the subject. This phallocentrism establishes an implicitly normative account of the subject, equating it with characteristics associated with masculinity. This normative commitment, in our View, blocks any well-meaning attempts by socialist feminists to find a place for women in Marxist theory, or alternatively, drastically to change the theory's outer shell while adhering to its basis principles. In the last resort, this leads to adopting the tacts of representation that Marxism utilizes – globalizing and totalizing difference in the service of an assumed sameness.

The concept of subjectivity in Marxism

It has been generally assumed since Althusser's work on ideology and subjectivity that any form of humanism is anathema to Marxism. Whereas earlier versions of Marxism (and Marx's own 'pre-scientific' writings) may have adopted concepts of a basic human nature and an unalinated essence of human existence, the development of 'scientific' Marxism meant that the determination of any human essence must be rejected as a form of idealism. Reference to a definite human nature is criticized for being bourgeois or ideological, since it is claimed that needs, desires, beliefs, and meanings are a historically determined to suggest that these might have a definite form or contents is seen as contrary to the goals of socialism.

Yet, a form of essentialism remains undetected in even the most rabid anti-humanist version of Marxism, since this so-called empty category of human nature nevertheless does have some given characteristics.

Human existence is still ultimately defined by the basic

activity of the production of material goods by labour. All social relations derive, in the final analysis, from economic relations (the only material relations that fill the category of subject). Apart from the fact that what is material is narrowly defined to include economic relations but to exclude linguistic, libidinal, and other forms of power relations, this simply assumes that the condition of labour – is the prerogative of men. The domination over nature and the creation of consumable and exchangeable goods through labour, i.e. production as meaningful activity on a world in order to transform it, has in fact been a description of the place accorded to men in patriarchal culture. What counts as labour and as production is narrowly defined in such a way that generally only the activities of men (and those of women in o far as they are the same a men) count.

Although Marxism holds that there is not determinate human nature in terms of the beliefs, wishes, aims, and project of subject, prior to any social determination being grafted onto it. Marxism assumes a subject as the raw material for a process of social stratification that permits no difference sand is therefore a neutral subject. This subject operates in the same manner as the subject of reason. The fact that there is such a collection of undifferentiated subjects is a presupposition of the idea of a socialist or communist revolution. Communism can become a future reality because, basically, if al the social conditions are equalized and evenly distributed, individuals must themselves be equalized, the same. This leveling is possible because of suppressed assumption of sameness, which perhaps represents the desire of the theorist or intellectual; to reduce the amorhous mass to a manageable category of 'universal human being. 'In this way, underneath it all, the theorist = the worker = everyman, and Marxism becomes the universally true representation of the *telos* of human existence and human potential.

Our point here is not to enter the debate between humanist and antihuman it versions of Marxism but to examine the truth effect of a discourse which functions on the basis of a universal singular, unified, and implicitly masculine entity, just as much as it is necessary to examine the truth effect of the anti-humanist position which speaks of structures and agencies rather than subjects. Both views pre-empt a scrutiny of the politics of representation which denies the sexual specificity of women in the interests of men. Both sets of discourses block a claim to difference, denying or regard in insignificant the *sexed* nature of human beings and the sexed nature of mode of representation and knowledge in patriarchal societies. It is only on the assumption that the naturalness of patriarchal relations between the sexes is an incontrovertible fact that the effect of both humanist and anti-humanist Marxism as universal representations of human existence and a covering over of female specificity is possible.

Marxism has been prepared to admit, given its views on subjectivity and agency as being determined by social and economic relations, that it has no adequate theory of the subject. It is at this point that the relevance and usefulness of psychoanalytic theory is acknowledged. The incorporation of the psychoanalytic account of the development of subjectivity has helped Marxism to explain the constitution of consciousness, by reference to the structure of the (bourgeois, patriarchal) family and the processes of socialization it develops for the (unconscious) production of subjects. The concept of the unconscious fits rather neatly (although in a form that distorts Freud's use of the term) with the Marxist epistemological requirement of a dichotomy between knowledge and ignorance. Today it is not so much the concept of 'false consciousness' but the unconscious that is used to explain why the masses are ignorant of their own real interests, why they suffer from bourgeois, individualist, or liberal tendencies. In other words, psychoanalysis has provided the basis of a theory of ideology, or of the production of a suitable bearer of capitalist relations. Moreover, the fact that the subject cannot know its own truth- the unconscious – other than through the mediation of the analyst reproduces the same truth effect as Marxism: namely that knowledge is not derived from experience or consciousness so its own conditions of existence, but comes from elsewhere, from outside. The truth of Capital and the truth of Oedipus together represent the truth of the primary determining term. Both theories take the male norm for granted, assume a universal determination, one in terms of masculine relations of production, the other in terms of a universal complex that takes the phallus as its primary determining tem. Both theories take the male norm for granted. However, the fact that psyhoanalysis bases its theory of the subject on the question of the differences between the sexes has provided Marxist feminist and other with the possibility of inserting a 'gender specification onto the subject of capitalism. Probably the most striking example is Juliet Mitchell's Psychoanalysis and feminism (Harmondsworth: Penguin 1975) which attempts to bring Marxist and feminist theory together using psychoanalytic precepts. Unfortunately, Mitchell (and a number of others) affirmed, in occurrence with Freud, that the female is a lack in relation to masculine, phallic fullness. Hence there can be no question of overcoming the patriarchal unconscious for women other than by an initiation into the male, rational norm, which implies an uncritical adoption of the universal truths of Marxism and psychoanalysis.

The outcome of Marxist interest in and use of psychoanalytic concepts is to a large extent guided, not by the details of psychoanalytic theory itself (for that, Marxists acknowledge, would be to accept an individualism that is contrary to them) but by the spectre of the twin evils of biologism and essentialism. Although psychoanalysis in its orthodox form embodies both of these assumptions, it is nevertheless claimed to be capable of being purified of its essentialist and biological traits and to provide the necessary elements for a Marxist theory of subjectivity. Anatomical differences between the sexes can be admitted, but hey can play no role in either modes of representation or in characterizing the type and form of subject, for these anatomical givens are outside of social and psychological spheres. To conflate them together is a form of biologism and reductionism. This implies a highly selective use of Frud's work: either his work on the unconscious is used to enhance or develop the concept of ideology, ignoring altogether the relations between the unconscious and sexuality; or else Freud's account f the distinction between the sexes is wholeheartedly adopted without any indication of the eternally oppressed position of women that his account entails.

What remains problematic abut any 'union' of Marxism and psycho-analysis is the presumption of masculinity as the norm of subjectivity. It is significant that what remains ignored by both Marxism and psycho-analysis is precisely the specificity of the female body, and the consequent differences in psychical functioning between the sexes. A recent critical questioning of psychoanalytic theory by feminists has been aimed at revealing the phallocentrism of psychoanalysis, seeing it as an express in of male a subjectivity, male desire, and male projections, rater than, as Mitchell did, as an accurate description of both sexes under patriarchy. Such a reading regards the construction of feminity as a lack not as a sociological fact, but as a programme established by male desires a based on the incapacity of men adequately to deal with the limits of their subjectivity. Women are represented in phallocentric discourse as the other, the lack that men cannot tolerate within themselves.

Power and the Sexually differentiated body

If Marxism and psychoanalysis have, as we have argued, developed a concept of the subject that is universal and neutral, then this subject is implicitly a male subject. The assumption of a universal category of subject, to which one can add a class, a race, or a sex, belies the already assumed structure of a male subject. Psychoanalysis explains this universal structuring of subjects by assuming a norm of subjectivity as phallic and, by virtue of the fact, assigns women to the category of un-phallic, that is, castrated. This homogeneous category of the subject is an effect of the levelling of all differences to the category of the same, which allows a comparative evaluation of the presence for absence of already valorized qualities, attributes, and capacities as they are distributed between men and women respectively. The most fundamental level of difference begins with the differences between sexed bodies.

One of the most striking elisions in Marxist theory is its neglect and ignorance f the role of the body in constituting consciousness and in characterizing exploitation and oppression. Admittedly, Marx does discuss the body of the worker as a locus of labour power, but his comments simply reflect a naïve positivist assumption of unity bodies as functional organisms which is inadequate to explain the complex place the body occupies in the social world. For Marxist theory, discussions of bodies and their specificities belongs to the realm of biology, and attempts to introduce them in social and political theory have to be regarded as biologism or essentialism. In this way Marxism has seriously arrested work done by feminists and others on specifying that particular forms of bodies and bodily processes mark out differences between subjectivities, that subjectivity is sexed. By simply dismissing all of this as biolgism and essentialism, the necessary analysis of biological existence and its representation in psychical life is neatly pre-empted, and the role of men in women's oppression is conveniently ignored.

This threatens to annihilate he specificity of women's

lived oppression, since that oppression is prevented from being represented in terms of the existence of sexually differenated bodies, and more particularly in their significance in psychic and social life. And yet, no explanation can be offered forwhy it is women's bodies and sexualities that operate as the site for this. The same blind spot characterizes psychoanalytic theory, although this theory at least openly admits it is in fact women's bodies and sexualities that serve, by their characterization as a lack deprivation, in the construction of the universal (male) subject. In other words, the body's specificity can be ignored by these Master-knowledges only because their concepts of subjectivity are already implicity masculine. The female body has already given up its 'use-value' in the process of exchange; its value is established by a phallic economy.

The point is that we are not disembodied subjects, consciousness distinct from bodies. Out psychologies and subjectivities are bounded by our morphologies, the psychical and libidinal relations we have tour bodies. The body as lived is what constitutes subjectivity, and structures and organizes consciousness. This implies that there can not be one or even two kinds of subject, but many different kinds, bounded not simply by the biological body but by its necessary social and individual signification. The body is not simply the 'seat' of subjectivity; it is also the target of technologies of power and forms of social control in all cultures. Its relations are not limited to capitalism, for even after a so-called socialist revolution, the cultural necessity of harnessing and inscribing the body as a social body remains – fact not often acknowledged in utopian conceptions of life 'after the revolution'. If, as we have suggested, thee are ireducible differences between sexed bodies and if any culture imposes itself b marking these differences, then the two sexed bodies require different technologies of power to organize and supervise the development of each.   Any theory that is based on the unquestioned assumption of a singular, non-differentiated concept of subjectivity denies these irreducible differences, blocking an understanding of the specific conditions which create the inscription and codification of bodies as sexually differentiated. Indicating sex differences cannot simply be a matter of a general model which differs only in its detail or by degrees, for the two sexes, but entails a radical rethinking of whether models, instruments, and discourses appropriate for describing male subjectivity are, in fat appropriate for female subjectivity. That Marxism takes little or no interest in these considerations is grounded in the fact that it is only interested in the subject as a reflection or product of ultimately economic demands - a tool in the service of capital - instead of recognizing the 'mediation' of sexual difference that helps structure consciousness and behaviour.

By suppressing the specificity of the body's morphology, and thus deny in sexual differences (only admitting it in so far as it can be explained by the mode of production in the last instances), capitalism and not patriarchy becomes the locus of all social power. Patriarchy can then either be reduced to an effect of capitalism, or alternatively to a functional prop for it, and the centrality of the Marxist paradigm is saved in the face of a threatening blow to its edifice. In other words, what can e parried in this way is the question how far the values and concepts of Marxism, and its 'natural' dominance over the left political field are, in fact, effects of the suppression of the problem of sexual difference. This evasion helps to relegate the debate about sex/class or capitalism/patriarchy continually to the 'private sphere' (where the relations between the sexes are admitted to the problematic) or to the catch-all phrase 'the sexual division of labour', which in itself hides male domination over this division into spheres. Moreover, since only capitalism represents power, Marxism prevents the possibility of questioning the relation between technologies of power on sexually differentiated bodies and power as the organizing principle of all social order. So, it is not just that Marxism is sex-blind, as so many recent socialist feminists recognize, but much more that it assumes (in union with the whole history of western cultural thought) the unproblematic primacy of one term of a dichotomy installed by patriarchy. In other words, it is phallocentric. The opposition between masculine and feminine constitutes a picture of subjectivity, the body, and social relations which, while it gives a place to women, does so only in terms of what they are not and never can become: independent categories of analysis. Feminity seen as deficient, variant masculinity. Women can only exist dependently. There an never be any question of a theoretical perspective which takes women as subjects, not takes its point of departure from women's specificity and feminity as an independent and autonomous category.

Different not equality

One ofth emajor effectis of th elevelling of th specificity of the female existence to male models is the reduction of feminist struggles for autonomy and self-detrmination to struggles for equality. The streategical evasion of th eproblem of th eody began with the introducton of gender, not the sex of the body,as the key term. Originally devised as a radicalfeminist resonse to reactionary theories about the natural inferiotiry of women,this sex/gender dichotomy has since been happily incorporated with Marxist feminist theories. This is not so surprising, since underlying the Marxist assumption that feminist theory needs completion, is the assumption that what all women are and should be after is equality with men. The various arguments about women's economic relations and familiar position imply that women need an equal share in production, reproduction, and consumption and an equal place in socialist struggles. If, however, the connection between sex and gender is an internal one, then the assumption tat the aim of women's struggles should be equality with men needs to be seriously questioned.

This equality is base don a denial of the sexed body as the defining men that they are part of the same struggles; and it is their reduction to a common denominator determined by masculinity that defines all struggles as ultimately one androgynous struggle. The leveling implied by the concept of equality works in conjunction with a number of familiar dichotomies in Marxist theory: subjective/objective ad political/psychological. Lived experience is equated with subjectivity, while structured, formalized knowledges derived, to from experience but form an analysis or synthesis of it, are equated with objectivity. This dichotomy allows men to speak the truth of women's experience because they are 'unattached' in their lived experience, and thus capable of 'objectivity'. This position completely denes the possibility of autonomy, of speaking for and of on self, and moreover involves a glaring disavowal of the male position within patriarchal grids of power and knowledge. This 'objective' discourse invalidates the truth of a different perspective, a different point of view, a different interest.

It is argued by Marxist feminists that autonomous forms of knowledge that are based on women's lived experience are already the effect of patriarchal domination. Assertions about feminity or female sexuality are always caught in the trap of unwittingly reproducing the 'eternal feminine', in so far as they are bound up with the body and its experiences. This argument presumes a pervasive and complete system of ideology and deception such that the oppressors position is completely absorbed by the oppressed in a passive, non-resistant way.

What we are suggesting here is that the autonomy of self-determined theories and practices is implicit in the ideal of difference. This autonomy is not simply taking up he right to determine one's own terrain and the extent of one's own oppression, but also the right to interpret and develop any there is, an politics, and any struggle from the position established by the lived oppression of women. So that, for example, the point is not simply to acknowledge the body existence, as Marxist-feminists are prepared to do, if only to acknowledge women's limitations, but to affirm and claim it as independently representable. To argue that such a feminist claim amounts to subjecting women to patriarchal power once against to miss the basic features of the claim to autonomy: namely that one form of challenge to patriarchal power is to reject its definitions and characterizations of feminity and to appropriate for itself the right to a self-determined and independent perspective on the world.

Conclusion

If, as we have claimed the morphology of the sexed body establishes the limits of lived experience and the socio-political meaning of that experience, then it seems justified to maintain that all non-feminist theories - those which do not start from women as such - including Marxism, are founded on masculine norms. Any bringing together of Marxism and feminism implies feminism's acceptance of these terms - adopting a male norm as universally applicable. This amounts to an unquestioned acceptance of phallocentrism as the unnatural and inevitable paradigm for all possible forms of being, thinking, and acting. The domination of Marxism over feminism cannot fail to result because even any presumed complementarity is necessarily governed by this principle of equality in sameness. 'My wife and I are equals' is the ruse of phallocentrism, as Wilden remarked.

The Unwillingness of Marxists and Marxist-feminists to recognize the need for a genuine autonomy for women's theories and practices - one which claims a positive difference - has led to some peculiar evaluations of the status and potential of feminist theory. Feminist theory is conceived in one of two ways either feminist theory is about 'women's issues' (abortion, rape, prostitution, pornography, domestic labor, sexuality, the family, health and welfare, and so on) – i.e. it is about women's place in a man's world; or it is seen simply as a form of critique of already existing non-feminist theories (Marx, Freud, etc.). Neither of these alternatives sees the possibility of a completely different perspective on problems of truth, reasons, reality, knowledge. Feminist theoretical work is assumed to attempt to overthrow, reverse, adapt, modify, deconstruct 'male' theory. Its methods must be adopted from elsewhere, no only from Marxism and psychoanalysis, but also existentialism, anarchism, aesthetics, semiotics, etc. Feminist theory is considered to be at most a critique of male theories, but never as capable of developing its own theories.

To see a feminist theory either as a critique or reworking of Master-knowledges or as an adoption of the other's theoretical tools is to underrate considerably what feminist theory has achieved and to consider it is limited terms. But what is perhaps more important is that it involves a reduction of the multiplicity and plurality of feminisms, equating differences here with oppositions once again. There is a wealth of feminist theory some good, some bad) that falls entirely outside the scope of this either/or split. Differences between women as well as women's difference from men need to be affirmed without reducing either to a common dominator. Because the concept of difference does not permit assumptions about commonness or meta-principles of a universalizing nature, it is well suited for acknowledging the specificity of any struggles by oppressed and exploited groups on their own particular terms.

In concluding, we are led by these considerations to ask whether there current emphasis on equality in Marxist politics does not, in the final analysis, have the effect, not only of bringing feminisms into line with Marxism. Nit pf reducing them to a commonness with it. The political and institutional power of Marxism is such that any feminism can only be tolerated in so far as it accepts Marxism's fundamental premises and modes of thinking. This amounts to a form of subjugation that can never provide the space for developing theories and practices independently. If feminism is a movement or series of them directed not so much at equality as at autonomy, then the coupling of Marxism and feminism together is problematic, to say the least. Perhaps what is at take is our capacity to adopt a conceptual separatism, i.e. the ability to take ourselves is the independent norm of our thinking and being. Such a conceptual separatism as nothing to do with tied old disputes about whether to work with or to relate to men. It simply means that any political or theoretical alliance with other radical movements, such as Marxism, cannot and never will involve an allegiance to concepts, categories, principles and modes of procedure that are derived form a negation of women' experience *as women*.

NOTES AND REFERENCES

1. At the time of writing this article, first published in the *New Statesman* (March 1980), Barbra Taylor had left her native Canada to research nineteenth-century utopian socialism in Britain (the results of which appeared in 1983 as *Eve and the new Jerusalem*, Virago) and described herself as active in the women's liberation movement.

2. With the assumption of theoretical hegemony by Marxism

CHAPTER EIGHT

Women in Judaism

"He dreamt that he saw a ladder, which rested on the ground with its top reaching to heaven, and angles of God were going up and down on upon it." Genesis 28:12

The title of this volume and its sequel, Religious Human Rights in Global Perspective, Presents us with both an anomaly and a challenge. On the one hand, the term 'religious," at least in the Western experience, in lines one to look to the heaven for the source of correct action.[1] Obligations stem from a lawgiving deity whose will has become known to us through various forms of revelation. In the other hand, the word 'human" is not simply an adjective describing the kind of rights began discussed, as opposed to, say, animal rights. Emerging in the early Enlightenment, the notion grounds our obligations to one another in the individual's humanity, an aspect of the person independent of his or her race, religion, or ethnic identity. The universalism inherent in this idea is one of the hallmarks of modernity, serving as the benchmark for treatment of minorities, prisoners of war, and criminals.[2] Therefore the term 'religious human rights' strikes us as a virtual oxymoron, for while religions focus on the top of Jacob's ladder, Enlightenment philosophers and ethicists are exclusively concerned with Jacob at its base.

Nevertheless, man of us, whether secular scholars of religion or religiously-committed scholars and laypersons, are involved in this project precisely because we do not see such an abyss separating he two realms. In our perception, there is a close, intimate connection between human rights and religion. Violations of human rights, whether locally or across the world, offend many of us as morally and religiously repugnant. On the positive side, advocates of human rights frequently link arms with priests, ministers, and rabbis, joining in common cause, such as in the American civil rights crusade of the 1960s. The dreams and goals of those who pursue and defend human rights are clear echoes of ancient prophetic voices which also hoped for an ideal society based on justice and truth. In short, the challenge of this volume and its sequel is that we want to be those angles, ascending and descending the ladder, some more easily than others, in an effort to better understand the connections and relationships between the two spheres.

This chapter concerns women's rights within wish communities. One way of approaching this subject is simply to list a woman's rights and obligations according to halakhah (Jewish law): what she is obligated to do for others, such as her spouse, children, and parents, and how, in turn, others are obligated to act with respect other. As in any legal system, there will be privileges as well as restrictions which developed over time, and which need to be seen from precisely that historical perspective. This, in itself, would be an ambitious project, and indeed is the necessary backdrop for any informed discussion of the topic. But if we are to be true to the challenge we believe this project sets before us, then we must sketch out, however theoretically, the potential contribution of viewing the issue from the perspective of human rights.

We should state, from the outset, that we are not merely engaged in the critical review of Jewish law by contemporary canons of human rights. This project was not established to expose aspects of religious traditions which affront and even violate accepted standards of recent human rights commissions and conventions. Not only would that undermine the spirit of cooperation which distinguishes this project, it would necessarily put the various religions on the defensive, forcing an apologetic posture that would preclude nay openness and candor crucial to our enterprise.

Nor is our aim to show, in the classical tradition of apologia, that a particular religious tradition anticipated or even served as the source of modern human rights, essentially claiming that contemporary views are simply redundant. Rather, our aim is to lay bare some of the assumptions and premises of each system, and them examine if any fruitful intersection is possible. We begin with a brief analysis of the different notions of right in each tradition followed by an overview of laws relating to women in halakha. We the take a particular case, considerably pressing on the contemporary jewish scene, and explore some ways that our discussion might illuminate that issue.

Jewish Law and Human Rights

The overlap of Jewish law and human rights in practical terms is an important starting point for our analysis of the respective assumptions of each system. *Prima facie,* the Jewish Bible's persistent concern for "the stronger, the orphan, and the widow" as well as for the poor persons, is an expression of the basic moral posture of Jewish law, insuring the care and equal treatment due every member of society regardless of economic condition or social status. The Rabbis continued in this vein, instituting laws and practices that would prevent abuses of these disadvantaged classes.[6] Medieval Jewish communities were almost universally characterized by locally supported institutions and funds established and maintained to help widows, orphans, and the poor—features that still distinguish modern Jewish communities across the spectrum. For those interested in human rights, Jewish history appears to stand proudly by its record of concern for the disadvantaged and unfortunate.

However, this practical intersection belies a fundamental theoretical difference between jewish law and modern notions of humanrights. Borrowing Robert M. cover's phrse.8 the 'narrative" behind the "nomos" of halakha is two-fold: first, it is the idea that all humans are created in the image of God, an idea which itself has two corollaries. One is that everyone is endowed with a measure of absolute worth, even sanctity, which obligates people to act with a basic degree of respect toward each other. The Genesi story refers to the first human as created with a divine image (1:26-27), and that this creation was "very good" (1:31). The Torah's imperative to "love your neighbour" (Leviticus 19:18) is predicated on the equal worth of every human being. For the Rabbis, this principle served as an in diction of the infinite value of human life; thus, witnesses in capital crimes were warned by the judges: "Anyone who destroys the life of a single person, it is as if her destroyed an entire world." When testimony is to have such potentially grave consequences, it is crucial to underscore the infinite worth of each individual. In rabbinic literature, the commandment not to leave an executed criminal hanging until dusk (Deuteronomy 21:22-23) is presented as a basic expression of the divine image of the person, even one who violated the law.

The notion that mankind is created in God's image has a further, perhaps more significant, corollary for human action: the imperative to imitate God. As beings with a divine aspect, persons are enjoined to live up to their potential and act in divine ways toward one another. The Pentateuchal injunction "you shall be holy, for I, the Lord your God, am holy" (Leviticus 19:2) is an echo of this notion, as is the rabbinic interpretation of Exodus 15:2: "Just as He is merciful and compassionate, so you shall be merciful and compassionate." These are the clearest expressions of the ideas that human beings are under the obligation to actualize their own divine image by acting ethically.

Secondly, the biblical account of the exodus from Egypt functions, already in the Torah itself, as the ultimate equalizer. As an epilogues to a lengthy chapter on how one is to treat the poor, especially those who are forced to sell either their inherited land or even themselves, the torah states: "for it is to Me that the Israelites are slaves, they are My slaves, whom I brought out of Egypt; I am the lord your God: (Leviticus 25:55). Economic lordship is the most common form of "subjugation" in a society; the law insists on protecting, the dignity of those who are forced to depend on others. For a nation which owes its collective existence to a benevolent and undeserved act of divine redemption, all members stand in equal relation to God. With god at the vertx, all jews are equal.

These two religious conceptions of equality are in marked contrast to the philosophical basis of modern human rights. For while the opening sentence of the American Declaration of Independence, in a desistic mimickry of the biblical stance, states "All men are created equal," in fat the 18th century notion of mankind' equality wan simply the latest incarnation of an iea which trees its origins to the Greek Sophists, and whose heirs were Machiavelli, Hobbes, and Locke. Broadly speaking, all these thinkers express the idea that the basic equality of people is their capacity—and willingness—to destroy everyone else in the unchecked pursuit of each person's own self-interests. Hobbes' famous description of humanity's pre-civilized state as 'the war of all against all" is the necessary consequence of seeing people as individuals engaged in the ceaseless and elentless pursuit of power. Echoing the Sophists, Locke as well asserts that the sole significance of a person as regards others is his or her being a source of potential danger. The critical corollary for Lokcke is that the primacy function of government (and law) is to protect citizens from one another, restraining the innate but subdued aggression which is constantly threatening to surface. This pessimistic, naturalistic view of humankind is in stark contrast to the predominant view in Judaism which both sees the person as a being with divine qualities, and portrays the role of law and government to be the nurturing of a person's moral character within a society actively cooperating to attain a higher idea.

In this light, the modern notion of human rights is not just a reconceptualization of an ancient moral impulse, formulated in immanent rather than transcendent terms. The descent down Jacob's ladder from religious obligations to human rights suggests a fundamental transformation of the social significance of persons. For the biblical word view, humans are created in the divine image and as such deserve dignity and respect as equals to every other person. People are obligated to help one another both to improve collective conditions are to assist in the other's material and spiritual development. In contrast for the modern Weltanschuung, "human rights" refers to one's claims against society—amen acing group of self-interested individuals who literally endanger one's well-being. For obvious reasons, minorities, women, children, and the handicapped required the protection of Human rights, for they are most vulnerable in a society formed solely to prevent the natural aggression of which all human's are capable and which they are willing to use.

We now turn to the issue of the rights of women in Jewish law. We will briefly sketch the general contrours of women's right and obligations, highlighting the rules and procedures which were instituted over time both to insure a woman's dignity and to protect her from potential abuses implicit in the unequal relationships in which most women found themselves: father-daughter and husband-wife.

Women in Jewish Law: An Overview

"I find womenmore bitte rtha death: (ecclesiastes 7;26). "he who finds a wife has found happenings (proverbs

18:22). Tehse two biblical passages formthe Ketuvim (the Writings) alert us to the multiplicity of voices contained in the Jewish tradition. Raely does one find only one opinion on a subject withinthe sources of Judiasm,even on such jundamental issues as idolatry or martyrdom. Froma methodological standpont, then, it is difficult to draw general conclusions about any subject from traditional Jewish law. Its authoritative texts apan millennia, from the Bible to contemporary codes and rabbnc responsa. The tradition is self-consciously exegetical and interpretive, using careful analysis of prior texts and codes to yield solutions to may problem. Historically, the majority of Halakha's earliest and most authoritative sources date from the rabbinic period, roughly spanning form about the second century B.C.E. to the sixth or seventh century C.E. During the time, an immense body of legal material evolve in the oral culture of the academies, initially summarized in the Mishnah in the late second-early third century C.E. by the patriarch Rabbi Judah, and later redacted with greater detail and commentary in the Palestinian and Babylonian talmuds. We shall focus on these sources in reviewing the legal status of women in Jewish law.

In matters of civil or criminal law, men and women are essentially equal, whether they be victim or criminal. Thus, Halakhah forbids harming a man or a woman, and both are held liable for assault. The consequences of harming a slave were identical whether the slave was male or femal. According to biblical law, both parents were due equal respect, and striking either parent was punishable by death. Both partners to an illicit sexual union were executed. And in contract to other ancient Near Eastern codes, such as the of hammurabi, neither the class nor the sex of the victim affected compensation.

While women enjoy access to all legal forms of redress, they are restricted from its process. They can serve neither as witnesses in criminal proceedings nor as judges in any court of law. This exclusion from public life extends to all areas of communal service in its official forms. Historically, however, women were not absent entirely from the public sphere. Both Talmuds are replete with legal cases involving women engaged in serious, even large-scale business transaction, and are often represented as possessing their own land.

It is with respect to ritual law where the clearest distinction between men and women is evident. According to the Mishnah, women are exempt form all positive laws which are of a time-bound nature, this encompasses most festival laws unless a specific exegesis re-obligates women in the observance, such as eating unleavened bread and at the Passoverseder. This exemption had wide-ranging consequences, for according to jewish law, in "verbal" laws such as prayers and blessings, one can discharge one's responsibility by listening to another recite the required formula as long as the two persons were of equal obligation. While women were permitted to recite the prayers. The time-bound nature of praying (morning, afternoon, and evening) meat that women were essentially exempt, and thus could not discharge a male's obligation. Women were not counted in the quorum for prayer, thus excluding them from synagogue services except as spectators. According to the Talmud, women were allowed to be called up to the Torah when it was publicly read, but subsequent rabbinic legislation excluded them form this sphere as well due to "the congregation's honor, a vague yet certainly unflaterignnotion.

This exemption from time-bound commandments is generally taken to be based on the social need to have the woman available at all times to meet the needs of there husband and children. Imposing an additional set of demands would simply be unfair. However, even this theory, reasonable from a socio-historical standpoint, is not universally accepted. Given a woman's obligation in several time-bound commandments, such as hearing the Scroll of Esther on Purim, lighting Hanukkah candles, and others, this explanation is not adequate. Moreover, this account should lead to the conclusion that single women, or elderly women with no children or husbands any longer, should still be obligated. Due to these objections, Saul Berman has argued that what truly underlies this exemption is the perceived needs of Jewish society, which the rabbis believed were best served by keeping women in the family context.[28] the critical distinction between the commandments, according to Berman, is those which can be performed at home and those which must be performed in the communal sphere. The primary goal of this exemption was family stability, a go a best achieved if the woman was not given the chance to choose between familiar duties and communal performance.

Berman's theory may also account for the other significant exemption of women in Jewish law: they are not obligated to study orah. For traditional Jews, the Torah is not merely a set of rules and laws, but the embodiment of the divine word, the record of god's revelation to the Jewish people. The oral tradition as which developed around it are the essence of rabbinic Judaism, and being left out of the enterprise could, arguably, deprive a jew of connecting with there people's spiritual heritage. Nevertheless, torah study, particularly in the rabbinic period, left the familial realm of parent to child Deuteronomy 6:7, 11:19) and entered the academy, where one first beard tannaim recite the oral traditions of previous scholars. Torah was no longer a family affair but a communal one, and, one again, women were excluded from that sphere.

Even this explanation, however, does not explain why the exemption was extended to all women, even those who presently are not, or are no longer, in the context of the traditional family. Moreover, given the temperament of many men today, these fathers' involvement in family duties should exempt them as well from some time-bound commandments rather, what we have here is, as Berman suggests, a fundamental split between the private and the public spheres. However, when this functional distinction is mediated through laws and is expressed in legal language (the only one available to the rabbis), many consequences which flow from the original distinction are sacrificed to create a clear and easily implemented system. These legislative concerns led the rabbis to exclude all women form the public realm in order to facilitate the situation of most of them—a concern law school professors often appreciate but the man (sic) in the street does not.

Thus, in certain respects, women enjoyed there same rights as men, while in others, particularly in ritual and academic settings, women were excluded and consigned to the home. This mixed image, where women and men are sometimes treated equally by the law and sometimes not, is even more noticeable in the next realm we will examine: marriage and divorce.

Marriage and Divorce

"A bad wife is as hard (to bear) as a stormy day." "If your wife is short bend down to listen to her." As these two passages indicate, an analysis of Jewish attitudes and practices in the realm of marriage and divorce demonstrates there has been significant development over the centuries, virtually all of its designed to enhance the status of the woman and to make her less vulnerable. These changes reflect both the dynamic quality of Jewish law and a basic attitude towards the woman as a person. As will be demonstrated, this almost inherent dynamic quality has not been marshalled to address a situation in which many Jewish women today suffer abuse and extortion to simply bring an end to their marriages.

The first chapter of Mishnah *Kiddushin*, which deals with issues of betrothal and property, opens with the statement that a women is "acquired by three different means: money, document, or sexual intercourse." Some contemporary scholars, focusing on the word "acquired" (*niknait*) and the first two transactional means mentioned in this Mishnah, have argued that this rendere the woman a form of property. There was, they contend, virtually no difference between acquiring a woman and acquiring other kinds of property. Their argument is strengthened by the fact that the subsequent paragraphs in this chapter of the Mishnah deal with the acquisition of other forms of property, such as slaves, animals, real estate and portable objects.

One can only speculate about the nature of marriage in pre-rabbinic times; there are simply too few sources of only dubious reliability. In any event, by the time of the Mishnah's redaction, the Rabbis had already significantly moved away from the concept of women as chatte, if it ever obtained at all. They did so in a number of ways. First, the amount which was used to effect the marriage was so minimal that it is hard to consider this transfer of funds a purchase. It was in essence a symbolic payment to recognize the man's "acquisition." What the husband was acquiring in this transaction was the sole right to have sex with this woman. In contrast to the purchase of property, before a marriage could be arranged, the consent of the woman had to be obtained. Moreover, the man could not sell a woman he acquired for a wife, nor could he compel her against her will to do certain things, as was the case of English law until the end of the nineteenth century. Nor could he treat her as an animal: though wife beating was recognized as a form of chastisement, it was considered by many Rabbis as grounds for compelling a man to divorce his wife.

Furthermore, on two occasions, the Bible records the payment of a bride-price (*mohar*) to the father for his daughter. This seems to reflect the prevalent custom in the ancient Near East custom of actually buying a bride. In the Second Temple period, however, economic conditions prevented young men from amassing sufficient sums to pay the *mohar* in advance. This led to the conversion of the *mohar* into a marriage settlement for the bride (not her father) providing for her in the event of divorce or widowhood. R. Simeon ben Shetah, the leader of the Pharisees in the Hasmonean period (mid-second century B.C.E.) strengthened the settlement by introducing the husband's pledge of all his possessions as security. The substance of the settlement is embodied in the marriage contract (*ketubah*) which witnesses sign before a wedding, attesting to the husband's acceptance of the obligation. In general, the sum of the settlement is roughly the equivalent of living expenses for one or two years. Subsequent rabbinic legislation insured the protective capacity of this settlement by prohibiting any couple from marrying without a *ketubah*; if it were later lost, rabbinic law forbad their living together until a new one was written and signed by witnesses. Further more, if the *ketubah* has to be collected, she was to receive the money before any other distributions were made from his estate. If the inheritance was insufficient, the rabbis ruled that the sons were to go begging allowing the mother and the daughters to be maintained by whatever funds ere available in the estble. These enactments collectively had the impact of rendering marriage easier and divorce more difficult.

Finally, he paragraph in Kiddushin which speaks of the "acquisition" of the wife is, in fact, the last time the Mishah uses the term niknait, "acquired," in reference to a marriage. All subsequent references use the term kiddushin, "exclusively designed," but also connoting an aura of holiness. In Judaism something that is holy is set aside of special use. In terms of marriage, kiddushin denotes exclusivity. According to the Rabbis the man was sanctifying the women to himself, that is, for his sole access to her sexual functions. While this was the husband's privilege, it was not his prerogative to allow others to "use" his wife, even by the seemingly legitimate means of divorce and subsequent remarriage.

While the rabbinic portrayal of betrothal was clearly dissimilar to the acquisition of chattel, it was particularly the rabbinic understanding of marriage and the mutual obligations it entailed that reveal true sensitivity and concern for protecting the woman. The Mishnah enumerates and the Gemara expands upon an entire series of rights and protection accorded the wife. Recognizing that from a social and economic perspective, the wife was the dependent partner in the relationship, the tradition provided her with a host of protections. Hena wife fell sick the husband had to provide for her. Should he die she could not be evicted from the marital residence. Most significantly, the Mishnah recognized that she has certain emotional and social needs. Her husband could not arbitrarily prevent her from visiting her parents of attending community gatherings such as weddings or funerals. If he did attempt to do so, he was obligated to grant her freedom. By divorcing her and granting her the funds promised her in theketubah. One thousand years later, Maimonides, who insisted on her right to visit her parents' home as well as her friends and neighbours observed that 'she is not an in prison from which she cannot come and go." Most importantly, her husband was liable for her support, burial, and ransom should she be kidnapped. All these practices are manifestations of her dependency on him and his responsibilities towards her.

A wife had certain reciprocal obligations towards her husband. According to the Mishanah, she was obligated to wash his face, hands, feet, make his bed, and pour his wine. The Talmud expanded and contracted these to reflect those acts which according to local custom are performed by a wife for her husband. Thus, today washing feet would not be in be included. In certain places, she was obligated no only to raise the children and perform household duties, but also to spin, weave, and sew the family's clothing. If she had the means, either from her husband's wealth or her own assets, she was allowed to hire others to do these chores for her, though Rabbi Eliezer cautioned that she should not remain idle but should be compelled, if necessary, to undertake certain tasks because "idleness leads to promiscuity."

Furthermore, the husband's financial responsibilities to his wife granted him rights to her earnings while they were married, and to the usufruct from the fields she brought into the marriage. But even in this regard, the husband's rights were limited. In contrast to Anglo-American law, any assets she brought to the marriage remained her property and were returned to her in the case of a divorce. While he controlled what was done with these during the marriage, he could not sell them without her consent.

Perhaps the true test of a woman's rights within society according to Jewish law is the status of the *unmarried* woman. In contrast to the traditional patriarchal system, there are entire classes of Jewish women who have total control over all aspects of their lives. While the dependent women—the minor daughter, wife, and levirate widow—have a nexus of rights, some of which have been enumerated here, their person is greatly controlled by the men upon whom they depend. In contrast, the divorce, the widow, and the adult unmarried daughter (after age twelve) are totally independent. There is extensive anecdotal evidence of these women arranging their own marriages, conducting business affairs, and functioning in all but the realm of ritual as autonomous and independent beings. Though a wife was forbidden from selling her own property without her husband's permission, a divorce could have the court compel her former husband to seel his property in order to gain what is due her as enumerated in the *ketubah*. The widow had even greater latitude. Not only did she control her own property, but she did not need court approval to sell portions of her late husband's settle. Moreover a widow who was not a levirate could marry whom selver she wished. The adult single daughter could engage in all sorts of business transactions without obstacle, for she had sole claim to her property. This belies claims made by those such as Simone de Beauvoir that Judaism is a pure patriarchal system. Only in the realm of ritual and Torah study were thee otherwise independent women curtailed in their activities. Perusal of both the laws and the general statements about marriage in the Talmud offers valid grounds to argue that the tradition considered marriage as a complex set of entitlements and obligations each partner had towards the other. As Judith Hauptman concludes, the Talmud considered marriage to constitute a relationship between two human beings each with his or her own set of needs and responsibilities. The man was clearly the dominant partner in this relationship, owing to a variety of social, economic and religious reasons. But her personal rights were protected in a sophisticated arrangement of reciprocal duties and privileges.

Reciprocity, however, does not imply equality, and this is the crux of the matter. In the biblical and rabbinic conception, marriage is not the union of two adults mutually consenting to spend their lives together—although the Rabbis did insist that both partners agree to the marriage. Rather, marriage is the man's acquisition of exclusive legal claim to his wife's sexual function. The only Pentateuchal reference to either marriage or divorce is significant in this regard:

When a man takes a wife and has intercourse with her, and if she fails to please him because he finds something obnoxious about her, her should write her a bill of divorce, hand it to her and send her away from his house. She will leave his household and [may] become the wife of another man. [If] this latter man rejects her, writes, ill of divorcements, hands it to her, and sends her away from his house, or [if] the man who married her last dies. Her first husband who divorced her shall not take her to be his wife again...

The expression in the first severe, "and has intercourse

with her," is the essence of the marital relationship. In Hebrew, the words for husband derives from the same root as "to have intercourse"—b.'a.l. to be sure, even these rights were limited by Halakhah: rbbinic tradition recognized rape within marriage, and forbad it. Even more for reaching was the notion that intercourse was a wife's right and a husband's duty, and a man could not withhold conjugal rights as part of a stipulation of marriage—in sharp contrst to other ancient near Eastern traditions.

What these verses make clear is that the model of marriage was unilateral acquisition of sexual rights, perhaps requiring, (as the Rabbis later did) the women's consent. And if this is how marriages are forged, then there exists only one way to dissolve them: the man must surrender the rights he possesses and return them to the women. This explains why the verse concentrates on the husband's dissatisfaction with his wife (for whatever reason), and not the reverse; only he can initiate a diverse, so only he can initiate a marriage.

Once again, it is rabbinic tradition which went very far in protecting the woman from the abuses inherent in a system where only one party has control. Even a brief survey of Jewish divorce law will reveal that the rabbis acted to enhance her clearly vulnerable position by making it avenues to safeguard a wife from a capricious and vengeful husband who, because of jealousy or instability, would try to wreak havoc with her life. The harder it was to divorce her, presumably, the more protected she would be.

The vast majority of the tactate of the Mishah on divorce is concerned with the technical matter of standardizing the get, the writ of divorce. The bill had to be written with certain kinds of ink, on particular forms of paper, and by a scribe. These various requirements were apparently intende to prevent the husband form sitting down in anger and simply scribbling a few lines which would radically affect his wife. It is striking that in rabbinic law, marriage entails for fewer technical details than divorce, reflecting both the preference of marriage (and the desire to facilitate it), as well as the bias against divorce ,ad the belief that the woman needed protection.

According to Jewish law, a married woman who committed adultery was executed, and if there were children form the act, they had the status of a *mamzer*, which prohibited them from marrying anyone but another *mamzer*. Given these serious consequences, the rabbis went to pains to make sure that the divorce was genuine and that the woman was clear about her own status. Rabban Gamliel, patriarch of the second century C.E., therefore enacted that if a man sends a get through an agent to his wife (a common practice if he happened to be far away from her), he is not allowed to canel that agency in a court. The *mishanah*, declares that Rabban Gambliel did this "for the betterment of the world" (*tikkum' olam*), and the Talmud offers two reasons for this enactment. One opinion maintains that if the nullification of the agency were allowed to be valid, then the wife might receive the divorce, mistakenly assume it was valid (even though it had been conelleled), and proceed to marry some one else. The children of this second marriage would then be *mamzerim*, a consequence to be avoided at all cots. The other possible situation, maintained by a different scholar, was that women, fearful that their husbands have celled the writ, might be paralyzed into inaction after receiving any writ of divorce through an agent. These women might never re-marry, fearful that they were still legally married to their first husbands.[65] It is not at all clear whether this was a prevalent practice, or whether Rabban Gamliel was merely preventing an anticipated abuse. In any event, according to one view, it was the women's future which was the patrirch's primary concern.

Nor could the husband's control extent beyond the termination of the marital relationship. Thus, one a woman had her get, she was free to marry whomever she wished.

Her first husband could not stipulate either during the marriage or in the get that he divorced her on the condition that she would not marry a specific person. Divorce meant total liberation from the first husband.

The Rabbis of the Babylonian Talmud, concerned to produce greater equity in the entire procedure, established a means for the woman t sue for divorce. In a variety of situations, she could turn to a Jewish court and ask it to force her husband to grant her a divorce: if her husband was afflicted by a physical condition which made him repulsive to her, if her did not uphold his obligation to maintain or support her as he stated he would in the *ketubah*, or if she found him sexually repulsive and could not have relations with him. Maimonides formulation vividly portrays the Halakha's sympathy for the woman caught in an unbearable marital bond:

> [She] should be questioned as to the reason for her rebelliousness [that is, her refusal to have relations with her husband]. If she says, "I have come to loathe him and I cannot willingly submit to his intercourse," he must be compelled to divorce her immediately, for she is not like a captive women who must submit to a man who is hateful to her.

Medieval rabbinic cauthorities added other grounds on which to sue for divorce, such as wife-beating or the husband's frequenting prostitutes. Divorce initiated by the man, however, was strictly a matter of individual judgment and discretion.

But ven this rabbinic effort to redress the inequity of divorce proceedings could not change the biblical character of divorce: a unilateral action by the husband. At best the court could compel him to give her the get if it found her suit legitimate. The man's consent was the *sine qua non* of the entire process.

Two other steps were taken in the early Middle Ages

to balance the powers in divorce, and both are credited to Rabbi Gershom of Mainz (960-1028): One banned polygamy on penalty of social excommunication (herem), the other forbad divorcing a woman against her will. These two rulings marked the end of the man's absolute right of divorce, for not only was her consent now necessary, but the man no longer had the option of ignoring his first wife and marrying another women. Divorce had to be effected before he could move on with his life. Prior to this ruling, the only leverage available to the woman was the financial consequences of divorce for the husband, the amount having been pre-set in the *ketubah*. In general, only the wealthy could afford a divorce, since the *ketubah* granted her the legal right to claim her dowry even if it meant 'taking the shirt off his back."

However, the method by which Rabbi Gershom instituted these rulings inherently contained a loophole: a rabbinic ban can be overridden if the dispensation of one hundred rabbis (*heter me'ah rabbanim*) is obtained. Thus, if a man's wife became mentally unbalanced, preventing her from accepting a get, the husband could secure the agreement of one hundred rabbis and marry a second wife, provided is first wife's needs were met. This strategy is, in fact, available to any an whose wife refuses to accept the bill of divorce for what are deemed illegitimate reasons, a decision rendered by the rabbinical court involved. In this scenario, the husband actually writes a get and deposits it in the court, appointing the members of the court as his proxies to deliver the get to his wife wherever she chooses to come to the court and accept it. Thus, the *heter me'ah rabbanim* does not leave her chained, but allows him to go on with his life even if she is recalcitrant and refuses to accept the get. No such recourse, however, is open to her; if her husband was beset by a mental illness, or refused to write the bill of divorce, she became an *agunah*, a chained woman, unable to remarry.

The unfortunate situation of the agunah is well-known in Jewish law, and was already addressed by the rabbis of the Mishnah. The typical case was a husband who never returned from traveling abroad, and while the precarious nature of travel justified a presumption of death, hard evidence was lacking which would clearly establish this fact and free her to re-marry. To prevent this, some Rabbis suggested writing a conditional form of divorce, whereby the writ would become valid if the husband did not return by a specified time. In the event that the husband did not have this foresight, the Rabbis were prepared to relax the rules of evidence, which normally require two witnesses to establish fact, and accept the testimony of only one witness, the Rabbis were even willing to accept the testimony of those who would, under normal circumstances, be disqualified, such as a woman, a minor, or even the wife herself despite her vested interests.

The more insidious type of agunah is the woman whose husband refuses to grant her a divorce. Whether out of anger, revenge, or spite he will not give her the document which will allow her to terminate the marriage and re-marry. Traditionally, rabbis treated this situation, known as "the recalcitrant husband," with familiar and tested methods to force him to divorce his wife. Various social pressures, ranging from public declarations and humiliation in the synagogue to outright social excommunication were at a rabbi's disposal to compel the husband to release his chained wife. These options, however, were effective when Jewish communities were fairly independent entities with virtually complete control over their internal affairs. If a man did not grant his wife her freedom, the court could socially excommunicated him and make it impossible for him to live in that community. Because people were far less mobile, the community could also more easily monitor his movements and warn other communities not to have any dealings with this married man who refused to accede to the court's ruling and issue his wife a divorce. Today, however when the rabinic courts do not possess such power, and men are free to travel far to communities unaware of their recalcitrance, the plight of the agunah has become quote severe. Even in the State of Israel, where rabbinic courts enjoy exclusive jurisdiction over marital matters, including the right to jail recalcitrant husbands.[77] There are nevertheless men who prefer to suffer this punishment rather than issue their wives a get. To be sure, for many cases it might be a simple matter of legislation, enacting a law which makes the consequences of recalcitrance much more severe, such as freezing assets, garnishing wages, and the like. Nevertheless, the procedural rules of divorce themselves present rescuing the women whose husband ignores all these punitive measures and remains recalcitrant. He, alone, an grant her freedom to re-marry, and his refusal to grant the get necessarily chains her to him for life.

More significantly, many women are able to secure a divorce only by meeting the extortionate demands of their husbands. Thus, women regularly find themselves subject to severe financial, custodial, and other sorts of stipulations in order to have their husbands agree to grant them a divorce. To avoid becoming permanent agunot, some women agree to pay their spouses exorbitant sums of money or to forgo child support. Inequitable divorce settlements are reluctantly agreed to, at times involving serious and delicate custody issues, in order to secure the get. Most regrettably, some rabbis have even come to see this kind of conduct by the husband as acceptable, providing the demands are not extraordinary. This kind of abuse is endemic to a divorce procedure which places the full responsibility of divorce on one party alone, and given today's world, social pressure will solve only a handful of the most severe agunah cases. The overwhelming majority of women will either capitulate to their husband's demands or suffer in silence and solitude.

There are, in essence, two sets of problems here: attitudinal and halakhic. For a long time, the traditional community denied that there was a problem. As recently as the late 1970s, many modern Orthodox rabbis and much of the Orthodox community dismissed the problem as one of little significane. Today, however, increasing numbers of rabbis are willing to acknowledge that this a serious problem. In part, their recognition of the problem is rooted in the fact that their daughters and granddaughters have faced this difficult situation. The problem of the recalcitrant spouse has increasingly been recognized by Orthodox rabbis as a problem which must be resolved. There are still those who believe that, while it is a tragedy, nothing essentially can really be done to change the situation. Men must simply be pressured to agree to the Rabinic Court's ruling. Some of the rabbis who take this position argue that the woman who finds herself in this situation somehow deserves it. In contrast, one rabbi publicly conceded that this situation was a tremendous Hillul Hashem, a desecration of God's name.

Rabbis of the Conservative movement have adopted their own solution. They have relied on the conditional vorce, inserting a clause in the marriage agreement which makes the marriage null and void if a civil divorce is not followed by a Jewish divorce within six months. The other Conservative strategy has been to have the rabbinic court annual the marriage if they deem it necessary to do so in the interests of justice. They justify this action on the passage in the Talmud "everyone who betroths does so at the discretion of the Rabbis." This is understood to men a that there is an implicit condition in every Jewish marriage that it is subject to annulment by Jewish legal authorities.[85] the Reform movement has simply done away with the need for a religious divorce altogether.

The Orthodox community does not accept the validity of the Conservative movement's solutions, finding technical halakhic difficulties both in the concept of a conditional marriage, and in the applicability of the Talmudic prerogative of annulment which, admittedly, was only rarely used historically.[86] Many within the Orthodox rabbinate diagnose the problem in a much different way. The faul lies not in the halakhic system per se; the fact that a large number of agunot have appeared only recently is evidence that the existing system is sufficiently viable. What these orthodox leaders bemoan is the changing conditions which have rendered traditional methods of coping with this problem essentially useless. The reliance on social pressure assumes both a tight-knit community and the individuals need for a community to supply his identity. Neither of these conditions obtain for the average Jew, excepting those who have chosen to live in the ulter-Orthodox community, particular the Hassidic sects. Given the mobility of people and their willingness either to join a different community or simply not to identify with an orthodox community altogether, the old strategies will not longer work. New methods must therefore be proposed to meet the challenges posed by the *agunah* problem.

Since secular governments have assumed many of the legal and social functions previously held by the autonomous community, the Orthodox rabbinate naturally first turned to these authorities to address the problem of *agunol*. This approach was tried in the State of New York which, given the large population of Orthodox Jews, heard many cases of *agunah*. The New York legislature passed a law that would withhold a civil divorce from a couple until "all barriers to the other party's remarriage" are resolved. Barriers to remarriage specifically include "any religious or conscientious restraint or inhibition imposed on a party to a marriage, under the principles of the denomination of the clergyman or minister who has solemnized the marriage, by reason of the other party's commission or withholding of any voluntary act." In 1992, this law was expanded to permit judges of civil courts to take into consideration a husband's refusal to grant a get when deciding the distribution of marital assets. A judge could withhold portions of the assets from the husband until he grants the divorce.

This New York law on divorce, however, has been challenged as unconstitutional. Moreover, other states have refused to adopt such legislation precisely because it compels a party to engage in a religious act on pain of withholding civil relief—a prima facie violation of the religion clauses of the First Amendment to the Untied States Constitution.

The opposition to this solution is not just constitutional in nature. Many Orthodox feminists find the efforts to rely on the secular authorities "insufficient" at best and a Hillul Hashem (desecration of God's name), at worst. These women, many of whom have been deeply involved in the struggle on behalf of agunot, regard reliance on decular authorities as a concession that Jewish law is incapable of ensuring justice for Jewish women they also contend that turning to the secular authorities for help is a strange decision for a community which has always believed its legal system to be the keystone of an all encompassing way of life.

Over the years, segments of the Orthodox community have proposed a range of solutions, many of which have not been widely accepted. Recently, the pre-nuptial agreement, used by couple son an ad hoc basis for years, has been standardized ad adopted by the Rabbinical Council of America, the organization of Orthodox rabbis. Under the terms of this agreement, the husband commits to maintain and support his wife until such time as the marriage is properly terminated. Both spouses agree to let the rabbinic court adjudicate any attempts to dissolve the marriage. (That provision protects the husband from a wife who procrastinates in order to be supported.) The major advantage of such an agreement is that it avoids the court as an instrument of religious coercion; the secular authorities are involved only in the enforcement of a civil contrast signed by two parties. However, all rabbis must demand that every couple sign such an agreement before marrying for this to serve as an even partial solution. Some rabbis are uncomfortable raising such practical concerns related to divorce with a couple presently planning a life together; some couples even refuse to listen. More significantly, the pre-nuptial agreement nevertheless requires the woman to hire a lawyer to sue her husband for the conditions stipulated in the contract. This is an expense which, in addition to all the expenses of a divorce, may make the prenuptial agreement of little value for some women in economic distress. Furthermore, this arrangement obviously leaves out all those women who were marriage without such an agreement but who nevertheless find themselves *agunot*. Thus, this new strategy must be tested overtime to see if it will achieve serious results in even a majority of *agunah* cases.

Understanding the Jewish Response to the Agunah

In light of our earlier analysis of human rights, the situation of the *agunah* and the rabbinic responses to there plight point to a disturbing trend in contemporary Jewsh law. In a word, contemporary halakha has become increasingly Lokean. For much of its formative history,halakha had opeated with the self-conscious aim of leading the communityto a higherplane of mutual respectandconcord. It not only anticipated abuses that lay in the technicalities of law and pre-empted them; it also resecribed actiosn that were delibertelydesigned to improve the interpersonal relations betweenmen and women, between adults and minors (particularly orphans), and between Jews and non-Jews. To be sure, there were rabbinic enactments that only addressed specific inequities once they had been perpetrated, although the historical extent of these abuses is rarely clear and usually incapable of verification. Nevertheless, the overall trajectory of Jewish law, particularly in the rabbinic period, was to create a covenantal society guided by the revealed law of God and predicated on the infinite worth of the individual who was created in the divine image. This, as we explained earlier, was in sharp contrast with the Hobbesian-Lockean pessimism regarding human nature.

In recent years, Jewish law has seen its role as primarily reactive, a trend the case of the *agunah* highlights quite well. Rather than preventing abuses which are only theoretically possible, many halakhic authorities wait until a problem reaches a certain intolerable level, and then address it, if at all. Obviously, there are exceptions, such as Rabbi Abraham Kock's *heter methirah* which allowed Jewish farmers to work the soil of Israel during the sabbatical year, a year during whih th eland is required to lie fallow. However, most rabbinic leaders (across the denominational divide) have allowed certain conditions which they acknowledge as lamentable to continue even as many Jews—usually in the minority—suffer. For instance, families willingly subject themselves to extreme economic hardship in an effort to conduct family celebrations at a level of extra vagence dictated by social custom and pressure. The increased affluence among Jews, especially in America but now even in Israel, has created a matrialistibent that imperials the more traditional values of modesty and humility, and more seriously forces those less endowed to forgo their dignity and seek assistance just to prevent the greater embarrassment in their own communities of having a sub-standard affair. Many rabbis address these regrettable social developments in sermons and other exhortatory media, but they remain reluctant to institute measures that could genuinely reverse these disturbing trends. In a liberal, capitalistic environment, where all pursue their own desires unfettered by moral restraints or social considerations, law is seen as interfering in the individual's freedom to spend money as he or she wishes, unless actual aggression or harm is being caused. But this is far form the ideal of nurturing a holy community, the traditional task of Halakha.

Of course, there are many reasons which may account

for this passivity: rabbinic authority is in fact a small shadow of what it once was, regrettably forcing many rabis to consider popular opinion before enacting certain rulings; the lak of institutional and social cohesion in the Jewish community makes it very difficult to implement significant changes or monitor their observane, and within Orthodoxy, which has defined itself over and against the Reform and conservative denominations precisely in its commitment onto to change the law, there is self-imposed restraint to implement any far-reaching halakhic changes, as necessary as they may be furthermore, we cannot discount that the Jews' very presence in a Locken system, especially in America, has influenced their views of Halalha. In defending Jewish law before the bar of contemporary culture, many have adopted the terminology and conceptual apparatus of secular law in their apologia. For mot legalists, Jewish law is not different from American law (or any secular, liberal system), and it need only intervene when the level of aggression of one against another becomes intolerable.

While many of these factors are external to halakha, it is noteworthy to mention a possible internal cause: the increased codification of Jewish law. When discussing the history of halakha, one must be aware that the legal and textual landscape did not remain the same. Aside from the relative social insularity of medieval Jewish communities, the halakhic system itself was extraordinarily pluralistic, with toleration of virtually any opinion which could find support or sanction in the rabbinic sources. In fact, it is not clear that one can refer to a "halakhic system" at all during this period. There was wide latitude within Jewish law, and some rabbis employed this latitude to institution rules and laws which would benefit their communities.

However, already during the Middle Areas, there were attempts to reduce the diversity of halakha and to codify only one or two positions on a given subject. Given the multiplication of vies, this is quite understandable; limiting options helps to unite a community and to sharpen itself-definition, particularly in the face of schismatic challenges. Codes were also preferred within Islam inclining those in its orbit to pursue a similar enterprise. Thus, in the twelfth century, Maimonides composed a major code of Jewsih law, partially intended to emulate his Muslim peers and partially intended to delegitimize the Karaites who rejected many rabbinic interpretations of the Torah. The codificatory trend continued (interestingly in Spain and the Middle East but not in Northern Europe) with the Araba'ah Turim of Jacob Ben Asher in the fourteenth century, and the Shulhan Arukh of Joseph Karo in the sixteenth century. Due to a variety of reasons, Karo's code combined with the glosses of Moses Isserlss, within a century of its initial printing achieved worldwide acceptance a the authoritative code of Jewish law. On most issues, only one or two positions are cited, thus removing other opinions from the domain of 'legitimate," that is, normative,views. Attempting to enact rulings which are not explicitly sanctioned in Karo's code is systemically difficult, inclining contemporary authorities to seek only those solutions which have some basis in the codes. Given the dramatically different set of religious and social circumstances it is unlikely that an answer will be found that addresses the widespread abuses of the agunah in a fundamental way.

Over the last several decades, divorce rtes have steadily increased throughout the industrialized world. And the religiously-committed community has not be immune to this trend. Unfortunately, in the Jewish case, the legal fallout of this phenomenon has been the widespread use of extortion by the husbands before granting their wives the get they so desperately need in order to close this agonizing chapter in their lives and move on. The worth tragedy is the *agunah* who remains in perpetual limbo, married yet single, unable to enter serious relationships because there prior marriage has not been officially terminated.

The aim of this chapter has not been to offer practical solutions to a clearly vexing problem. We chose not to review the legitimacy of existing legal options or to propose new ones, for that is neither within our expertise nor appropriate to this forum. Rather, in the spirit of this project, we have sought to shed light on a contemporary crisis with in the Jewish community by informing an otherwise insular discussion with the philosophical refection and comparative analysis which a meeting of scholars affords. For only by greater insight and deeper understanding will Jacob be able to ascend the ladder hitherto reserved for angles alone.

CHAPTER NINE

The Sex/Gender Distinction

This distinction is used in both confused and confusing ways and it is the purpose of this chapter to clarify first, what the theoretical basis of this distinction is, second, to ascertain whether or not it is a valid or coherent distinction, and finally, to consider the political effects of the use of this distinction by various political groups. This tripartite task will involve overlapping considerations of feminism's relation to socialist and homosexual politics. The tale of the uncomfortable alliance between feminist and socialist politics and feminist and homosexual politics has recently surfaced in a way that is potentially productive for all parties.

A critical appraisal of past and continuing alliances is the least one expects from radical theorists who value dialectical and historical analysis. It is in this spirit that the question of the viability of analyses located at the intersection of 'sex' and 'class' can be addressed. The difficulty of reconciling sex and class, or feminism and Marxism, despite the intervention of a third party, psychoanalysis,) has' been well demonstrated. In this context, the introduction of 'spot-lighting' of gender, as an analytical tool which purportedly yields high explanatory returns (as opposed to the barren category of 'sex') offers occasion for comment. Over the past five years or so, feminist theory, of an Anglo-American orientation, has taken up the notion of 'gender' with considerable interest and mixed intent influential journals and texts such as *m/f, Ideology and Consciousness, Feminist Studies, The Reproduction of Mothering, The Mermaid and the Minotaur* and *Women's Oppression Today,* share if nothing else, this enthusiasm for the notion of 'gender' as a central explanatory and organizing category of their accounts of the social and familial and/or discursive construction of subjectivity. In general, the favouring of the category 'gender' over the category 'sex' is defended in terms of the 'dangers of biological reductionism'.

Theorists who favour analyses based on gender argue that it is indispensable to see 'sex as a biological category and gender as a social one Additionally, it would appear that the role of prior or current political commitment to anyone of a variety of 'left' politics plays a decisive role in this preference for 'gender'. Given that the category 'gender' commands considerable theoretical centrality in contemporary feminist and socialist-feminist theorizing as compared with its peripheral employment in the early seven-ties, it is appropriate, at this time, to critically reassess its credentials. It is in the area of political analysis and practice that the recent proliferation of the sex/gender distinction becomes most worrying.

The distinction has been used by groups as diverse as: Marxists; (usually male) homosexual groups; and feminists of equality. The effect of the use of the sex/gender distinction by the three groups outlined above, though clearly they display discernibly distinct political and theoretical motivations, has been to encourage or engender a neutralization of sexual difference and sexual politics. This neutralizing process is not novel, it can be traced to nineteenth-century liberal environmentalism where're-education' is the catchcry of radical social transformation. Much of contemporary radical politics is, perhaps unwit-tingly, enmeshed in this liberal tradition. A feminism based on difference rather than on *a priori* equality is representative of a decisive break with this tradition.

What I wish to take to task in implicit and explicit investigations of gender theory is the unreasoned, unargued assumption that both the body and the psyche are a post-natally passive *tabula rasa.* That is, for theorists of gender, the mind, of either sex, is a neutral, passive entity, a blank state, on which is inscribed various social 'lessons'. The body, on their account, is the passive mediator of these inscriptions. The result of their analyses is the simplistil solution to female oppression: a programme of re-edueation, the unlearning of patriarchy's arbitrary and oppressive codes, and the relearning of politically correct and equitable behaviours and traits, leading to the whole person: the and rogyn. It is precisely this alleged *neutrality* of the body; the postulated *arbitrary* connection between femininity and the female body; masculinity and the male body; and the apparent simplicity of the a historical and theoretically naive solu-tion, viz. resocialization, that this paper proposes to challenge.

Before proceeding to present a critique of the proponents of the sex/ gender distinction I should clarify what I take to be the central issue at stake. It would appear that one of the most burning issues in the contemporary women's movement is that of sexual equality *vs* sexual difference. It is arguable that this debate brings to a crisis both feminism's association with socialism and feminism's association with (male) homosexual groups. Both associations are often predicated upon an assumed 'essential' or possible equality, in the sense of 'sameness' between the sexes. It is against the backdrop of this question that this chapter is situated. I would maintain that the proponents of sexual equality consistently mischaracterize and distort the position of those feminists who favour a politics of sexual difference". The fault may well lie with those feminists who have not made clear what such a 'politics of difference' amounts to. This chapter is an attempt to amend this situation and, in addition, to quell, once and for all, the tired (and tiring, if not tiresome) charges of essentialism and biologism so often levelled at theories of sexual difference[9] Critics of feminists of difference tend 10 divide the entire theoretical field of social enquiry into an exclusive disjunction: social theory is *either* environmentalist *or* it is essentialist. In Therefore, and it follows quite logically from this premise, if feminist theories of difference are not environmentalist then they must be essen-tialisl. The task remains, then, to reopen the field of social theory from its forced containment in this disjunction and demonstrate the practical and theoretical viability of the politics of difference. The latter task shall be effected indirectly, by way of a critique of the proponents of 'degendering'

The Degendering Proposal

The problem of the relationship between sex and gender is, of course, not a new one. Freud grappled with the problem of finding a suitable definition of masculinity and femininity and their relation to men and women in the 'Three Essays' published in 1905'" However, the authoritative source for the recent prominence of writings centring on gender is not Freud but Robert J. Stoller, a contemporary psychoanalyst. Stoller published a book titled *Sex and Gender,'*2 in 1968, a text wherein he reports the findings and theses arising out of his research and involvement with the Gender Identity Research Clinic at UCLA.

Stoller studies first various *biological* anomalies (for example, neuters and hermaphrodites) in order to ascertain the- relationship between sex and gender, and second he considers the biologically normal but *psychologically* disturbed individual (for example, the transsexual). He claims, at the completion of his research, to be able to account for the aetiology of both the transvestite and the transsexual - although his account is self-avowedly more complete in the case of *male* transvestites and transsexuals than in the (much rarer) cases of female transvestites and transsexuals. He claims to be able to account for these psychological anomalies largely in terms of the distinction which he develops and systematizes between sex and gender.

The explanation is as follows. The biological sex of a person has a tendency to augment, though not determine, the appropriate gender identity for that sex (i.e. masculinity in the case of the male sex; femininity in the case of the female sex). However, a person's gender. These psychological influences on gender identity, he claims, can completely override the biological fact of a person's sex and result in, for example, the situation of the transsexual.

Stoller takes the genesis of transsexual ism to be wholly social, that is, not biologically or physically determined. He posits, as the cause of male transsexualism, the mother's attitude to the child from birth. He reports that in all normal infants there is an initial period of symbiosis with the mother but that this symbiosis must be broken, particularly in the case of the boy, if normal masculinity or femininity as a separate (and in the case of the boy, different) and independent identity is to develop.

Stoller posits, in the case of the male transsexual, an unwillingness on the part of the mother to allow the child to separate from her and develop as an individual. It must be stressed that it is not only a matter of how long the child is held close to the mother's body but also in what manner. If the mother sees the child as a part of or extension to her own body, then the child will respond by not developing an iden-tity separate from the mother's (or developing it at a critically late stage) and so, in the case of a male child, will feel himself to be a woman trapped in a male body.

The details of Stoller's work are not terribly important for the purposes of this paper. What is important is that his work was generally heralded as a breakthrough in the area of sexuality and socialization. As such it was quickly taken up by feminist theorists as offering theoretical justification for the right to equality for all independently of sex. His work has been used by Greer, Millett, Oakley, and more recently by Chodorow, Dinnerstein, and Barrett, to name a few.

Millett, writing in 1971, and acknowledging Stoller as support or 'proof' of her view, offers the speciously reasoned conclusion that since 'Psychosexually (e.g. in terms of masculine and feminine, and in contra-distinction to male and female) there is no differentiation between the sexes at birth. Psychosexual personality is *therefore* postnatal and learned.' Millett's contention that 'patriarchal ascriptions of tempera-ment and role' to the sexes are arbitrary leads to the inevitable and naive feminist tactic of the re-socialization of society. She writes since patriarchy's biological foundations appear to be so very insecure, one has some cause to admire the strength of "socialisation" which can continue a universal condition *"on faith alone"*, as it were, or through an acquired value system *exclusively*. What does seem decisive in assuring the maintenance of the temperamental differences between the sexes is the conditioning of early childhood.

Greer and Oakley pursue the same line of reasoning, with idiosyncratic differences.

The initial appeal of the implications of Stoller's research, in the late 1960s and early 1970s, is consistent with the social context of liberal humanism. Education or re-education, at that time, scemed a particularly viable programme for radical social change. Ten years later, howevcr, both the context and the sentiment have altered considcrably. Previous demands and strategies of the women's movement have 'back-fircd' or proved to be co-optable. It is in this context that we need to examine. very carefully, both the 'politics of equality' and sentiments originating with the liberal humanists of the eighteenth and nineteenth cel1luries. The unproblematic assumptions of Stoller's research by contemporary writers, such as Chodorow and Barrett, warrants careful scrutiny.

In order for a programme of 'degendcring' to be successful or even theoretically tenable, one would have to allow the validity of at least two unargued assumptions central to the thesis put forward by Stoller and assumed by the 'degendering feminists'. These are: i) that the body is neutral and passive with regard to the formation of consciousness. consciousness is primary and determinant - implicitly a rationalist view; and ii) the important effects of the historical and cultural specificity of one's 'lived experience' is able to be altered, definitively, by consciously changing the material practices of the culture in question. If the validity of these assumptions is allowed then one could claim that cultural and historical significances or meanings receive their expression in or are made manifest by an (initially or essentially) neutral consciousness which, in turn, acts upon an (initially) neutral body. One could claim, in addi-tion, that masculine and feminine behaviours are arbitrary forms of behaviour, socially inscribed on an indifferent consciousness that is joined to an indifferent body.

However, the above-mentioned assump-tions warrant no such validity. To clarif.):he problem in other words, socialization theory, which posits the social acquisition of a particular gender by a particular sex is, implicitly, a rationalist account, an a historical account, and an account which posits a spurious neutrality of both the body and consciousness. In order to substantiate this position *vis-a-vis* the resocialization feminists who uncritically adopt Stoller's account, these two assumptions, outlined above, will be treated in detail. Although they are obviously interrelated, they will be treated separately for the sake of clarity and manageability.

Sex/Gender and the Rationalist Conception of the Subject

It is in the area of the heredity *vs* environment debate that the extreme difficulty of avoiding conceptualizing the person as a split body/ consciousness is most apparent.

The sex/gender distinction is situated in such a debate and, it will be argued, is deeply entrenched in the problems of confused terminology and conceptualizing that characterize that debate. The sex/gender distinction is understood, by socialization theorists, as a body/consciousness distinction. This is not to suggest that this understanding does not have an immediate, commonsense validity but rather that such an understanding commits its user to a series of assumptions that, historically, have proved untenable.

Theorists who uncritically use the mind/body distinction consistently characterize the subject as either predominantly (or wholly) determined by biological forces, i.e. heredity or predominantly (or wholly) determined by the influence of social or familial relations, i.e. environment. Both these positions, the latter being the one that would best characterize reo socialization feminists, posit a naive causal relation between either the body and the mind or the environment and the mind which commits both viewpoints, as two sides of the same coin, to an *a priori*, neutral, and passive conception of the subject. If we conceive of the body as neutral and passive and of consciousness as socially determined, then we are at least halfway to a behavioural conception of subjectivity. It is unclear if the behaviourist conception of conditioning, which is based on various experimental hypotheses in animal ethology, has any valid application in the sphere of human behaviour. The stimulus-response model of conditioned behaviour assumes a passive and non-signifying subject who can be trained to respond appropriately and who can be relied upon to *consistently* respond appropriately. Psychoanalysis read as a *descriptive* theory of the constitution of subjectivity in (western, industrialized) patriarchal society, seriously undermines the behaviourist conception of 'conditioning' and the assumed passivity of the subject.

The problem of the interrelation and interaction of the body and the mind is by no means an archaic theoretical preoccupation. It is c): of this problem that psychoanalysis arose. The Freud of 1889, that is, Freud the neurophysiologist, was perplexed by the phenomenon of hysteria, a disorder- he once described as representing a 'mysterious leap from the mind to the body'. Since Freud's early work on hysterics with Charcot and Breuer both physiological and psychoanalytic understandings of the socalled mind-body problem· have altered drastically. 25 A cogent and theoretically useful account posits that there is one unitary reality underlying two (or more) distinct levels of theoretical abstraction and that the 'mysterious leap' is actually a leap from one kind of discourse, say the psychological, to another, the physiological. 26 It remains to integrate this insight into everyday and theoretical conceptions of the person - a task not always achieved even by those who offer acknowledgement of the necessity of such integration.

Freud stressed, from his earliest papers, that even perception cannot be regarded as passive but rather is an active process.[27] He argues further that consciousness cannot be equated with the perceptual system and that, in fact, most of what is perceived never even enters consciousness but remains pre-conscious or unconscious This implies an activity, and not necessarily a conscious activity, on the part of the subject that cannot be accounted for by the behaviourist. Perception can be reduced to neither the body nor consciousness but must be seen as an activity of the subject.

Concerning the neulrality of the body, let me be explicit, there is no neutral body, there are at least two kinds of bodies; the male body and the female body. If we locate social practices and behaviours as embedded in the subject, as we have with perception, rather than 'in consciousness' or 'in the body' then this has important repercussions for the subject as always a *sexed* subject. If one accepts the notion of the sexually specific subject, that is, the male or female subject, then one must dismiss the notion that patriarchy can be characterized as a system of social organization that valorizes the masculine *gender* over the feminine gender. Gender is not the issue; sexual difference is. The very same behaviours (whether they be masculine or feminine) have quite different personal and social significances when acted out by the male subject on the one hand, and the female subject on the olher. Identical social 'training', attitudes, or, if you will, conditioning, acquire different significances when applied to male or female subjects.

This is largely a result of the activity of the subject and its drive to master social relations and meanings· Each gesture, attitude, percep-tion, that enters human consciousness, does so charged with significances that relate to all that has gone before. That the male body and the female body have quite different social value and significance cannot help but have a marked effect on male and female consciousness.

The orthodox account of the gender/sex distinction claims that the social determination of personal identity operates at the level of ideas, the level of 'the mind'. What this account fails to note is the obvious divergence between feminine behaviour, experience, lived out by a female subject and feminine behaviour, experience, lived out by a male subject (and vice versa with masculine behaviour). This claim does not imply an commitment, on my part, to a fixity or essence of the social significance of bodily functions, events, or experience. Signification, and its con-stitutive role in the construction of subjectivity is curiously absent from the writings of the proponents of degendering. This is likely to be an effect of their implicit commitment to a behaviourist conception of the person and the resultant stress on passive conditioning and socialization rather than the active process of signification.

While explicitly wishing to distance this paper from a historical and *a priori* accounts of the social significance of the sexed body and its behaviour, I would suggest that some bodily experiences and events, though lacking any *fixed* significance are likely, in all social structures, to be privileged sites of significance. Various anthropological, ethological, and historical evidence would seem to support this claim. For example, menstruation is likely to be one of these privileged sites. The fact that menstruation occurs only in (normal) female bodies is of considerable import for this paper. Given that in this society there is a network of relations obtaining between femininity and femaleness, that is, between the female *body* and femininity, then there must be a qualitative difference between the kind of femininity 'lived' by men. H To take again the example of menstruation, in our culture it is associated with shame and modesty - both characteristically feminine attributes. An interesting speculation is whether this shame could be connected to the more general shame involved in the failure to control one's bodily fluids, excretions, wastes, given the high store put on this control in our culture. Freud's neglect of the effect of the menses on the pubertal girl's psyche is significant. That the flow of blood would have profound psychical significance for her is dear and that this significance would centre around ideas of castration, sexual attack, and socially reinforced shame is highly probable. The female's first act of coitus would probably also bear on this.

The point is that the body can and does intervene, to confirm or to deny, various social significances in a way that lends an air of inevitability to patriarchal social relations. A thorough analysis of the construction of the specificity to female experience, which takes account of the female *body*, is essential to dispelling this 'air'. To slide from 'male' and 'female' experience to 'masculine' and 'feminine' experience further confuses the issue. The 'feminine male' may have experiences that are socially ascribed as 'feminine' but - and this is the relevance of the body and its specific social value and meaning - in a way that must be *qualitatively* different from female experience of the feminine. He is parasitically dependent on the female body, more particularly the mater-nal body, by a process of identification. This point shall be elaborated further.

It has been the purpose of this section to argue that the view that consciousness is wholly socially constituted and inscribed by means of a passively conditioned socialization which in turn acts upon a neutral and passive body is untenable. I have argued that the conception of a passive subject (supported by various behaviourist-oriented assertions), central to the programme of degendering is demonstrably inadequate to account for human behaviour and, in particular, the activity of signification.

Contextual Specificity

A most common claim made against feminists of sexual difference is that their theories are essentialist and *a priori*, in short, ahistorical. This claim

operates like the infamous blade that cuts both ways. The irony of the accusation is that feminists who propose degendering propose it outside of history and without considering the extreme resilience of expressions of sexual difference and the network of language and other systems of signification that both constitute and perpetuate this difference. Again, Chodorow provides us with the stereotype of this claim. She states 'To see men and women as qualitatively different kinds of people, rather than seeing gender as processual, reflexive, and constructed, is to reify and deny relations of gender, to see gender differences as permanent rather than as created and situated.' Note the slide from sex to gender in this passage - from biological terminology (men, women) to psycho-logical terminology (feminine, masculine). What is quite remarkable in her article is that she does not write about the body at all, except in a footnote where she does little more than acknowledge this (convenient) 'oversight'. She writes there:

We cannot know what children would make of their

bodies in a non-gender or non-sexually organised world, what kind of sexual structuration or gender identities would develop. But it is not obvious that there would be *major* significance to biological sex differences to gender difference, or to different sexualities.

This kind of speculative phantasy is merely veiled rhetoric - the point is that we are historically and culturally situated in a society that is divided and organized in terms of sex - an historical fact. The charges of essentialism and ahistoricism can be made both ways. The recognition of the historicity of the significance of sex and gender can be shown to be of prime importance to theories of sexual difference. It is this historicity, this specificity that the analysis is based upon. Theorists of sexual difference do not take as their object of study the physical body, the anatomical body, the neutral, dead body, but the body as lived, the animate body - the *situated* body.

It is striking that the body figures in socialization theory only as the biological anatomical or physiological body. There is little analysis of the body as lived: of the body's morphology or of the imaginary body. If one wants to understand sex and gender or, put another way, a person's biology and the social and personal significance of that biology as lived, then one needs an analysis of the imaginary body. It is here that the importance of the feminist rereadings of Freud's work in terms of a theoretical description of how it is that male and female biologies are lived as masculine and feminine subjectivities in patriarchal culture is located.

As I indicated at the beginning of the preceding section, it was largely due to Freud's early work with hysterics that the discipline of psychoanalysis arose. What Freud posited as crucial in order to understand the hysteric's symptom was an understanding of the emotional and libidinal investment obtaining between the subject and her (or his) body.J9 This insight opened the way for future advances in the still prevalent mechanism of dualist conceptions of the subject. Contem-porary French psychoanalytic research, in particular the work of Laplanche and Lacan, can be seen as such advances. In Lacan's formulation of the 'mirror phase' he claims to have shown 'an essential libidinal relationship with the body-image'.

In both papers where Lacan treats, specifically, the genesis of the ego, he stresses the importance of the mirror phase in relation to both hysteria and the imaginary body. He writes:

> To call these (hysterical) symptoms functional is but to confess our ignorance, for they follow the pattern of a certain imaginary anatomy which has typical forms of its own. In other words, the astonishing somatic compliance which is the outward sign of the imaginary anatomy is only shown within certain definite limits. I would emphasise that *the imaginary anatomy referred to here varies with the ideas (clear or confused) about bodily functions which are prevalent in a given culture.*

The existence and operations of the imaginary body are most clearly demonstrated by the aetiologically related phenomena of 'phantom limb' and hysteria. What these phenomena illustrate is a libidinal or narcissistic relation of the subject with its body. This relation defies mechanistic or purely empirical explanation along either rationalist or behaviourist lines. The dispute concerning the experience of the unity of the body tends to centre around what this experience is predicated upon, and whether it is an experience given immediately in perception or developed in a milieu of social meaning and value. There is abundant evidence to favour the latter description. Schilder maintains that both 'phantom limb' and hysteria can be understood only if we take into account the fact that all healthy people are, or have, in addition to a material body, a body-phantom or an imaginary body. This psychical image of the body is necessary in order for us to have motility in the world - without it we would not be intentional subjects. The imaginary body is developed, learnt, connected to the body-image of others, and is not static.

Hysterical symptoms have a demonstrably clear relation to the (cultur-ally specific) imaginary body. Hysterical paralysis, for example, conforms to the culturally and linguistically delineated imaginary body. Hysterical paralysis of the arm does not correspond to the anatomical or physiological organization of the body but rather to the anatomically naive conception of the body, where the arm ends at the place where the shirt-sleeve meets the shoulder seam. Or again, there is an intimate relation of equivalence between the mouth and the vagina" that is, in the case of Dora:" used to express her unconscious desire via the symptom of *Tussis nervosa.* Knowledge of the particular form of the culturally constructed imaginary body is essential in order to understand the social (rather than individual) character of hysteria. The surprising homogeneity in the expression of the hysterical symptom, such a, *anorexia nervosa,* within a given culture, signals the social character of the imaginary body. The imaginary body is sociallv and historicallv specific in that it is constructed by: a shared language; the shared psychical significance and privileging of various Lones of the body (e.g. the mouth, the anus, the genitals); and common institutional practices and discourses (e.g. medical, juridical, and educational) on and through the body.

It is by way of an analysis of the imaginary body that it can be shown to be the site of the historical and cultural specificity of masculinity and femininity. It is to the imaginary body that· we must look to find the key or the code to enable the decipherment of the social and personal significance of male and female biologies as liven in culture, that is, masculinity and femininity.

In this connection it is also clear that there is a contingent, though not arbitrary, relation between the male body and masculinity and the female body and femininity. To claim this is neither biologism or essentialism but rather to acknowledge the extremely complex and ubiquitous network of signification and its historical, psychological, and cultural manifesta-tions. To deny this network and the specific historical form of femininity and masculinity and their relation to female and male subjects and to favour instead a conception of the subject as essentially neutral or neutered and further, to base one's political practices on this conception, can only lead to the reproduction, at another site, of these relations.

When Freud describes femininity and masculinity as end results of a developmental chain, he is Quite explicit. The respective tasks of women and men in our culture are, for women, to 'take over' the place of the object, passive, castrated, the feminine, and, for the man, to 'combine' the values of subject, active, phallic, masculine: Among the traits that epitomize femininity for Freud (and our culture) are: passivity, maso-chism, narcissism, envy, shame. What I suggest is that these feminine behaviours are not merely the result of patriarchal socialization and conditioning, the strength of which Millett was so admiring, or a discur-sively constituted category lacking a referent, but additionally are modes of defensive behaviour that utilize the culturally shared phantasies about biology - that is, they are mahifestations of and reactions to the (conscious and unconscious) ideas we share about our biology.

Freud saw the biology of women and men to be unproblematic - the ovum is passive, the sperm active - the problem for him was the psychology of masculinity and femininity which 'mirrors' this biology: the man actively penetrates the passive vagina. However, and this is the role of cultural and historical specificity, it is not given *a priori* that the penis is active, the vagina passive. This concept has to do with the imaginary anatomy, where the vagina is conceived of as a 'hole', a 'lack' and the penis as a 'phallus'. One could just as well, given a different relational mode between men and women, conceive of the penis as being enveloped or 'embraced' by the active vagina. In this context an interesting addendum is provided by recent biological research which maintains that the ovum is not as passive as it appears - it rejects some sperm and only allows entry, or envelops, a sperm(s) of its 'choice'.

Masculinity and femininity as forms of sex-appropriate behaviours are manifestations of an historically based, culturally shared phantasy about male and female biologies, and as such sex and gender are not arbitrarily connected. The connection between the female body and femininity is not arbitrary in the same way that the symptom is not arbitrarily related to its aetiology. Hence, to treat gender, the 'symptom', as the problem is to misrecognize its genesis. Again, we can here note parallels between behaviourist psychology and 'degendering'. The therapeutic techniques of behaviourism - systematic desensitization, behaviour modification, and so on - treat the symptom only.

In the above analysis of the two assumptions taken to be crucial to the theory of degendering, it has been argued that masculine and feminine forms of behaviour are not arbitrary inscriptions on an indifferent consciousness which is joined to an indifferent body. To speak of 'acquiring' a particular gender is to be mistaken about the significance of gender and its intimate relation to biology-as-lived in a social and historical context. The account of difference' that has been affected only indirectly, is an ongoing project and as such is both tentative and incomplete. However, even at this stage we can oppose the naive simplicity of degendering and its questionable theoretical basis.

Transsexualism Reconsidered

It has been argued throughout this paper that the

relation between masculine behaviour acted out by a male subject and masculine behaviour acted out by a female subject (or feminine behaviour acted out by a female subject and feminine behaviour acted out by a male subject) cannot be symmetrical. In other w0rds, it has been argued that masculinity and femininity do not differ with regard to the sexes in terms of quantity only, but *qualitatively*. If this thesis is correct then to suggest the degendering of society as political strategy is hopelessly utopian, ahistorical, and functions theoretically and practically as a diversionary tactic. Additionally, it has been argued that the programme

Of degendering is based on a misunderstanding of" patriarchal social relation. This all hut concluding section is titled 'transsexualism reconsidered' because it is the case of the transsexual that most clearly demonstrale, the dissymmetry between masculinity/femininity and male/female. An understanding of the determinant ion 0 I' male and female transsexual ism not to be found in the sex/gender distinction or in an analysis of the acquisition of gender identity. It was mentioned early in this paper that Stoller's account of transsexualism is more complete in the case of male transsexuals than female transsexuals. Contrary to Stoller's hopes,"' it clear that the same account will not cover both cases. It has been suggested that the male transsexual can be understood only if we first understand the genesis of the primitive ego and the notion of the imaginary body. The male transsexual, due to his primary relations to hi, mother, is in the situation of being constituted in such a way that his (primitive) ego connicts with his imaginary (and biological) body, leading to his subjectivity being conceived by him as 'female-in-a-male-body'. Brieny this would involve the non-resolution of the misrecognition of the body of the other for one's own", that is, the male transsexual's primitive (bodily) ego is predicated upon a female body (i.e. the maternal body)"" and he docs not develop, until comparatively late, a separate identity from his mother. His transsexualism, in fact, is evidence that this separa-tion is never adequately achieved. The desire of the mother is active in this non-resolution or critically *late* resolution.

The case of the female transsexual cannot be symmetrical. The relation of the female infant to the mother's body is not and can not be problematic *in the same way.* This may partially explain the relative rarity of female transsexualism. (Though the extremely common phenomenon of the 'tom-boy' is transsexualism, of a sort.) Female transsexualism is much more likely to be a reaction against oppression, that is, against the socially required forfeit of activity that was once enjoyed and socially tolerated. This possibly is overlaid by the desire of the mother to make a husband-substitute of the girl and/or the mother's own resemment of the female role in patriarchy_ The transsexual knows, most clearly, that the issue is not one of gender but one of sex. It is not masculinity *per se* that is valorized in our culture but the *masculine male.*

On another level, this dissymmetry between the sexes is renected in feminist musings concerning whether women are excluded (or all but excluded) from certain professions *because they are prestigious* or whether those professions are prestigious *because women are excluded.* The implication being that it is not what is done or how it is done but who does it that determines its value. The problem is not the socializa-tion of women to femininity and men to masculinity but the place of these behaviours in the network of social meaning and the valorizing of one (the male) over the other (the female) and the resultant mischar-acterization of relations of difference as relations of superiority and inferiority.

There is another aspect to the theory of gender that is also important to consider, and that is the political use to which the sex/gender distinc-tion is put.

The Effect of the Sex/Gender Distinction in Political

Analysis and Action

The commitment to economism or humanism in many Marxist accouI1lS of the social and political status of women each, in their different ways, effects the neutralization of sexual difference. Economism by its privileg-ing of the relations of production over psychical and social forms of subjectivity that are prior to or inadequately captured by the capitalist mode of production. Humanism by its adherence to an *a priori* and universal conception of human nature that, also, takes no account of sexual difference. A coherent account of the construction of male and female subjectivity under patriarchy and capitalism is indispensable for effective political strategy. However, to shift the site of amihsis from 'male' to 'masculine', from 'female' to 'feminine', claiming by the shift priority to gender in the construction of men and women, rather than avoiding the problems of 'individualism' merely presents us with another set of problems. For example, masculinity and femininity and their constitutive role in sexual difference are often, on this account, reduced to the status of a *deus ex machina*.

M. Barrett in *Women's Oppression Today* uses the category of gender to argue that socialism and feminism are compatible and 'that the ideology of masculinity and femininity has a crucial role in the division of labour as it has developed historically' Barrett's extensive and central use of the category gender is problematic in that she does not state, support, or defend its theoretical status, but rather assumes that there is general agreement concerning its, apparently transparent, explanatory merits. She writes: 'The processes by which gender, and particularly femininity, is socially constructed in capitalist society have been extensively explored. This topic falls within the well-researched area of 'socialization studies' in sociology and has also been a major focus of feminist accounts.' It has been argued, at some length, in this paper that both the explanatory value and theoretical adequacy of 'socialization studies' are extremely tenuous.

The question arises then, 'why would a theorist, familiar with the implications of psychoanalytic theory for socialization theory, adopt the use of gender, knowing it is based on questionable theoretical grounds?' A likely explanation is that prior political investments and allegiances lead some feminists to neglect casting their otherwise critical eye in the appropriate direction.

Recent issues of the local journal *Gay Information* reveal a similar commitment to the centrality of the category. Gender in sexual politics,. What Carrigan and others'" argue is that the diversity of preference and practice is such that a biological distinction, male/female. is inadequate to account for forms of sexuality. There is no quarrel here. However, to introduce gendered forms of sexuality lakes us out of 01lL' hiatus into another. This move adopts, in keeping with socialization theory, only a quantitative distinction between masculinity and femininity and their relation to the construction of male and female subjectivities. Again, the body is neutral and *a priori,* consciousness a passive *tabula rasa..*

It is in the above context that I maintain that the programme of degendering put forward initially by feminists such as Millell and OaklC) and taken over by Chodorow, is based on a misunderstanding (originat-ing with Stoller's mistaken thesis of the genesis of transsexualism) of masculinity and femininity as conditioned forms of behaviour. Rather, I would suggest that 'masculinity' and 'femininity' correspond at the level of the imaginary body to 'male' and 'female' at the level of biology. It bears repetition that this statement does not imply a fixed essence to 'masculine' and 'feminine' but rather an historical specificity.

What has brought equality feminists and difference feminists into the present sharp confrontation is, partly, the so-called 'crisis' in Marxism and the withdrawal of the labour of many feminists from Marxist-oriented research.

Also, at another level, the influence of French feminism has been instrumental in the formulation and defence of a politics of difference, which is often placed in opposition to the politics of Marxist-feminism.

One could also argue that the gradual demise of the call for sexual equality and the rise of the insistence on sexual difference can be accounted for in purely pragmatic terms, that is, trial and error - we asked for equality and it didn't work, let's insist on difference. Prac-tically, this has been the case in a number of areas. For example, the demand for equal legal status is now thought by some to be counter-productive. The feminist campaign for the acquittal of the cases of Roberts and Krope were argued on the grounds that the law of provoca-tion did not take account of the, in general, disproportionate strength of men and women.[58] Likewise, many feminists have pointed out the abuse by men of the recently introduced anti-discrimination legislation.

However, there are also, and more importantly for the purposes of this paper, several theoretical determinations of the tactical shift from -equality to difference. The most important of these I take to be [he growing belief in the inefficacy of key theoretical concepts in various analyses and understandings of oppression (whether racial, class.

The early feminist contribution to this social change is typified by the challenge to the notion that the sexual division of labour is natural, claiming rather that it is ideological - the implication being that alongside the struggle against capitalism should be the struggle against patriarchy, that the struggle for male emancipation was not, necessarily, compatible with or inclusive of the struggle for female emancipation. The stumbling block to the proposed 'equal society' was (either or both) women's reproductive capacity and the responsibility of childrearing. These feminist claims represented the first 'crack' in the edifice of the homogeneity of radical and/or socialist politics. However, this 'crack' was quickly sealed, often by feminists themselves, by recourse to the claimed necessity of the neutralizing of sexual difference. For example, Firestone's 'cybernetic communism', proposed the literal neutering of bodies by means of the complete technologization, and hence socializa-tion, of the reproductive capacity. So, in effect, the edge of sexual -difference and the denial of sexual neutrality was quickly, but not effec-tively, blunted by the call to neutralize the difference.

What is overlooked in this megalomaniacal phantasy, leaving aside the desirability or otherwise of its details, is that the implied neutrality is not a neutrality at all but a 'masculinization' or 'normalization' (in a society where men are seen as the norm, the standard) of women - a making of 'woman' into 'man'. 61 This move has many echoes in discourse and politics, as many feminists have tirelessly pointed out. An assumption implicit in the aim of neutralizing the body and to thereby allot primacy to the ideological is the total passivity of the body. What this analysis yields, at best, is the predominantly Anglo-American crass empirical equation between patriarchal sex-role socialization and patriarchal consciousness.

It is the revival, or continuation, of the above problematic that the proponents of the sex/gender distinction seek. In addition to the neutralization of sexual difference, the sex/ gender distinction lends itself to those groups or individuals whose analyses reveal a desire to ignore sexual difference and prioritize 'class', 'discourse', 'power', or some other 'hobby-horse'. Their accounts attempt to co-opt or trivialize feminist struggles and feminist theory at its peak, reducing sexual politics to gender difference and positing as primary the relations obtaining between genders and power, gender and discourse, or gender and class - as if women's *bodies* and the repression and control of women's bodies were not a crucial stake in these struggles.

Feminism and the Problem of Gender Identity

Lacan never tired of repeating that *Totem and Taboo*

(1912) was wrong, and that the Oedipus complex was Freud's own neurosis. Lacan offered instead his own theory of the paternal metaphor and the Oedipal structure which make use of his innovative concepts of the Phallus, Castra-tion, Desire, and *jouissance.* By recasting Freud's realist picture of the Oedipal complex away from both myth and biology, Lacan introduced the concept of a structure which is formed by the intervention of a third element into the original infant-mother dyad: the Law of the Name-of- the-father. Moving from the realm of the Freudian sexual triangle to that of symbolic effect, Lacan leaves the scene of the incest taboo to dramatists and anthropologists. Sexual identity is not based on biological gender, or any other innate factor, but is learned through the dynamics of identification and language.

One finds two different systems of meaning within Lacan's epistem-ology, each complete in its own sphere: the one of language, and that of an unconscious discourse. In the unconscious system which Lacan calls the Other discourse, meaning does not come from substance or essence, but from structural associations and signifying effects. Within this context, not only the Oedipal myth, but myth in general is simply 'the attempt to give epic form to that which operates itself from struc-ture'. In the early 1950s Lacan used the word 'structure' to mean that which functions *like* a language: i.e. by transformations. In the same way that speech and lexicon are governed by the fundamental laws of language which Roman lakobson names as metaphor and metonymy, Lacan has depicted an unconscious which transforms its representational networks of imagistic relations through analogous procedures of combination, condensation, substitution, and displacement] In light of Lacan's structural picture of the unconscious, any direct linking of his Oedipal structure to biology through body configuration, gender, genital experience, or its 'resolution' in genital satisfaction, is a complete mis-interpretation of a symbolic, representational, transformational drama.

Lacan saw the effect of the Oedipal nexus as that which decides the assumption of sex, where sex is correlated with identity rather than gender: One might describe his Oedipal structure as t he obligation every child is under to submit his or her sexuality to certain restrictions and to the laws of organization and exchange within a sexually differen-tiated group, and in this way find her or his place within that society.; The Oedipal crisis occurs, not because a child wants to possess its mother sexually, but when the child comprehends the sexual rules in a society. The crisis is resolved when the rules are accepted and acceded to. These rules are conveyed by what Lacan calls the Symbolic order, but by 'symbolic' he does not mean that which is representative of a second hidden thing or essence. Instead, he means that order of life which includes language, cultural codes, and conventions, and whose principal function is to differentiate one thing from another, and to mediate between non-verbal experiences - the Imaginary order of identifications - and real events - the Real. In other words, the Lacanian Symbolic order interprets, symbolizes, articulates, and universalizes both the experiential and the concrete, which it has in paradoxically circular fashion already shaped.

In a meeting of Lacan's Seminar Twenty (1972-3) he suggested that perhaps one of the women should write a 'book entitled *Beyond the Phallus,* ironically punning on Freud's *Beyond the Pleasure Principle* (1920). 'That would be lovely,' Lacan said, 'and it would give another consistency to the women's liberation movement. A pleasure or ecstasy *(jouissance)* beyond the phallus.'6 Lacan's 'beyond the phallus' phrase is striking because it encapsulates the growing controversy surrounding his theories on the Phallus and Castration in their relationship to the structuring of gender identity and sexual personality. Later on, I shall consider the reasons for the seemingly ironic tone of Lacan's joke-cum-challenge. Certain feminists do not take Lacan's theories as a joke, however, and have attacked his thought, alleging him to be a phallocrat. On the contrary, I believe that Lacan's thought provides a key for understanding the socialization and symbolization processes which have shaped woman's specificity through the ages.

Lacan located the source of sexual identity in a pre-Oedipal period which occurs even earlier than the one Freud proposed. The structural cornerstones on which any identity is built are Desire and Law. In this way the roots of identity are ethical, not ontological. 7 But none of this makes sense except in light of Lacan's innovative view of human iden-tity; what we usually call the ego or self or personality. For Lacan, iden-tity does not derive from genetic predispositions, nor from an unfolding of neurophysiological developmental sequences; nor is it the product of a war between biological and cultural forces, nor the reflection of collective archetypes. Identity is built up as a composite of images and effects - i.e. mental representations - taken in from the outside world from the start of life, which are developed in relation to the Desire for recognition and the later social requirements for submission to an arbitrary Law.

Born premature in terms of physiological functions by comparison with other animals, the human infant is more dependent on the world around it. The human neonate transcends its helplessness and insufficien-cies by fusion with others, principally the main Other - usually mother - of early feeding and care." In this way the mother becomes the 'centre' of identity the infant lacks by serving as the mirror form with which the infant mimetically identifies. Lacan calls this period between six and eighteen months of age the mirror stage. At around eighteen months two major changes occur. The child begins to use language somewhat coherently, and also becomes aware that the father's presence - or any other third person - is a prohibiting force to the infant's merger with the mother. The infant begins to perceive its own separateness from the mother, only when forced to such awareness by what Lacan calls the phallic signifier or the paternal metaphor. But by 'signifier' Lacan means something different from Saussure. The Lacanian signifier resembles the Saussurian sign. The combination of sound and concept which acquire meaning in relation to other sounds and concepts -articulated speech in other words - is what Lacan means by signifier. By signified he refers to the cumulative effects caused by the signifiers that are repressed into the unconscious, but later surface as the fixed identity themes of a person's being.

The phallic signifier of difference imposes a sense of limitations and 'self' -boundaries on a mirror-stage psychic illusion of symbiotic wholeness. At the same time the phallic signifier introduces the possibility for reflective self representation through naming. Playing on the French words *non* and *nom,* Lacan says that the father's Name appears to mean 'no'. Language then works to re-inforce the phallic injunction to differentiation by offering substitutive possibilities in compensation for the loss of natural spontaneity. Culture has, thus, begun to impose itself on nature.

The learning of psychic differentiation from the (m)other is so painful that Lacan describes the experience as Castration; i.e. the infant feels incomplete, broken, an *hommelelte."* But one must not take this term literally. No incest wish is being punished here by fear of organ loss. The fear is more global; fear of loss of 'self' -continuity. Paradoxically, language both creates an unconscious space in being - a permanent sense of loss or Otherness - by introducing a deferral of 'lived' experience, but also becomes a mechanism for helping human beings to master their own incompleteness. The infant represses the pain of separation, and also internalizes the phallic signifier. The residue of this drama is what Lacan has named Desire: a structural inadequacy in the human subject which drives individuals to strive forever, to seek new ways to compensate for the elemental loss of a psychic illusion of unity. People, language itself, material goods, meaning and belief systems, all play substitutive roles In displacing the lost object(s) along a signifying chain of Desire. Lacan equates Desire with libido, but locates the source as a lack of the Other -a lack which seeks to overcome itself - rather than in biological or sexual drive. As individuals become ever further alienated into the objectifying rules and norms of language, codes, and social laws, and ever further away from the pre-Oedipal dyadic sense of oneness, they feel a want-in-being *(manque-ii-elre)* which is neither existential, nor real, nor metaphysical, nor material. It is a 'subversion of the human subject which makes him or her aim, not at renunciation or repression, but at the realization of Desire, in other words, at the refinding of a pre-social self.'

By a 'subversion' of the subject Lacan means that the unconscious experiences of fusion and separation - Desire and Law - circumscribe consciousness and language, and thereby subvert perception and inten-tionality from the domain of objectivity and willed action to that of struc-tural effect and dictate. The conscious, speaking subject seeks the roots of its own unconscious formation by the mere fact of using language, but more specifically through the whole symbolic system of substitution. The goal sought is a repetition, the replacement of the pleasure *(jouissance)* in the illusion of wholeness which was characteristic of the pre-phallic period. *Jouissance,* a word which Lacan recommends that one not even translate into English, means orgasm, or the purely sexual release of tension experienced in *plaisir.* Abstractly speaking, *jouissance* becomes the temporary pleasure afforded by the recognition of others, substitutes for the original Other. But substitutes are of necessity imperfect, for the gap or lack in being *is* the unconscious which, by definition, is unknown.

In direct contradiction to the prevalence of ego

psychologies in Anglo-American thought, Lacan shows the human subject as neither unit whole, nor autonomous. Split between language and individuality, between 'saying' and 'being', the subject is operated by the structures of Desire and Law which are both explicable in mathematical terms. The mirror-stage duality of mother - infant symbiosis is experienced by the infant as a singularity or unity, and is only perceived as the dyad it actually is from the perspective of Oedipal triangularity. This humble mother-infant-father drama places the foundation of human ontology on a structural split. It introduces a permanent drive towards identification with, and recognition from, others - in an effort to deny the unwelcome insights of the tenuousness of being, with their implicit intimations of death, i.e. a gap in being; an identity composed of fragments.

The human tendency to seek unities through love, meaning, belief, and so on, derives from the mirror-stage experience of taking on an alien identity and Desire as our own and then repressing it. The paradoxically opposite and equally strong tendency is to strive for difference in order to bow to the forces which first divided the subject along lines of social and personal parts. Such structural underpinnings denote the Imaginary order of identification and homogeneity, and the Symbolic order of individuation and heterogeneity. These connictive inclinations will always delimit human behaviour to unitary strivings and binary displacements and substitutions.

Although the specific meanings attached to the structures of Desire and Law vary according to personal experience and historical context, the experiences themselves shape both History and personal trajectory. The 'enemy' which feminists must confront, then, is neither class-structure, not patriarchy *per se,* but the mirror-stage process by which a human subject takes on its essential form and fixations in a mathe-matically formalizable equation. In so far as the primordial sensation of sameness is attached to the (m)Other, Desire - cum lack - is elementally linked to the female. In so far as the secondary experience of individua-tion or difference is attached to the father, Law is linked to the male. Freud's error, according to Lacan, was to mistake this symbolic, struc-tural drama for a biologically based, natural one.

One of the most prolific French feminist writers on the contemporary scene is Luce Irigaray. Like the philosopher Gilles Deleuze, and the psychoanalyst Felix Guattari, Irigaray sees the Lacanian Symbolic order as enemy territory, ruled by phallocrats, patriarchs, and pederasts. It is an order to be resisted if women are to gain the freedom of their own specificity. But Irigaray reads Lacan ideologically and substantively, and therefore accuses him of making prescriptive statements. By equating the phallic signifier with patriarchy, she substantivizes the concept biologically such that Phallus = penis = male. But she only harks back to older biological determinisms by implying that males and females have 'natural' psychic attributes in keeping with gender. By failing to see that the phallic signifier is intrinsically neutral, meaningless in its own right, and only takes its power from associations catalysed in the Oedipal drama, Irigaray does not understand that Lacan is describing first causes, not approving them.

In *Speculum de I'autrejemme* (1974) Irigaray accuses psychoanalysis of a 'masculine bias', of being arrested in the phallic phase, and equating female sexuality with motherhood. 15 In *Ce Se.xe qui n 'en est pas un* (1977) she portrays Lacan as a profiteering cynic who gains pleasure, power, and love from being a Master. 16 In her rejection of the Lacanian theory of a phallic fixing of a child's sexual destiny, Irigaray treats the mirror stage as implicitly male. His mirror becomes the most recent version of a philosophical topos whose *raison d'etre* is to valorize sameness and visibility, she says. I? In Lacan's case the standard of sameness is the Phallus. Irigaray asks: '*And as jar as the organism* is *concerned, what happens when the mirror reveals nothing to see?* No sex, for example, as is the case for the little girl.' 18 Although Irigaray offers no 'other' perception *Speculum,* she does advance some ideas of her own in *Ce Sexe.* She concludes that Lacan's theory of a phallic fixing of sexual identity is homosexual in its exclusion of otherness, with heterosexuality merely as a mediate homosexual form in its exchange of women between men. As a foil to a phallic sexual economy, she proposes woman's subtlety and pliancy, her 'feeble resistance'.

What I find particularly disturbing in Irigaray's analysis i~ her 'resistance' to getting Lacan 'right'. Because she misreads Lacan, she misses the chance to use his theories to either transcend his own limita-tions (as other feminists have done with Freud), or to make sense of suggestions that Lacan has purposely left unresolved. I n her depict ion of the Lacanian mirror stage as the earliest in a series of historical stages which oppresses women, lrigaray reduces this stage to the literal and biological. In fact, Lacan's mirror-stage concept is a metaphor for a mimetic process which occurs in inter-social relation~ with or without a mirror. Initially, the mirror stage refers to the representation of a visual, corporal unity with which the infant identifies, in contrast to the inner tumult felt because of motor-skill and neurological prematuration at birth and for some months after. I n the first six months of Ii fe, Lacan hypothesizes that infants merge perceptually with images and objects in the outside world, actually become them in their elemental fantasies. Lacan denotes this primordial perception by Frege's mathematical O. When the infant identifies with the human form - its (m)Other's and its own in a mirror - it has passed cognitively from 0 to I. But by identifying a centre of unity outside itself, by taking an-Other to be itself, human perception of difference starts out based on a lie - on a disjunction or asymmetry - whose later effects range from the production of a double as in the *Doppelganger* phenomenon, to a bodily disintegration such as that depicted by Hieronimus Bosch's figures. In adult life, the repressed mirror-stage structure functions dynamically to diffract the supposed unity of the speaking subject, and keeps people from feeling 'one' with themselves. And this victimization by an-Other discourse which serves as the repressed centre of being, haunts males, as well as females.

Irigaray's confusion of the fixing of a Gestalt during the six- to eighteen -month mirror-stage period, with the phallic fixing of sexual identity which occurs after the mirror stage, blinds her to what I find most important for feminist theory: that Lacan's epistemology comes the closest of any to demystifying the basic causes and differences of sexual personality. His description of the structures underlying the patriarchal order is certainly not an ideological support for maintaining that order. The essential drama is one of structural effect. The confusion of sexual organs and gender is a secondary occurrence, which is solidified and substantified in language, enshrined in myth, and passed on as 'natural' truth.

The French philosopher lean-Marie Benoist has described (he phallic or Oedipal function as a semantico-syntactic operator of Desire. As the absent - i.e. figurative or metaphorical - operator of the unconscious, the phallic signifier traps the subject in the Symbolic, teaches the limit of Desire, and permits any triangular social configuration to symbolize itself (Benoist, pp. 226-8). It also coincides with the learning of language, thereby linking *logos* to Desire and Law. The Oedipal complex which Freud defined as the organized ensemble of loving and hostile desires felt by the child towards her or his parents, has been recast by Lacan to account for the evolution that little by little substitutes the father for the mother. This is what Irigaray refers to as the phallic fixing of sexual iden-tity. In the summary of French psychoanalyst Serge Leclaire, the mother is taken as the central and primordial character in the complex, and the father as the principal and ultimate reference. The mirror-stage identifica-tion with a unified, corporal image of 'self' corresponds more or less to identification with the (m)Other's body. Gradually, the child identifies as well with the object of the (m)Other's Desire. Wishing to be all for her, the child wants to be the signifier of her Desire: i.e. (he Phallus in the symbolic and signifying sense of that which replaces lack. For from an Imaginary perspective, the Phallus is the signifier of the lack inherent in Desire. In this context, the first signified for an infant is the paternal metaphor. But since a child does not know what the (m)Other's Desire really is, the first and only real and concrete signifier is the child's Desire to fuse with - i.e. please - the (m)Other. Thus, children quickly detach themselves from any primal identification with whatever will replace the (m)Other's lack, for they see that despite their efforts to be what (m)Other wants, she still remains dissatisfied.

This fact points a child towards otherness,):e. the referentiality of the father. And so the first metaphorical or 'pure' signifier is the Name-of-the-father which spells out prohibition, separation, difference, compromise, i.e. Castration. At this stage, the (m)Other is the mediator who opens the way to permit the birth of Desire and Law: the child cannot fill all her wants. In this phase, the child learns the relation of the (m)Other to the father's name. I n the third phase, the father's real sexual organ is equated with having the Phallus or not; i.e. with being lacking or not. The psychic evolution of the Oedipal complex is an identificatory reshaping of the subject, then, which is complete when the child fixes a sexual identity by identifying either with the (m)Other or the father. The gender complications of this drama mean that when a child renounces identification with the possibility of being 'all' for Mama, that concern is transferred into making social sense of gender difference.

Even though the Lacanian Phallus does not refer to the real father, or to the biological organ, this term does underline the idea that t he real father, the penian part-object, and the phallic differential function are confused in language. An identificatory logic locates the phallic signifier at the origin of culture, and arbitrarily links the male - *qua* father - to the prin-ciples of Law and reality, setting him in opposition to the mother-linked principles of Desire and subjectivity. The Shakespearean ontological crisis of being could be understood in Lacanian terms as a completion of the sentence as 'to be or not to be, the Phallus'. The historical plight of woman has been the linguistic and representational misunderstanding which translates 'be' as 'have' and Phallus as penis. In defence of the theory that there is no natural causality to sexual identity, Lacan says that man and woman exist as pure signifiers, the nature of things being the nature of words (*Seminaire* XX, p. 68). But Lacan does not mean that words make up the unconscious discourse in any transparent or one-to-one way.

The influence of modern linguistics on Lacan's thought is well known. Saussure taught that language is an ever-flowing, referential, differential, arbitrary system. Lacan adds to this what Saussure's theory lacks: a context. Language is not, as Freud believed, a set of simply received sounds. It is an all-encompassing network whose effects create impressions and reactionS", and later attribute meanings and labels, which ultimately link up with mirror-stage networks of perceptual images and relations.

We see that for Lacan language is not a static, transparent medium through which to unveil hidden meanings. Nor will its depths be plumbed by a proper clarification of all its potential codes and organizatory mechanisms. Nor is it merely a series of untruths, awaiting Derridean deconstruction. Language is a dense and opaque body which struggles to embody Real and Imaginary experiences and symbols, which it can only ever approximate because of its intrinsically representational and deferred nature. Thus, while philosophers place themselves in conscious thought and language, seeing themselves as its correlate, Lacan situates himsel f within unconscious meaning which makes normative language 'mean' more than it says. He speaks of the efforts of the unconscious to both know and deny its own messages and structures through the material elaborations of conscious language systems. Under Lacan's moulding hands, language can no longer be seen as a pristine means to translation of thought, but has itself become the 'royal road' to the unconscious, and a paradoxical bridge back to consciousness. What the French psycho-analyst offers feminist theory, then, is a picture of the place of man and woman within a history of structuration, symbolization, and meaning *(Seminaire* XX, p. 69).

In scrutinizing woman's history of oppression I would offer the concept of a double Castration. At the level of primary Castration, both males and females experience loss, and gain an unconscious and a social personality. At a secondary level, this structural drama is substantivized, interpreted, explained. Since the (m)Other within is the dark-faced part of us all, the idea of unseen dominance or secrct power is displaced onto woman. She becomes someone to fear, deny, ignore, fight, conquer, or conversely worship and enshrine. Whether extolled or denigrated, people indirectly take a position towards their own unconscious truths in their fundamental stance towards woman. The myths that have grown up to elaborate this symbolic drama are then propounded as 'natural' truths, finding their validity in theology, biology, genetics, science, politics, economics, mythology, and so on.

One can well understand that feminists who take Lacan's ideas at face value would reject his argumentation as finalistic and deterministic. I find, on the contrary, the theoretical basis for a continued feminist rewriting of the Other's discourse and Desire, one which prescribes change in light of informed comprehension of structural cause and effect. I would make a distinction here between femininity and feminism, however. I see femininity as allying itself with the archaic corporal (m)Other, as well as the (m)Other as a principle of loss. In this picture masculinity becomes a flight from the feminine, a rejection of the pain of loss and Castration. At the same time, the mirror-stage (m)Other remains as an internalized principle of sensuality and corporal experience, thus raising the issue of female sexuality to a problematic level for both men and women. Whether woman is feared as a seductress, sought as a sex object, or idealized as a mother, her *primary* value is supposed to reside in her physical being. The pervasiveness of the equation of the feminine with the sexual explains, in part, why feminists threaten the very sexual economy on which gender identity is established.

Lacan maintained that one of the many functions of language is to compensate for psychic division undergone through the Oedipal split. Although there is not a one-to-one link between conscious and unconscious 'language', a person's unconscious experiences will later govern their use of language in an invisible intentionality. For example, a person who iden-tifies with phallic forces will use language to represent his or her ego on the slope of the master: one who bases authority on 'knowing'. The hysteric, on the contrary, poses the very question of being by addressing her or his discourse to the master (*Seminaire* XX, 'A Jakobson'). Although the intentionality which informs these discourse structures is not sex-linked, the patriarchal order tends to make masters of men, and hysterics of women. But, by master, Lacan does not think of one who does 'know'. He describes a discourse based on ignorance and opinion, one which masks the truth of the unconscious.

By denying Castration, the master discourse perpetuates the denial and suppression of the split in the subject, and thereby retains an unchallenged belief in conscious autonomy, and unity of being. Lacan locates the hysteric's discourse close to the analyst's, that is, close to the search for meaning in terms of the truths of the unconscious. Whether master, hysteric, analyst, or academic, people speak to master the signifiers hidden in the discourse of the Other. In this sense, to speak risks making oneself visible at the level of unconscious inten-tionality. Discourse-wise, anatomical difference is a correlative of different uses of language, then. That is, gender characterizes itself by specific modes of entry into general discourse as a positioning of onesel f towards the paternal metaphor. It should not be surprising, from this point of view. that many feminist literary critics have found that women writers 'speak' a different language from their male counterparts· At a macro-level, however, I would contend that literature itself - not literary criticism - is a subversion of the phallic order, and as such is on a feminine and hysterical slope.

There is no 'beyond the phallus', then, if one means beyond differentia· tion, society, language, Law, and reality. The Symbolic order keep~ it, subjects from plunging headlong into incestuous lures and hallucinatory desires, psychosis being total submersion in the Imaginary order of the Other. Primary Castration, seen as differentiation from the (m)Other, is unavoidable and universal if people are to live in sanity. Secondary Castration attributes meaning to this drama in terms of gender difference·. Generally speaking, men set out on a quest to try to be the Phallus, to embody power and prestige. And women try to marry as high up the phallic ladder as possible. Yet, no one can be the Phallus, for it is only ever a signifier: something that represents a subject for another signifier. For men as well as women, the climb to power - whether directly held or held by association - entails compromise submission, and association.

The Symbolic order codes and linguistic descriptions change all the time.

As new economic and historical realities continue to reflect the change in sex roles, and in gender possibilities, the secondary meanings attached to Castration mirror new realities. Such changes bring many questions to mind. If the mirror-stage separation trauma were to be less gender-related, what impact would this have on sexual identity? Would the Oedipal drama come to centre on individual, as opposed to sexual, differences? Can loss ever *not* be associated with the (m)Other unless we live in a 1984-type fantasy world? Lacan has never said, as Freud did, that female sexuality is an outcome of thwarted phallic strivings. Nor does Lacan attribute female gender specificity, as did Heinz Kohut, to a natural biological development. Instead, it is to the double effects of Castration on women that he points to, first through separation, and then thmugh an arbitrary linking of power-penis-Phallus, and conversely, loss-no penis-Castration. direction of disrupting the history of Other repetition, of sowing disunity among standard social codes, practices, and linguistic commonplaces, as well as by altering the structure of •object relations. I rigaray's effort to create a language according to what she calls the 'laws of the feminine' is certainly one kind of step in that direction. But it is Lacan's thought which gives us the basis of a new theory on which to continue rewriting our history.

In conclusion, I submit that feminist efforts to change the social, linguistic order encounter a circular dilemma. Although mirror-stage iden-tification and phallic differentiation are not biologically determined along sexual lines, their effects are predictable. If Lacan is right, then we know what must be restructured. And it is not by overthrowing patriarchy *cum* capitalism that human beings will gain the freedom of Desire which Deleuze and Guattari foretell, nor that feminists will eradicate phallocractic - i.e. power-based - values even if they live in exclusively female groups. For any group evolves its own phallocratic structure, because recognition and power needs inhere in the structure of the human subject itself. Within a Lacanian context, then, there can be no tomorrow of communist egalitarianism which will eradicate power structures, and no Utopia where woman's superior values will replace man's tarnished ones. But there can be a tomorrow where differentiations are

CHAPTER TEN

Philosophy of Women Power

Feminists have made in developing criticisms of the apparent sexual neutrality of the so-called 'queen of knowledges', philosophy. Because philosophy sees itself, and is seen by others, as providing both an explanation for and a critique of the presumptions and forms of arzument used in other knowledges, and because many disciplines rely on philosophical positions to justify themselves (whether they recognize this or not), feminist interventions into philosophy may be of major strategic significance in the assessment and transformation of both philosophy and other academic disciplines.

Moreover, well-placed criticisms of the discipline may exert a ripple effect on related or dependent knowledges: if basic questions regarding methods, criteria, and underlying assumptions are questions within philosophy, then both the sciences and the humanities may also be implicated. Genevieve Lloyd's chapter comes from her detailed and sustained analysis of the ways in which reason has come to be conceived as an inherently and (usually) implicitly male enterprise throughout the history of philosophy. While her book ranges from the period of Greek philo-sophy to the modern period, culminating in the work of Sartre and de Beauvoir in the twentieth century, her third chapter, reprinted here, concentrates on the ways in which the threshold of modern philosophy, usually marked by the advent of Descartes' work, sets up a series of methods, goals, and presumptions which will negatively or positively characterize all of contemporary philosophy as well. In this chapter, she pairs the rationalism associated with Cartesian philosophy, with the empiricism attributed to Hume. Rationalism and empiricism are today seen as two competing and opposed positions; the former presumes the priority of mind over matter and privileges reason over perception and observation; the latter, by contrast, positions sensation, observation, perception, and matter in a position of priority over pure reason or conceptual processes in the allainment of knowledge.

Although in this sense, rationalism and empiricism can be seen as opposites, each prefer-ring opposed sides of the binaries mind/matter, subject/object, and reason/perception, in another sense, they can be seen merely as two sides of a single coin, as participants in a struggle over one and the same intellectual territory. Lloyd focuses largely on the most privileged concept within the history of philosophy and of Descartes' treatment of it - the notion of reason. For Descartes, reason is not to be understood as a variable mode of apprehending objects (objects are. after all, highly variable and a reason based on the specificity of objects would have to be as variable as those objects); rather, it is a specific and singular form of the operations of the knowing subject's mind. It is an ordered and rigorous set of intellec-tual procedures, 'certain and simple rules', that are designed to ensure that truth can be guaranteed.

Descartes concentrates on providing a set of methodological foundations or guarantees that will yield truth independent of the objects investigated. In this sense, his method i, abstract and general: its goal is to be applicable to any object of investigation, whether this be the purely abstract notions provided by mathematics and geometry, the empirical and conjectural contents of the physical sciences, or the day-to-day knowledge of subjects provided by perception. His method would, Descartes hoped, provide a single, cohesive unity to the disparate forms of knowledge, showing them all to be the products of a unified and self-knowing mind.

His aspiration to provide a single unified method for all forms of knowledge is, Lloyd argues, based on a rigid separation, indeed dicho-tomization of mind and body. Where the body, and those pragmatic knowledges based on the body's capacities are disparate and varied, where, for example, the method needed to produce a good carpenter is quite different from that needed to produce a good ballet dancer, the mind is singular and unified. The arts, based on the body's various skills and capacities, are thus to be dramatically distinguished from the sciences and humanities, in which the mind and reason are pre-eminent.

The mind was considered to be a natural or innate source of truth, if only its proper functioning, independent of the accepted and taught dogmas of tradition, could be ensured. This meant sweeping aside the false and constricting overlay of opinion and prejudice in favour of allowing the uncluttered and unobstructed mind the disciplined use of its own facilities and techniques.

Descartes thus formulated what he considered to be a few simple and direct procedures to remove the varivous obstacles to the mind's proper functioning: his method involved the breakdown of complex mental processes into their simplest components - clear and distinct ideas - and then a method of synthesizing the ideas thus analysed using an orderly and logical form of recombining, a kind of conceptual process of building or reconstruction. By using this method, t he mind could be guaranteed access to the truth into whatever matters it enquired.

The clarity and distinctness of ideas, their 'purity', comes, not from perception or from the information provided by the senses or the body - for the senses can be mistaken, and perception often provides confused rather than distinct ideas - but from the rational and controlled use of the mind. The body is thus regarded as a kind of impingement on, a sullying of, the ideas that are the raw materials of knowledge. It is not the senses, he argues, that perceive wax, because wax is so empirically changeable and dependent on various conditions; it is the mind that perceives its underlying identity. Descartes, Lloyd argues, aligns the distinction between the mind and the body with the opposition between reason and non-reason. It is only in so far as the mind is capable of clearing itself of the extraneous interferences of the body that it is capable of transcending the accidents and errors of perception.

Lloyd argues that Descartes' separation of the mind from the body had an ambiguous relation to women's access to the production of philosophy. On the one hand, by taking reason out of the hands of educators and a scholastic pedagogical tradition from which women had been excluded, and by making reason quite independent of the specificities of bodies, there was no *a priori* reason why women should be excluded from philosophical activities. If bodies have no direct rela-tion to and influence on minds, then women's minds are as philosophically inclined as men's. He thus presumes an egalitarianism, or at least an egalitarian potential, to the operations of mind.

Yet, on the other hand, Descartes none the less leaves the division of labour so prevalent in patriarchal societies still intact. While women are not actively excluded from the operations of reason, neither can they be included as women. It is only in so far as women have neutral, sexually indifferent minds that they have access to reason. Moreover, in spite of his own objectives in securing for the individual a private or conceptual access to reason, independent of its subjective particularity, Descartes nevertheless affirms women as the guardians of the sphere of everyday life, in which reason, emotions, mind, and body, are interrelated:

Women's task is to preserve the sphere of the intermingling of mind and body, to which the Man of

Reason will repair for solace, warmth and relaxation. If he is to exercise the most exalted form of Reason, he must leave soft emotions and sensuousness behind; women will keep them intact for him. (Lloyd, p. 50)

In recognizing the implicit masculinity in the concept of reason as it is received by the philosophical community, Lloyd does not advocate the abandonment of reason by feminists. To affirm that philosophy has up to now functioned to oppress and subordinate women does not necessarily mean the abandonment of philosophical principles, the refusal of logic. Truth, or validitv. The critique of reason posed by many feminists can, Lloyd argues, be seen as pan of an ongoing tradition of auto-critique, a critique sustained by philosophers themselves in their relations to past or prevailing philosophical positions and systems.

In short, while reason is a male-dominated concept up to now, there is no reason to suppose that philosophical notions of reason cannot themselves be reformed so that transformations compatible with feminist principles can themselves become part of the philosophical enterprise. Philosophy is itself open-ended enough to be radically transformed. Lloyd retains the belief that feminists need not abandon reason in devising critiques of it. Indeed, through the interventions of feminists, philosophy could itself become a genuinely human rather than an exclusively male endeavour. Lloyd's position entails questioning the ways in which the discipline of philosophy conceives of itself, its underlying and unrecognized mascu-linity which parades as universality. In investigating its masculinity, women's access to the discipline can no longer be regarded as a matter of individual struggle and achievement, but must be seen as a series of political struggles against philosophical systems for the rights of self-definition and a philosophical perspective. These are also the issues concerning Gatens in her paper.

Gatens sets out to examine the ways in which women

have been posi-tioned in the discipline of philosophy. She focuses not so much on women's passive placement by the discipline as on the ways in which feminists have, in recognition of philosophy's misogyny, attempted to reconstruct a philosophy able to include, speak to, and about women. However, certain strategies developed by feminists have themselves fallen into some of the misogynist traps lying within philosophy: in particular, the strategy of extending philosophy so that where it had previously excluded women, it was now capable of including them. Recourse to universalisms or humanisms, in which women's activities are added to those of men to provide a 'complete picture' of human activity involves the strategy of neutralization (or neuterization), including women only in so far as they are the same as men, on men's criteria.

Gatens, for example, sees de Beauvoir as *more than* a faithful adherent, an acolyte; her claim is that de Beauvoir has actively transformed existentialism from an individualized account incapable of dealing with corcepts like oppression to a dynamic (if problematic) account of the oppression of women. De Beauvoir has not only rewritten existentialism, but more relevantly in this context, she has not recognized the substantial overhaul of Sartre's posi-tion she has undertaken: she herself has seen her work as an addendum to his. In other words, she has rendered her own work invisible.

The third strategy Gatens outlines which implies the recuperation of critical feminist challenges to mainstream philosophical texts is a project of reformulaling misogynistic philosophy from within. In adhering too closely to the criteria governing philosophical assessment and credibility (clear, logical argument, statements in principle translatable into logical form, etc.) feminist philosophers risk submilling heir feminism to the primacy of philosophy instead of reordering philosophy according to principles.

Gatens examines the ways in which feminists have

struggled against philosophy's resolute containment of women, making clear that the task is not as straightforward as it seems. If philosophy or, for that mailer, other academic disciplines, are not to be abandoned altogether, then feminists must negotiate a series of manoeuvres that ill no[only cast feminist principles in philosophical terms, but will submit philosophy itself to feminist scrutiny and transformation. This would involve ques-tioning many of the most basic assumptions of the discipline, it, arbitrary division from other forms of knowledge, its goals, means, and criteria of assessment. Gatens advocates an open-ended philosophy, one capable of admitting its absences, accepting its limits and its partiality. Only such a broad and open field would enable women's differences, their specific interests to find philosophical expression, to be discussed, contested, transformed - a recognized and valued part of philosophical history rather than its unspoken underside.

Reason as attainment

In *The Philosophy of Right,* Hegel contrasted the 'happy ideas, taste and elegance' characteristic of female consciousness with male attainments which demand a 'universal faculty'. 'Women arc educated - who knows how? - as it were by breathing in ideas, by living rather than by acquir-ing knowledge. The status of manhood, on the other hand, is attained only by the stress of thought and much technical exertion.' I These kinds of connection between maleness and achievement are not confined to Hegel. In western thought, maleness has been seen as itself an achieve-ment, attained by breaking away from the more 'natural' condition of women. Attitudes to Reason and its bearing on the rest of life have played a major part in this; a development that occurred in the seven-teenth century has been particularly crucial.

In the illustrations, in the last chapter, of Reason's superiority over other aspects of human nature, it was seen as a distinctive human trait, with ramifications in all areas of life - the practical, no less than the contemplative - even if, as with Augustine, this was regarded as an inferior diversion of Reason. In the seventeenth century, Reason came to be seen not just as a distinguishing feature of human nature, but as an achievement - a skill to be learned, a distinctively methodical way of thinking, sharply differentiated from other kinds of thought - and its relationships with other aspects of human nature were also transformed. The most thoroughgoing and influential version of Reason as methodical thought was the famous method of Descartes. Something happened here which proved crucial for the development of stereotypes of maleness and femaleness, and it happened in some ways despite Descartes' explicit intentions.

Descartes' Method

In its Greek origins, the basic meaning of 'method' was a road or path to be followed; and the metaphor of a path whose goal is understanding recurs throughout the entire philosophical tradition which grew from Greek thought. The method which proceeds without analysis, says Socrates in Plato's *Phaedrus*, is 'like the groping of a blind man'.' The follower of true method is preserved from such blind wanderings by understanding the reason for which things are done in a certain order. Descartes used the same metaphors. In expounding his 'rules for the direction of the mind', he attacked those truth-seekers who 'conduct (heir minds along unexplored routes, having no reason (0 hope for success, but merely being willing to risk the experiment of finding whether the truth (hey seek lies there'. It is, he says, as if a man seeking treasure were to 'continuously roam the streets, seeking to find something that a passer-by might have chanced to drop,] But, although t he description of the goal remained much t he same, Descartes com-pletely transformed the relationship between Reason and method which had been central in the intellectual tradition since the time of Socrates.

The original Socratic ideal of method, illustrated by the definition of love, is expounded in the concluding sections of the *Phaedrus*. Right method, says Socrates, involves processes of generalization, the 'survey of scattered particulars, leading to their comprehension in one idea'; and processes of division into species, 'according to the natural formation, where the joint is, not breaking -any part as a bad carver might'. These processes are aids to speaking and thinking; they belong in the art of rhetoric. But they are also supposed to be guides to truth, helping those who practise them to discern a 'one and many' in Nature.

Most of the ingredients for later developments in the idea of method can be found in these brief *Phaedrus* passages: the idea of an orderly procedurly; of an analysis to be conducted in relation to an end to be achieved; the connec-tions between method and teaching; the importance of understanding the nature of the soul, in which persuasion is supposed to be induced. The ability to impart the Socratic art of rhetoric involves grasping its nature and relating its parts to the end which is supposed to be achieved in the soul. However, Socrates' general description of the art of rhetoric passed into the tradition as a general rubric which could be extended to any art: the teacher must have an understanding of what the art deals with and be able to analyse and evaluate its parts in relation to the achievement of its end.

Aristotle developed the idea of a systematic treatment of the art of arguing and debating into a concern with a rational way - a reasoned procedure - for arriving at sound conclusions. But the relation of reason to the 'way' or 'method' was similar to the original Socratic version. Reason - whether applied to the art of persuasion, to other arts, or more narrowly to the investigations which are supposed to yield truth - was incorporated into method. Method was a reasoned way of pursuing an activity; and it was the grasp of this internal reason which was supposed (0 enable the activity to be taught.

In Descartes' system, in contrast, method became not so much a reasoned way of proceeding - a path to be followed rationally - as a way of *reasoning:* a precisely ordered mode of abstract thinking. And the right order of thought was to be determined not by the variable subject -matter and ends of the activities at issue, but by the natural operations of the mind itself. Descartes' actual definitions of method are on the surface not very different from earlier ideas of method. By a method, he says in his *Rules for the Direction of (he Mind,* he means certain and simple rules such that, if a man observe them accurately, he shall never assume what is false as true, and will never spend his mental efforts to no purpose, but will always gradually increase his knowledge and so arrive at a true understanding of all that does not surpass his powers:

To see what is really distinctive and important about Descartes' method we must see it in the context of the metaphysical doctrine for which he is most notorious - the radical separateness of mind and body - and also in the context of his immediate predecessors in the development of ideas of method.

Descartes' method, he insisted, is unitary and yields truth regardless of subject-matter. He criticized his Aristotelian scholastic predecessors for holding that the certainty of mathematics was unattainable in other sciences and that the method of each science should vary with differences in the material it investigated. A single and identical method, he thought, could be applied to all the various sciences, for the sciences taken together were nothing else but the very unity of human reason itself. This vision of the unity of the sciences as reflecting that of Reason arose directly from Descartes' radical separation of mind and body. Where body is involved, the formation of one habit inhibits that of others. The hand that adapts itself to agricultural operations is thereby less likely to be adept at harp playing. But the sciences consist entirely in the cognitive exercise of the mind. The traditional conception of a multiplicity of methods for different subject-areas thus rests on a faulty assimilation of mind to body. The sciences do not share in the inevitable multiplicity of the bodily arts. Knowing one truth does not have the restricting effect that is the consequence of mastering a bodily art; in fact it aids us in finding out other truths. So the sciences, taken all together, are identical with human wisdom, which always remains one and the same, however applied to different subjects.[5]

All this is strongly opposed to what Descartes saw as the arbitrariness of the prevailing scholastic curriculum divisions. This concern was not new. Descartes' humanist predecessors had also been dissatisfied with the arbitrary methods of presentation of the traditional disciplines which, they thought, created needless difficulties for students. In the sixteenth century. Peter Ramus had devised 'one simple method' to bring order to the subject taught in universities. Ramus' method proceeded from universal and general principles down to the more specific and, singular. an order which he supposed to reflect the different degrees of clarity among the parts of a discipline. The clearer was to precede the more obscure, following the order and progression from universal to "Ingular Aristotle had distinguished what is prior in Nature and what is prior I" us. Ramus' idea was a right order and progression of thought, which would reflect the priority in Nature of the universal over the particular. But there was no real justification for his conviction that what was priol in being should also be clearer to students."

For Descartes, the idea of a right order of thought was grounded in an understanding of the nature of the mind. The correspondence between the basic structures of human thought and the order of the world, he argued, is divinely guaranteed. To find and to follow the mind's most basic operations was for him not just a prerequisite for ease in learning. His organization of subject-matter in accordance with what is more apparent to an attentive mind was not just a pedagogical device. Clarit) and distinctness were the marks of truth. His method was directed to uncovering those basic ideas whose truth was assured by the fact that a veracious God created both the mind and the material world. Method was not confined to pedagogy; it was linked with criteria of truth.

As a development in the politics of learning, the significance of this approach to method cannot be overestimated. Earlier Renaissance reforms of educational procedures often found themselves in conflict with those who saw following the 'natural' processes of the mind as less important than following approved methods of strict de')1nstration and proof, however difficult these may have been to impart 10 students. Descartes' method undercut this conflict. Its aim went beyond the transmission of an already established art or the successful pursuit of a course of study; it aimed at valid knowledge. It should not be seen, he insisted, as a means of persuasion, belonging in the art of rhetoric; it belonged, rather, with the discovery of new truth. But such discovery was assured precisely through following the natural processes of thought. At the same time, Descartes' grounding of this unified method in the unity of Reason itself, accessible through introspection, enabled him to separate method entirely from the realm of public pedagogy and disputation.

The implications for Reason of thus severing the links between method and public procedures of discourse, debate, and successful argument were far-reaching. The right ordering of ideas was no longer associated wit h the best arrangement of the school curricula, but with private abstract thought, which can be pursued quite independently of public educational structures and procedures. Persuasion was internalized as what is clear and apparent to an attentive mind - the mark of truth itself. Reasoning in accordance with this new method does not demand conformity with the subtle forms of argument accepted as valid in the public disputations of the schools. The emphasis is entirely on unaided Reason. Descartes presented the method as simply a systematization of the innate faculty of Reason or 'good sense' - the power of 'forming good judgement and of distinguishing the true from the false'. And this natural light of Reason is supposedly equal in all. 7

Descartes saw his method as opening the way to a new egalitarianism in knowledge. In a letter written shortly after the publication of the *Discourse on Method,* he commented that his thoughts on method seemed to him appropriate to put in a book where he wished that 'even women' might understand something.[8] From our perspective, this tone may sound patronizing, but the remark is to be understood against the background of associations between earlier Renaissance versions of method and pedagogical procedures. By and large, it was only boys who were given systematic formal education outside the home. The exclusion of women from method was a direct consequence of their exclusion from the schools in which it was pursued. Descartes' egalitarian intentions come out also in his insistence on writing the *Discourse on Method* in the vernacular, rather than in Latin, the learned language of the schools. The work, he stressed, should appeal to those who avail themselves only of their natural reason in its purity. The point was political as well as practical. The use of Latin was in many ways the distinguishing mark of the learned. Women, being educated mostly at home rather than in the schools, had no direct access to the learned, Latin-speaking world. The teaching of Latin to boys thus marked the boundaries between the private world of the family, in which the vernacular was used, and the external world of learning, to which males had access. The accessibility of the new method even to women was thus a powerful symbol of the transformation which it marked in the relationship between method and autonomous, individual reasoning.

In place of the subtleties of scholastic disputation, which can only, he thought, obscure the mind's natural clarity, Descartes offered a few supposedly simple procedures, the rationale of which was to remove all obstacles to the natural operations of the mind. The general rubric of the method was to break down the more complex operations of the mind into their simplest forms and then recombine them in an orderly series. The complex and obscure is reduced to simple, self-evident 'intuitions', which the mind scrutinizes with 'steadfast, mental gaze', then combines in orderly chains of deductions. II Anyone who follows this method can feel assured that 'no avenue to the truth is closed to him from which everyone else is not also excluded, and that his ignorance is due neither to a deficiency in his capacity nor to his method of procedure'.

Descartes' method, with its new emphasis on the privacy of the mind's natural operations, promised to make knowledge accessible to all, women. Such was his intent. The lasting influence of his method, however, was something quite different, though no less a product of hi, radical separation of mind and body. In the context of association already existing between gender and Reason, his version of the mind- body relationship produced stark polarizations of previously existing contrasts. This came about not through any intellectual move made within his system, but as a by-product of his transformation of the rela-tions between Reason and its opposites. Descartes strongly repudiated hi, medieval predecessors' idea of a divided soul, which had Reason - iden-tified with the authentic character of a human being - struggling with lesser parts of the soul. For him, the soul was not to be divided into higher (intellectual) and lower (sensitive) parts; was an indivisible unity, identified with pure intellect. He replaced the medieval philo-sophers' divisions between higher and lower pans of the soul with the dichotomy between mind and body. In this limited respect, Descane,' system echoed the thought of the early Plato. In place of the older divi-sions within the soul he introduced a division between the soul - now identified again with the mind - and body; the non-rational was longer part of the soul, but pertained entirely to the body.

There is within us but one soul, and this soul has not in itself any diversity of parts; the same part that is subject to sense impressions is rational, and all the soul's appetites are acts of will. The error which has been committed in making it play the pans of various personages, usually in opposition one to another, only proceeds from the fact that we have not properly distinguished its functions from those of the body, to which alone we must attribute everything which can be observed in us that is opposed to our reason.

The drama of dominance between human traits persisted in Descartes' philosophy, but it was played out as a struggle between the soul itself -equated with pure intellect - and body. He saw the encroachments of non-intellectual passion, sense, or imagination as coming not from lower parts or aspects of the soul, but from altogether outside the soul - as intrusions from body. Descartes' method is founded on this alignment between the bodily and the non-rational. It involves forming the habit of distinguishing intellectual from corporeal matters. And this search for the purely intellectual - the clear and distinct - made possible polarizations of previously existing contrasts, which had previously been drawn within the boundaries of the soul. Those aspects of human nature which Reason must -dominate had not previously been so sharply delineated from the intellectual. The distinction between Reason and its opposites could now coincide with Descartes' very sharp distinction - than which, as he says, none can be sharper - between mind and body. Descartes' alignment between the Reason-non-Reason and mind-body distinctions brought with it the notion of a distinctive kind of rational thought as a highly restricted activity. Augustine had presented the mind's dealings with practical matters as a diversion of a unitary Reason from its superior function of contemplation.

This diversion was at risk of entanglement with sense, but it was not thereby different in kind from the Reason employed in contemplative thought. Descartes separated thought of the kind that yields certainty much more sharply from the practical concerns of life. It was for him a highly rarefied exercise of intellect, a complete transcending of the sensuous - a highly arduous activity which cannot be expected to occupy more than a very small part of a normal life. In the *Discourse on Merhod,* he stressed the contrasts between the demands of enquiry into truth and the attitudes appropriate to the practical activities of life. The foundations of the enquiry into truth demand that the mind rigorously enact the metaphysical truth of its separateness from body. This securing of the foundations of knowl-edge is a separate activity from the much more relaxed pursuits of every-day life, where mind must accept its intermingling with body. Descartes' separation of mind and body yielded a vision of a unitary pure thought, ranging like the common light of the sun over a variety of objects. Its unitariness, however, served also to separate it from the rest of life.

Pure thought of this rarefied kind secures the foundations of science. However, most of scientific activity itself involves exercise of the imagination rather than of pure intellect; scientific investigation, although it demands sustained effort and training, occupies an inter-mediate position between pure intellect and the confusion of sense. The rest of life is rightly given over to the sway of the senses, to that mudated zone of confused perception where mind and body intermingle. In his correspondence with Princess Elizabeth, Descartes again stressed that arduous clear and distinct thought, of the kind that secures the foundation of science, can and should occupy only a small part of a well-spent life. If we can take seriously his autobiographical remarks to her - as he insists she should - it is something to which he himself devoted only a few hours a year.[14] It is through pure intellect, trans-cending the intrusion of body, that we grasp the separateness of mind and body on which true science is founded. The greater part of the life of a Cartesian self is lived in the zone of con fused, sensuous awareness. However, it is sustained there by the metaphysical truth, which pure thought can grasp, of the absolute separateness of mind and body; and by the possibility of a complete science grounded in this truth. Underly-ing the confusion of the senses, there is a crystalline realm of order, where sharply articulated structures of thought perfectly match the struc-ture of intelligible reality. These clear, matching structures of mind and matter underlie the confused realm of the sensuous produced by the intermingling of both. Individual minds can rest assured that there is an underlying right order of thought, which provides a secure underpinning for lives lived predominantly in the realm of the sensuous; the confusions of sense and imagination hold no ultimate threat.

Arduous as the grasp of the metaphysical basis of Descartes' method may be. the method itself was supposed to be accessible to all. And within the terms of the system there is. in all this, no differentiation between male and female minds. Both must be seen as equally intellectual substances, endowed with good sense or Reason. The difference in intellectual achievement between men and women, no less than that between different men, must arise not from some being more rational than others, but 'solely from the fact that our thoughts pass through diverse channels and the same objects are not considered by all'. 15 But removing method from the restraints of public pedagogy did not, in prac-tice, make knowledge any more accessible to women. Descartes' method may be essentially private and accessible to all. But for him, no less than Bacon, the new science was, none the less, a collective endeavour. It is by 'joining together the lives and labours of many', he says in the concluding section of the *Discourse on Method,* that science will progress.' It is through a corporate exercise, however non-corporeal may be its ultimate metaphysical foundation, that the new science will advance, rendering humanity the promised goal of becoming 'masters and possessors of nature'. Descartes thought his account of the mind opened the way to a newly egalitarian pursuit of knowledge. But the channels through which those basically equal resources of Reason had to flow remained more convoluted, even for noble women, than for men. Elizabeth poignantly expressed the situation in one of her letters to Descartes:

> the life I am constrained to lead does not allow me enough free time to acquire a habit of meditation in accordance with your rules. Sometimes the interests or my household, which I must not neglect, sometimes conversations and civilities I cannot eschew, so thoroughly deject this weak mind with annoyances or boredom that it remains, for a long time afterward, useless for anything else.'[8]

The realities of the lives of women, despite their supposed equality in Reason, precluded them, too, from any significant involvement in the collective endeavours of science, the developing forms of which quickly outstripped the private procedures of Descartes' method.

It is not just impinging social realities, however, which militate against sexual equality in this new version of Reason's relations with science. There are aspects of Descartes' thought which - however unintentionally - provided a basis for a sexual division of mental labour whose influence is still very much with us. Descartes' emphasis on the equality of Reason had less influence than his formative contribution to the ideal of a distinctive kind of Reason - a highly abstract mode of thought separable in principle, from the emotional complexities and practical demands of ordinary life. This was not the only kind of thought which Descartes recognized as rational. In the Sixth Meditation he acknowl-edged that the inferior senses, once they have been set aside from the search for truth - where they can only mislead and distort - are reliable guides 10 our well-being. To trust them is not irrational. He does not maintain t hat we are rational only when exercising arduous pure thought, engaged in intellectual contemplation, and assembling chains of deduc-tions. Indeed, he thinks it is not rational to spend an excessive amount of time in such purely intellectual activity.' None the less, through his philosophy, Reason look on special associations with the realm of pure thought, which provides the foundations of science, and with the deduc-tive ratiocination which was of the essence of his method. And the sharp-ness of his separation of the ultimate requirements of truth-seeking from the practical affairs of everyday life reinforced already existing distinc-tions between male and female roles, opening the way 10 the idea of distinctive male and female consciousness.

We owe to Descartes an influential and pervasive theory of mind, which provides support for a powerful version of the sexual division of mental labour. Women have been assigned responsibility for that realm of the sensuous which the Cartesian Man of Reason must transcend, if he is to have true knowledge of things. He must move on to the exercise of disciplined imagination, in most of scientific activity; and 10 the rigours of pure intellect, if he would grasp the ultimate foundations of science. Woman's task is to preserve the sphere of the intermingling of mind and body, to which the Man of Reason will repair for solace, warmth, and relaxation. If he is to exercise the most exalted form of Reason, he must leave soft emotions and sensuousness behind; woman will keep them intact for him. The way was thus opened for women 10 be associated with not just a lesser presence of Reason, but a different kind of intellectual character, construed as complementary to 'male' Reason. This crucial development springs from the accentuation of women's exclusion from Reason, now conceived - in its highest form -as an attainment.

Hume on Reason and the Passions

Descartes' method transformed Reason into a uniform,

undifferentiated skill, abstracted from any determinate subject-matter. This loss of differentiation gave rise to another crucial change. Reason lost the strong motivational force it had in earlier thought. In the lack of inner direction to specific ends, Descartes' Reason became an inert instrument, needing direction by an extraneous will. For him, the understanding lacked even the power to affirm or deny, and its polarization from the non-rational bodily passions deprived it also of the capacity to struggle directly wit h non-rational forces. Plato's Reason, in contrast, was presented as strain-ing of its own resources towards truth; and in the 'divided-soul' model. Reason deliberated about ends, decided between them, and struggled with the passions to determine which end would prevail. Aristotle, too, despite his repudiation of the divided soul, presented Reason as control-ling or subduing by its own force the emotional part of human nature.

For Descartes, Reason's origins ensured it a connection with truth and with human well-being, though one that depended on an extraneous divine benevolence. But if his supporting theological views are repudiated, the impotence of this methodical abstract thought becomes apparent. Spinoza, reacting against the passivity of Descartes' version of Reason, rejected the distinction between will and understanding, making Reason an active, emotional force, able - like the earlier Greek versions of Reason - to engage with passions in its own right. But it was Descartes' version of Reason that prevailed; and its inherent inertness and impotence appeared most starkly in Hume's version of Reason. For Hume, Reason has of itself no power to control passion or to deliberate about ends. Its motivating force lies always outside itself, in the driving force of passion. Under the aegis of different passions, it is directed to different ends. Reason has of itself no power to deliberate about ends or to choose between them; and it entirely lacks the affective force necessary to struggle with the passions. It 'is and ought to be nothing but the slave of the passions, pretending to no other office but to serve and obey them.

What are the implicating of this reversal for the male-female distinc-tion? We might expect I(to loosen the alignment between maleness and Reason, but what actually happens is a subtle reinforcement of the older pattern. To see how this is so we must look more closely at Hume's restructuring of the Reason-passion distinction, and at its repercussions in Kant's treatment of the role of Reason in morality.

Hume turned on its head the seventeenth-century rationalists' picture of the role of Reason in knowledge and, more generally, in human life. For him, all our beliefs about the world, all our knowledge of matters of fact, resolve into expectations of stability, predictability, and constancy arising from customary associations in the mind. Reason plays no part in all this;· belief is a function of our sensitive rather than of our cognitive nature. Reason can conjoin ideas in chains of necessary deduc-tion; but these cannot yield understanding of the real natures of things. Reason yields knowledge in strictly limited areas of thought, such as logic and mathematics, where all that is involved is a grasp of entirely formal relations between ideas; knowledge of 'matters of fact', however, is the province not of Reason, but of imagination. The understanding which delivers the world to us is reduced [0 'the general and more established properties of the imagination'. in contrast to the trivial suggestions of the fancy'.. Its reliability rest, entirely on the force our 'strong propensities', under the force of custom, to consider thing, in a certain way. For Descartes, conformity 10 Reason determined what is or is not to be regarded as 'natural'; for Hume, it was the other way round: Reason must rest on and conform to our natural propensities,. 'Where reason is lively, and mixes itself with some propensity, it ought to be assented to. Where it does not, it never can have any title 10 operate upon US. These strong inclinations are the left of what is, trustworthy in human thought, and provide the motivating force for a Reason which is of itself entirely inert.

A new and, at first sight, disconcerting picture emerges of the role of Reason in morality. Reason can still discover connections between things, but it has no role in how those connections affect us. Of itself it can never 'produce any action or give rise to volition'. Nor can it prevent volition, or 'dispute the preference' with any passion or emotion. The supposed pre-eminence of Reason above passion rests on a misunder-standing; the principle which opposes our passion is called Reason only in an improper sense. Hume's argument for this conclusion is not altogether persuasive. Passions, he points out, are not susceptible of agreement or disagreement with relations of ideas or matters of fact, and are therefore incapable of being true or false - a prerequisite for being in conflict with Reason. But what is important here is not Hume's justification of the point, but its import for his understanding of morals.

Where a passion is neither founded on false suppositions, nor chuses meaning insufficient for the ends, the understanding can neither justify nor condemn it. 'This not contrary to reason to prefer the destruction of the whole world to the scratching of my finger. 'This not contrary to reason for me to chuse my total ruin, to prevent the least uneasiness of an Indian or person wholly unknown to me. 'This as little contrary to reason to prefer even my own acknowledged lesser good to my greater, and have a more ardent affection I' or t he former than the latter.

Hume's point is not that any of these stances should be regarded a, acceptable to people of good sense, but rather that their being or not being so is in no way a matter of Reason. Moral distinctions are not the 'offspring of reason', which is wholly inactive. They derive from a moral sense grounded in feelings or sentiment. Hume acknowledged thai the idea that moral distinctions derive from passions, in relation to which Reason is utterly impotent, would meet with resistance. But he diagnosed this resistance as resulting from conflating with Reason what are in faci 'calm passions' - actions of the mind which resemble Reason in that thel operate with the same calmness and tranquillity, producing little emotion in the mind. Such calm passions as benevolence, the love of life, kind-ness to children, or 'the general appetite to good, and aversion to evil' influence the mind no less than the more violent passions of resentment, fear, or apprehension. What we call 'strength of mind' implies the prevalence of the calm passions above the violent; and this, Hume suggests, is what is 'vulgarly' called reason. It refers to affections of the same kind as the passions, but 'such as operate more calmly, and cause no disorder in the temper'. But their comparative tranquillity causes us to regard them as conclusions only of our intellectual faculties. Generally speaking, it is the violent passions that have the more powerful influence on the will. But it is often found that the calm ones, 'when corroborated by reflection, and seconded by resolution', are 'able to control them in their most furious movements'. This 'struggle of passion and reason', as it is called, Hume concludes, 'diversifies human life', making men different 'not only from each other, but also from themselves in different times'.

On the basis of this general distinction between calm and violent passions, Hume reconstructs the distinction between Reason and passion in terms of two forms of acquisitiveness or self-interest; he argues that the curbing of one by the other is the basis of civil society. The more primitive forms of the passion of acquisitiveness produce inevitable conflicts in large societies; for acquisitiveness combines destructively with partiality of affection - the tendency to give priority to our own interests and those of our immediate relatives. The 'first and most natural senti-ment of morals' is associated with this immediate preference for ourselves and friends above strangers. But it combines with the passion of acquisitiveness to produce inevitable social conflict. The resources available to satisfy the passion of acquisitiveness are limited; and the avid desire to acquire goods and possessions for ourselves and our nearest friends is 'insatiable, perpetual, universal and directly destructive of society'. So the 'partial and contradictory motions of the passions of different individuals' must be restrained, if society is to survive.

However, this passion - like all passions, according to Hume - can be controlled only by a stronger one; and the only passion strong enough to regulate and restrain it is acquisitiveness itself. It alone has sufficient force and proper direction to counterbalance the love of gain and render men fit members of society by making them abstain from the possessions of others. I f it is to play this restraining role, it must first undergo a change of direction. But this readily happens, Hume thinks, on the slightest reflection, since 'tis evident, that the passion is much better satisfy by its restraint, than by its liberty, and that in preserving society, we make much greater advances in acquiring possessions, than in the solitar and forlorn condition, which must follow upon violence and an univer-sal license.

The preservation of society thus rests on the control of acquisitiveness by a more reflective and far-sighted version of itself: 'whether the passion of self-interest be esteemed vicious or virtuous, 'tis all of a case; since itself alone restrains it: So that if it be virtuous, men become social by their virtue; if vicious, their vice has the same effect'

In this reconstruction of the old theme of the subordination of passion to Reason, control is exercised not strictly by Reason, but by a calm, reflective form of passion - an enlightened self-interest. But the resulting operations of justice in society can be ascribed to Reason in an improper sense, in that they involve considering objects 'at a distance'. From this more detached perspective, preference can be given to 'whatever is in itself preferable' - a principle that is 'often contradictory to those propensities that display themselves upon the approach of the object'.

Reason, as reflective passion, remains for Hume a weak and vulner-able force in comparison with more immediate forms of acquisitiveness. In the normal course of events, it does not prevail over the more intense attractions of objects close by. To have efficacy it must be embodied in externally imposed authority. The social remedy for destructive self--interest depends on making the long-term observance of justice the immediate interest of particular persons who take responsibility for the execution of justice. When the reflective form of acquisitiveness is embodied in institutions of justice, 'men acquire a security against each others' weakness and passion, as well as against their own, and under the shelter of their governors, begin to taste at ease the sweets of society and mutual assistance'

This, then, is Hume's version of the relationship between Reason and passion: immediate self-interest subjected to the control of a higher and more reflective version of itself. Reason in its 'improper' sense - whether it be 'calm' as against 'violent' passions, 'reflective' as against 'immediate' and 'partial' self-interest, or 'remote' perspective embodied in magistrates as against the pursuit of short-term interests - controls passion. And this relation of dominance or control is articulated in terms of a distinction between 'public' and 'private' interests. The public passion of acquisitiveness is given the role of curbing private interest in acquiring goods and possessions for the sake of the individual and his family.

Bibliography

Anika Lemaire, *Jacques Lacan,* trans. D. Macey (Boston: Routledge & Kegan Paul, 1977).

An operational definition: Wallace, Anthony F. C. 1966. Religion: An Anthropological View. New York: Random House. (p. 62-66)

A recent overview: A Scientific Definition of Religion. By Ph.D. James W. Dow

Barzilai, Gad; Law and Religion; The International Library of Essays in Law and Society; Ashgate (2007).

Descartes, René; Meditations on First Philosophy; Bobbs-Merril (1960).

Durant, Will (& Ariel (uncredited)); Our Oriental Heritage; MJF Books (1997).

Durant, Will (& Ariel (uncredited)); Caesar and Christ; MJF Books (1994).

Durant, Will (& Ariel (uncredited)); The Age of Faith; Simon & Schuster (1980).

Elisabeth Roudinesco, *Un Discours au reel: theorie de I'inconscient et politique de la psychanalyse* (Paris: Maison Marne, 1973), p. 200 (*Seminaire* inedit de Jacques Lacan, 1970).

Fitzhugh Dodson, *Tout se joue avant six ans,* trans. and ed. Robert Laffom (Verviers, Belgium: Marabout Service, 1970), p. 38.

Jacques Lacan, *Le Seminaire* (1954-1955), *Livre lJ, Le Moi dans la tMorie de Freud et dans la technique de la psychanalyse* (Paris: Seuil, 1978), p. 51.

Jacques Lacan, 'Of structure as an inmixing of an otherness prerequisite to any subject whatever', in *The Structuralist Controversy,* ed. Richard Macksey and Eugenio Donato (Baltimore: The Johns Hopkins Press, 1975), pp. 187-8.

Jacques Lacan, *Le Seminaire* (1953-1954), *Livre I, Les Ecrits techniques de Freud* (Paris: Seuil, 1975), p. 80.

Marija Gimbutas 1989. The Language of the Goddess. Thames and Hudson New York

Jacques Lacan, *Le Seminaire* (1972-1973), *Livre XX, Encore* (Paris: Seuil, 1975), p.69.

Jacques Lacan, *Le Seminaire* (1964), *Livre Xl, Les Quatre Concepts Fondamen-taux de la Psychanalyse* (Paris: Seuil, 1973), p. 35.

Gonick, Larry; The Cartoon History of the Universe; Doubleday, vol. 1 (1978).

Haisch, Bernard The God Theory: Universes, Zero-point Fields, and What's Behind It All — discussion of science vs. religion (Preface), Red Wheel/Weiser, 2006.

Lao Tzu; Tao Te Ching (Victor H. Mair translator); Bantam (1998).

Marx, Karl; "Introduction to A Contribution to the Critique of Hegel's Philosophy of Right", Deutsch-Französische Jahrbücher, (1844).

Saler, Benson; "Conceptualizing Religion: Immanent Anthropologists, Transcendent Natives, and Unbounded Categories" (1990).

Saint Augustine; The Confessions of Saint Augustine (John K. Ryan translator); Image (1960).

The Holy Bible, King James Version; New American Library (1974).

The Origin of Live & Death, African Creation Myths; Heinemann (1966).

Poems of Heaven and Hell from Ancient Mesopotamia; Penguin (1971).

The World Almanac (annual), World Almanac Books.

The Serotonin System and Spiritual Experiences - American Journal of Psychiatry 160:1965-1969, November 2003.

Selected Work Marcus Tullius Cicero

The World Almanac (for numbers of adherents of various religions), 2005

Religion [First Edition]. Winston King. Encyclopedia of Religion. Ed. Lindsay Jones. Vol. 11. 2nd ed. Detroit: Macmillan Reference USA, 2005.

On religion definition: The first major study: Durkheim, Emile (1976) The Elementary Forms of the Religious Life. London: George Allen & Unwin (in French 1912, English translation 1915).

Wilfred Cantwell Smith The Meaning and End of Religion (1962) notes that the concept of religion as an ideological community and system of doctrines, developed in the 15th and 16th centuries CE. A distillation of the Western folk category of religion: Geertz, Clifford. 1993 [1966]. Religion as a cultural system. pp. 87-125 in Clifford Geertz, The Interpretation of Cultures: Selected Essays. London: Fontana Press.

World Religions and Social Evolution of the Old World Oikumene Civilizations: A Cross-cultural Perspective by Andrey Korotayev, Lewiston, NY: Edwin Mellen Press, 2004.